SIERRA CLASSICS

100 Best Climbs
in the High Sierra

SIERRA CLASSICS

100 Best Climbs in the High Sierra

John Moynier
Claude Fiddler

Chockstone Press
Evergreen, Colorado

SIERRA CLASSICS: 100 BEST CLIMBS IN THE HIGH SIERRA

ISBN: 0-934641-60-9

PUBLISHED AND DISTRIBUTED BY
Chockstone Press, Inc.
Post Office Box 3505
Evergreen, Colorado 80439

Cover Photos
>Front: Claude Fiddler on Minaret Traverse; photo by Vern Clevenger
>Back: Mt. Conness; photo by John Moynier

WARNING: CLIMBING IS A SPORT WHERE YOU MAY BE SERIOUSLY INJURED OR DIE.
READ THIS BEFORE YOU USE THIS BOOK.

This guidebook is a compilation of unverified information gathered from many different climbers. The authors cannot assure the accuracy of any of the information in this book, including the topos and route descriptions, the difficulty ratings, and the protection ratings. These may be incorrect or misleading and it is impossible for any author to climb all the routes to confirm the information about each route. Also, ratings of climbing difficulty and danger are always subjective and depend on the physical characteristics (for example, height), experience, technical ability, confidence and physical fitness of the climber who supplied the rating. Additionally, climbers who achieve first ascents sometimes underrate the difficulty or danger of the climbing route out of fear of being ridiculed if a climb is later down-rated by subsequent ascents. Therefore, be warned that you must exercise your own judgment on where a climbing route goes, its difficulty and your ability to safely protect yourself from the risks of rock climbing. Examples of some of these risks are: falling due to technical difficulty or due to natural hazards such as holds breaking, falling rock, climbing equipment dropped by other climbers, hazards of weather and lightning, your own equipment failure, and failure of fixed protection.

You should not depend on any information gleaned from this book for your personal safety; your safety depends on your own good judgment, based on experience and a realistic assessment of your climbing ability. If you have any doubt as to your ability to safely climb a route described in this book, do not attempt it.

The following are some ways to make your use of this book safer:

1. **CONSULTATION:** You should consult with other climbers about the difficulty and danger of a particular climb prior to attempting it. Most local climbers are glad to give advice on routes in their area and we suggest that you contact locals to confirm ratings and safety of particular routes and to obtain first-hand information about a route chosen from this book.

2. **INSTRUCTION:** Most climbing areas have local climbing instructors and guides available. We recommend that you engage an instructor or guide to learn safety techniques and to become familiar with the routes and hazards of the areas described in this book. Even after you are proficient in climbing safely, occasional use of a guide is a safe way to raise your climbing standard and learn advanced techniques.

3. **FIXED PROTECTION:** Many of the routes in this book use bolts and pitons which are permanently placed in the rock. Because of variances in the manner of placement, weathering, metal fatigue, the quality of the metal used, and many other factors, these fixed protection pieces should always be considered suspect and should always be backed up by equipment that you place yourself. Never depend for your safety on a single piece of fixed protection because you never can tell whether it will hold weight.

Be aware of the following specific potential hazards which could arise in using this book:

1. **MISDESCRIPTIONS OF ROUTES:** If you climb a route and you have a doubt as to where the route may go, you should not go on unless you are sure that you can go that way safely. Route descriptions and topos in this book may be inaccurate or misleading.

2. **INCORRECT DIFFICULTY RATING:** A route may, in fact, be more difficult than the rating indicates. Do not be lulled into a false sense of security by the difficulty rating.

3. **INCORRECT PROTECTION RATING:** If you climb a route and you are unable to arrange adequate protection from the risk of falling through the use of fixed pitons or bolts and by placing your own protection devices, do not assume that there is adequate protection available higher just because the route protection rating indicates the route is not an "X" or an "R" rating. Every route is potentially an "X" (a fall may be deadly), due to the inherent hazards of climbing – including, for example, failure of fixed protection, your own equipment's failure, or improper use of climbing equipment.

THERE ARE NO WARRANTIES, WHETHER EXPRESS OR IMPLIED, THAT THIS GUIDEBOOK IS ACCURATE OR THAT THE INFORMATION CONTAINED IN IT IS RELIABLE. THERE ARE NO WARRANTIES OF FITNESS FOR A PARTICULAR PURPOSE OR THAT THIS GUIDE IS MERCHANTABLE. YOUR USE OF THIS BOOK INDICATES YOUR ASSUMPTION OF THE RISK THAT IT MAY CONTAIN ERRORS AND IS AN ACKNOWLEDGEMENT OF YOUR OWN SOLE RESPONSIBILITY FOR YOUR CLIMBING SAFETY.

Preface

"Climb the mountains and get their good tidings.
Nature's peace will flow into you
as sunshine flows into trees.
The winds will blow their own freshness into you,
and the storms their energy,
while cares will drop off like autumn leaves."

– John Muir

This project began as a simple guide to the finest climbs in the High Sierra. As we researched the book, we became fascinated by the personalities and stories involved with these climbs. Much of the history of Sierra climbing has existed as an oral tradition; stories told among climbers, handed down through generations, but never formally recorded.

We have recorded some of these tales and included them in the text describing these classic climbs. In the process, this book became a unique guide to Sierra climbing, offering both a sense of history and an introduction to the climbing potential of the range. It is our hope that it serves as an inspiration for those who choose to climb in this exquisite mountain wilderness.

– Claude Fiddler & John Moynier

Acknowledgements

We would like to thank the following individuals for their photos, detailed topos, route descriptions and advice: Scott Ayers, Allan Bard, Alan Bartlett, Dick Beach, Julie Brugger, Vern Clevenger, Gary Colliver, Will Crljenko, Peter Croft, Andy DeKlerk, Chris Falkenstein, John Fischer, Urmas Franosch, Nancy Gordon, Michael Graber, Al Green, Gary Guenther, Bob Harrington, TM Herbert, Jim Howle, Bruce Ingersoll, E.C. Joe, Malcolm Jolley, Jim Keating, Chris Keith, Bruce Lella, Richard Leversee, Pete Lewis, Chris Libby, Pete Lowery, Dave Nettle, Doug Nidever, Dave Page, Robert "S.P." Parker, Allan Pietrasanta, Michael Pope, Bob Rockwell, Steve Roper, R.J. Secor, Andy Selters, Gary Slate, Jim Stimson, Mike Strassman, Valentin Trenev, Bela Vadasz, Mimi Vadasz, Tim Villanueva, Todd J. Vogel, James Wilson and Gordon Wiltsie.

We would especially like to thank David Brower, Glen Dawson, Jules Eichorn, Richard Leonard and Rhea Voge for their stories, photos and historical background. We would also like to thank our publisher George Meyers of Chockstone Press, Dan McConnell of Speed of Light Photography for the photo reproductions, Rose Moynier for her help editing the text, Robin Ingraham, Jr, for his historical information and Nancy Fiddler, who worked as our contributing editor.

Foreword

I was blessed to be born beneath the vaulted eastern edge of California's High Sierra, and the once-endless days that I spent climbing, skiing and just admiring its craggy facade have indelibly shaped my everyday existence.

These are the mountains that kindled a love that has lured me to some of the wildest ranges on earth. But nearly every time I have struggled halfway around the globe to the Himalaya, the Alps, the Andes or Antarctica, I've found myself wondering why I hadn't just stayed home.

Here, in the spacious wilderness stretching between Mount Whitney and the Sawtooth Range, lie most of my fondest climbing memories, as well as my closest brushes with elements far more powerful than I. This landscape has humbled me and it has almost killed me. But mostly, it has inspired me to come *alive*.

Who could not become enraptured after wrapping fingers over the Sierra crest? Nowhere else will I ever find more joy than watching vast panoramas unfold below my feet on the Swiss Arête, Cathedral Peak or Charlotte Dome. And to every horizon, high above sparkling lakes and iridescent meadows, are endless other granite highways, with cracks and chickenheads leading straight into a sky so clear and blue that the sun is just a pinpoint.

These are mountains we can meet with just a rucksack and a ropemate, but they're also not to be taken lightly, looming with every element of personal challenge we might seek from the sport. I've learned many a frightening lesson from the bergschrund on Palisade Glacier, from runouts on long, blank faces, and from rocks that have teetered and tumbled when I expected them least. And benevolent as Sierra weather might usually be, I've felt my hair stand on end from lightning, and staggered miles through surprise summer snow. But even in the worst, endless bivouacs, when cold and a distant dawn gave rise to my deepest fears, I've never questioned why I climb there.

This is a range beckoning with a lifetime of discovery, and in revealing some of its finest, often-deserted byways, this book becomes a roadmap of the stairways to heaven.

– Gordon Wiltsie

Sierra Classics
100 Best Climbs in the High Sierra

Table of Contents

Introduction

"Then it seemed to me that the Sierra should not be called the Nevada or Snowy Range, but the Range of Light. And after ten years spent in the heart of it, rejoicing and wondering, bathing in the glorious floods of light, seeing the sunbursts of morning among the icy peaks, the noonday radiance on the trees and rocks and snow, the flush of the alpenglow, and a thousand dashing waterfalls with their marvelous abundance of irised spray, it still seems to me above all others the Range of Light, the most divinely beautiful of all the mountain chains I have ever seen."

– John Muir

The High Sierra, John Muir's "Range of Light," is a very beautiful place. These sublime mountains have also been called the "gentle wilderness." Compared to dramatic ranges like the Tetons, Bugaboos and Canadian Rockies, which present obvious mountaineering challenges, the High Sierra requires a more intimate and patient relationship from the climber before it reveals its secrets. The rewards to be found here, however, are just as satisfying as any of those more renowned ranges. The rock is clean, the weather amiable and there is a rich climbing history.

This is a friendly range whose charm lies in its familiarity and accessibility. Within the local climbing community, many climbers echo the phrase "travelling to distant ranges in an exercise in appreciation for the High Sierra."

Introduction

Climbers seeking to push their limits on short, hard sport climbs will be disappointed with the High Sierra. While there are a number of excellent big walls and technically difficult routes, the real attraction of the Sierra lies in long, moderate ridges and airy granite peaks. The climbing here is best characterized as being "fun." The hundred routes we have listed in this book represent the broad range of climbing experiences available in the High Sierra. These routes are the best of the best; the very finest climbs of the Range of Light.

"By far the grandest of all the ranges is the Sierra Nevada, a long and massive uplift lying between the arid deserts of the Great Basin and the Californian exuberance of grainfield and orchard; its eastern slope, a defiant wall of rock plunging abruptly down to the plain; the western, a long, grand sweep, well watered and overgrown with cool, stately forests; its crest a line of sharp, snowy peaks springing into the sky and catching the alpenglow long after the sun has set for all the rest of America."

– Clarence King

The High Sierra

The name Sierra Nevada literally means "snowy mountain range" – an appropriate name, as the higher elevations are covered with snow for much of the year. The Sierra Nevada range is California's topographic backbone, forming an uninterrupted span of nearly 400 miles from Tehachapi Pass in the south to near Mt. Lassen in the north. The section from Cottonwood Pass in the south to Sonora Pass in the north is considered the "High Sierra." This region stretches more than 150 linear miles and averages about 20 miles wide. Eleven peaks rise over 14,000 ft. and hundreds more top 12,000 ft. and 13,000 ft.

The major factors forming and sculpting the High Sierra have been erosion by rivers, glaciation and the slow quarrying of freeze-thaw action. The western slope is relatively gentle, but extensive vertical movement on the Sierra Nevada fault has produced an eastern escarpment that rises 10,000 vertical feet from the Owens Valley floor to the peaks on the crest.

Geologically speaking, the range is essentially one giant granite block 40 to 80 miles wide and part of the great Sierra batholith that has been tilted on its side by uplift. The granite is generally of excellent quality and often sports a profusion of feldspar knobs. The older, metamorphic cap rocks are present in a few areas, like the Kaweahs, the Ritter Range and the Devils Crags. This dark rock is often weathered into stunning gendarmes and towers and has a reputation for being quite loose.

Summer is the best time for extended trips into the range. The weather is generally stable, although there may be periods of intense afternoon thunderstorms and occasional tropical monsoons. The weather in fall is often unsettled and cold. Heavy winter snowfalls make the range relatively inhospitable from November to April. Winter storms may deposit between three and six feet of snow and are usually accompanied by high winds. Avalanche hazard during these times can be extreme. The weather in spring (April-May) is generally fine, but the lingering snowpack means that travel is usually best accomplished on skis. For a detailed study of the ecology of the range, consult *Sierra Nevada Natural History* by Tracer Storer and Robert Usinger.

Getting There

The crest of the Sierra Nevada runs from the northwest to the southeast, and access is generally best provided from the west or the east. The closest airports are in Fresno on the west side, and in Reno on the east. Small airports are found in Bishop and Mammoth, but the only regular air service to these is from Los Angeles. Bus service to the Sierra exists, but a car is much more practical.

The Sierra is flanked by parallel roads: U.S. Highway 99 on the west and U.S. Highway 395 on the east. All-season U.S. Highways 50 and 80, as well as California Highway 88, cross the Sierra near Lake Tahoe. U.S. Highway 6 gives access from the east to the Owens Valley, while California Highway 14 connects Highway 395 to Los Angeles.

California Highways 108 and 120 are the only roads to cross the High Sierra, but both of these roads are closed in winter, from the first of November until Memorial Day. Highway 108 links Sonora and Bridgeport via Sonora Pass and provides access to the Tower Peak area. Highway 120 links Yosemite Valley with the eastern Sierra via Tuolumne Meadows and Tioga Pass and provides access to the Yosemite high country.

Introduction

Many spur roads lead to the various west-side trailheads from Fresno and Highway 99. California Highway 198 accesses Mineral King and Giant Forest from the south via the towns of Visalia and Three Rivers. California Highway 180 reaches Kings Canyon and Sequoia National Parks. California Highway 168 leads east past Huntington Lake to trailheads at Lake Edison and Florence Lake. California Highway 41 leads north through Oakhurst and reaches Yosemite Valley, the spur road to Glacier Point, and Highway 120.

Bishop is located between Reno and Los Angeles on Highway 395 and serves as the hub for the east side. The smaller towns of Lone Pine, Independence, Big Pine, Mammoth Lakes, June Lake, Lee Vining and Bridgeport lie on or near Highway 395 and offers amenities including grocery stores, motels, showers and restaurants. Backpacking and climbing supplies, as well as current route conditions, can be found at Wilson's Eastside Sports in Bishop (619) 873-7520, Pat's Backcountry Shop in Mammoth Lakes (619) 934-2008, and Alpenglow in Tahoe City (916) 583-6917.

Using this Guide

We assume that you have a basic knowledge of climbing techniques and the proper use of roped belays and rappels. Depending on the peak and time of year, a basic understanding of glacial travel, snow and ice techniques and avalanche hazard awareness may be useful. A familiarity with the fundamental skills of wilderness travel, including the use of a compass and United States Geological Survey (USGS) topographic maps is also necessary.

The peaks in this guide are described from south to north, with the peaks west of the crest treated separately. The elevations of the peaks are based on USGS 15-minute topographic maps. The cardinal directions listed in this book are based on true north, as represented on these USGS topographic maps, and refer to the primary orientation of the feature, rather than the traditional name for a route.

Descriptions of each region are preceded by a USGS 15-minute topographic map of the area. This is followed by an introduction to the special characteristics of the area and pertinent information about the approaches. The individual routes are accompanied by a photograph, an anecdotal introduction and a terse written description. We have provided the essential information needed to reach, climb and descend a route, while trying to maintain a vital sense of adventure and self-reliance. Some of the technical climbs also include a sketched "topo" of the route, which provides more specific climbing information. All climbing directions assume you are facing the described feature.

For more detailed approach information, consult Starr's *Guide to the John Muir Trail and the High Sierra Region*. A more complete list of the climbing routes and passes of the range can be found in Steve Roper's *Climbers' Guide*

7.5 Minute Maps for the High Sierra
Area maps for *Sierra Classics* are highlighted

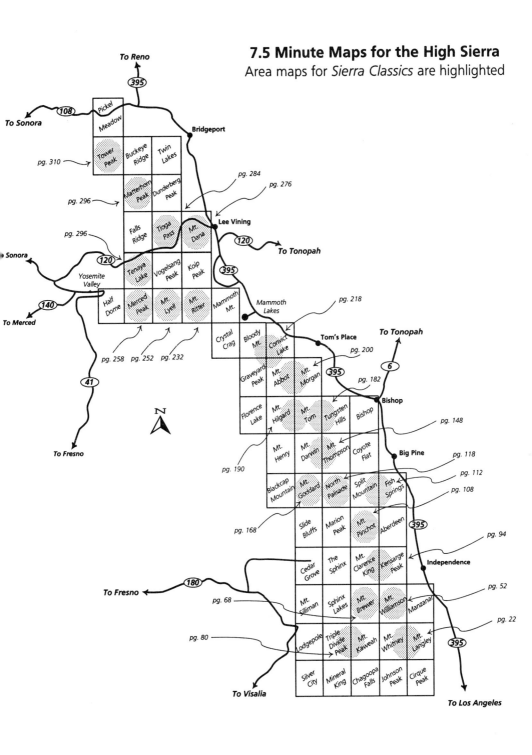

To Reno

395

To Sonora

108

To Sonora

Pickel Meadow

Bridgeport

Tower Peak — pg. 310

Buckeye Ridge

Twin Lakes

pg. 284

pg. 276

Matterhorn Peak — pg. 296

Dunderberg Peak

Lee Vining

Falls Ridge — pg. 296

Tioga Pass

Mt. Dana

120

To Tonopah

Sonora

120

Yosemite Valley

Tenaya Lake

Vogelsang Peak

Koip Peak

395

140

Half Dome

Merced Peak

Mt. Lyell

Mt. Ritter

Mammoth Mt.

Mammoth Lakes

pg. 218

To Merced

pg. 258 pg. 252 pg. 232

Crystal Crag

Bloody Mt.

Convict Lake

Tom's Place

To Tonopah

41

Graveyard Peak

Mt. Abbot

Mt. Morgan

395

pg. 200

pg. 182

6

Florence Lake

Mt. Hilgard

Mt. Tom

Tungsten Hills

Bishop

Bishop

pg. 148

N

pg. 190

Mt. Henry

Mt. Darwin

Mt. Thompson

Coyote Flat

Big Pine

pg. 118

pg. 112

To Fresno

Blackcap Mountain

Mt. Goddard

North Palisade

Split Mountain

Fish Springs

pg. 108

pg. 168

Slide Bluffs

Marion Peak

Mt. Pinchot

Aberdeen

395

pg. 94

Cedar Grove

The Sphinx

Mt. Clarence King

Kearsarge Peak

Independence

180

pg. 52

To Fresno

pg. 68

Mt. Gilliman

Sphinx Lakes

Mt. Brewer

Mt. Williamson

Manzanar

pg. 22

pg. 80

Lodgepole

Triple Divide Peak

Mt. Kaweah

Mt. Whitney

Mt. Langley

395

Silver City

Mineral King

Chagoopa Falls

Johnson Peak

Cirque Peak

To Visalia

To Los Angeles

to the High Sierra and R.J. Secor's *The High Sierra – Peaks, Passes and Trails.*
The Shooting Star Guides, written by Allan Bard, provide in-depth information
for the following classic climbs: the East Face and East Buttress routes on Mt.
Whitney, the Swiss Arête on Mt. Sill, the Southeast Buttress on Cathedral
Peak, and the North Arête of Matterhorn Peak. The annual issues of the
American Alpine Journal (AAJ), as well as individual issues of *Climbing, Rock
and Ice,* and *Ascent* magazines, are also sources of information for recent
routes.

Key to Route Descriptions

The header above the line at the top of the page refers to the 15-minute
USGS topo reproduced at the beginning of each section.

Mt. Russell	The name of the peak.
14,016 ft.	The elevation of the peak on the 15-minute map.
East Arête	The name of the route.
Class 3	The route's overall rating.
F.A. Norman Clyde; June, 1926	The climber(s) who made the first ascent of the route and the date of the climb.
F.F.A.	The climbers on the first free ascent (where appropriate).
Mt. Whitney Area Map:	Indicates the page at the beginning of that section where the area map is reproduced.
USGS Quad Maps:	The USGS 7.5-minute topographic maps needed for the approach and climb. These maps have replaced the 15-minute map series (some of these larger-scale maps are still available through Wilderness Press Maps).

*Below this summary information, the reader is provided with descriptive, his-
torical and/or anecdotal information, followed by:*

Route:	A terse written description of the route to be used in conjunction with the photos, USGS maps, other guide books and your mountain judgement.
Alternative Routes:	Other recommended climbs in the area.
Descent:	The recommended route off the peak.

Key to Reading Route Topos

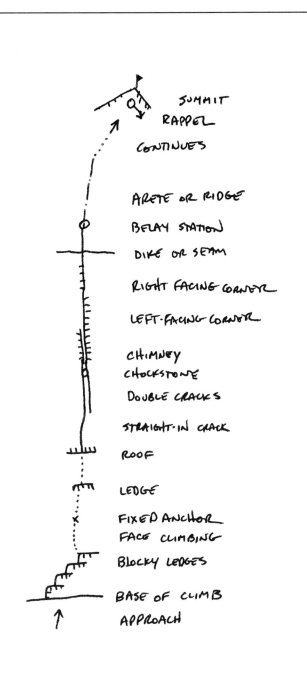

SUMMIT
RAPPEL
CONTINUES

ARETE OR RIDGE

BELAY STATION

DIKE OR SEAM

RIGHT FACING CORNER

LEFT-FACING CORNER

CHIMNEY
CHOCKSTONE
DOUBLE CRACKS

STRAIGHT-IN CRACK

ROOF

LEDGE

FIXED ANCHOR
FACE CLIMBING

BLOCKY LEDGES

BASE OF CLIMB

APPROACH

A Brief History of Climbing in the High Sierra

The climbing history of the Sierra Nevada begins with the first inhabitants of the range. The Native Americans living on both sides of the Sierra frequented the mountains on trading and hunting expeditions. Flakes of "worked" obsidian have been found throughout the range, especially on the known routes over Taboose Pass and Mono Pass (Bloody Canyon). Presumably, hunting for bighorn sheep led the Indians to many major Sierra peaks, as arrowheads have been found on or near the summits of Mt. Conness, Mt. Mendel and Mt. Langley, among others. Other than this, little is known of native climbing history.

In 1863 the California Geological Survey, under the direction of Josiah Whitney, began the first thorough exploration of the High Sierra, and formally named many of the major features. The Whitney Survey, as it was called, was responsible for many of the first recorded ascents of peaks from north of Yosemite National Park to south of Mt. Whitney. The team was comprised of field leader William Brewer, topographer Charles Hoffmann, geologists James Gardiner and Clarence King, and packer Richard Cotter. Their travels are chronicled in Brewer's *Up and Down California in 1860-1864* and King's romanticized *Mountaineering in the Sierra Nevada*.

On the first ascent of Mt. Brewer in July of 1864, Hoffmann and Brewer saw a group of peaks to the southeast, which they took to be the highest in the range. Cotter and King asked permission to try to climb the tallest of these. After an epic crossing of the Kings-Kern divide, the pair climbed Mt. Tyndall, only to find two other peaks equal in height, and two even higher, on the horizon. The tallest of these they later named Mt. Whitney. This peak was to become a nemesis for King; its first ascent was to elude him, despite his considerable efforts.

John Muir made his first trip into the Sierra in 1868, and the following summer came to call the range his home. He was a prodigious traveler and climber, and his accounts of these trips are full of flowery prose. Muir was especially impressed with Cathedral Peak, which he described as "a temple displaying Nature's best masonry and sermons in stone." The summit tower of this peak features a short, vertical crack. His 1869 solo first ascent was probably the most difficult climb made in the country at that time. He said, "I am forever and hopelessly a mountaineer."

Muir is credited with first ascents on many other peaks, including Mt. Ritter and Mt. Whitney. He wrote about climbing the highest peak at the head of the San Joaquin River, but whether this was Mt. Darwin or Mt. Humphreys is difficult to ascertain from his notes. Muir is perhaps better remembered as a father of the environmental movement and founder of the Sierra Club, a career that was inspired by his life spent wandering the Sierra. After a full season of exploring the range, the indefatigable Muir would write, "I feel eager and ready for another excursion."

Another early mountaineer and charter member of the Sierra Club was Theodore Solomons. As a young boy, he had dreamt. of a trail following the length of the crest. While exploring the route of the present-day John Muir Trail, Solomons made early ascents of the Seven Gables, Mt. Goddard and Mt. Ritter. He also named many features of the range, including the peaks in the Evolution group.

By the turn of the century, interest in mountaineering in the Sierra had grown, particularly among members of Muir's newly formed Sierra Club. It was at this time that the Sierra Club began taking extended outings into the high country under the leadership of William Colby. From the beginning, mountain climbing was an integral activity on these trips.

Some of the most prominent mountaineers of this era were Joseph "Little Joe" LeConte, James Hutchinson and Bolton Coit Brown. LeConte, like his father, was a professor at the University of California. His excellent maps and photographs of the range were among the first made of the High Sierra. During his travels, he participated in the first ascents of Mt. Gould, Mt. Gardiner, University Peak, Observation Peak and Marion Peak. In 1903, LeConte made the first ascent of North Palisade with his life-long friend James Hutchinson, who later became President of the Sierra Club and editor of the *Sierra Club Bulletin*.

In 1908, Hutchinson and LeConte teamed with another future Sierra Club president, Duncan McDuffie, to build on the work of Theodore Solomons in developing a high mountain route through the range. During their explorations, they made the first ascents of Mt. Mills and Mt. Abbot. Twelve years later, on August 11, 1920, Hutchinson, McDuffie and a packer named Onis Imis Brown made the first ascent of the formidable Black Kaweah. Hutchinson made many other climbs with his brothers Lincoln and Edward, including the first ascents of Matterhorn Peak and Mt. Humphreys.

Perhaps the most difficult ascent of the era was accomplished by Bolton Coit Brown, a professor of Fine Arts at Stanford University. After a failed solo attempt to reach the summit of Mt. Clarence King in 1895, he found success a year later using a rope sling for artificial aid to surmount the exposed summit block. Today, this pitch is rated 5.4 and has resisted solo attempts by many experienced mountaineers. Brown also made the first ascents of Mt. Ericsson, Arrow Peak, Mt. Woodworth and Mt. Stanford. He was often accompanied on Sierra trips by his wife Lucy, and later by their young daughter Eleanor.

Charles Michael was another solo climber who was confident on difficult climbs. It was said that he climbed everything that did not need pitons. A complete list of his accomplishments may never be known, as he usually climbed solo and was closed-mouthed about his travels. Between 1912 and 1920, Michael made the first ascents of Devils Crag #1, Michael Minaret and Michael Pinnacle in the Kaweahs. Many of his solo routes on these peaks are today rated moderate fifth class.

Sierra Club outings during the first quarter of the century provided a number of mountaineers with the opportunity to make extended trips into the Sierra. William Colby, Edward Parsons, Walter Huber, James Rennie, Francis Farquhar and Norman Clyde were among the most active participants. Colby was involved in these outings for more than forty years. His longevity was matched by that of Walter Huber, who made first ascents of peaks throughout the range, particularly in the northern Yosemite region. Farquhar also was active with the Sierra Club for many years, eventually becoming president of the club for two terms.

Legendary Sierra climber Jules Eichorn reflected about his frequent partner, Norman Clyde: "Norman had a quality of character that would not let anything interfere with his appointments with the mountains." No one else, before or since, has come close to matching his record of climbs and first ascents. He began his string of first ascents in 1914 and made his last in 1946. He wrote: "1914 was the first year that I did any climbing of any account in the Sierra. Climbing at that time was what mountaineers sometimes refer to as 'free climbing.' Ropes were seldom used and those that were, were not adequate and probably no one knew anything about using a rope in climbing. In the twenties, there was considerable change. Personally, I learned the technique of roped climbing from Swiss guides and the Canadian Alpine Club in the Canadian Rockies."

Photographer unknown

Norman Clyde

While most of Clyde's first ascents were made solo, he also served as guide and woodcutter on Sierra Club outings, leading hundreds of people up Sierra peaks. He continued to be active in the annual outings until just a few years before his death in 1972.

By the 1930s, a core group of young mountaineers had evolved within the Sierra Club which included Jack Riegelhuth, Raffi Bedayn,

Walter Brem, Lewis Clark, Richard Jones, Glen Dawson, Jules Eichorn, Hervey Voge, David Brower, Richard Leonard, John Olmstead, Bestor Robinson, Hans Leschke, Carl Jensen, Ted Waller and Oliver Kehrlein. Although this group made a number of quite difficult ascents without any formal training in the use of roped climbing techniques, they later agreed that many of these ascents had involved unjustifiable risks.

On a Harvard Mountaineering Club outing to the Canadian Selkirks in 1930, Francis Farquhar was introduced to modern rope management by Dr. Robert Underhill, a prominent eastern climber and a professor at Harvard. Farquhar was impressed by Underhill's climbing record in the Tetons and Canada and asked him to write an article for the Sierra Club Bulletin. This appeared in 1931, titled, "On the Use and Management of the Rope in Rock Work." Farquhar also invited Underhill to attend the Sierra Club's 1931 High Trip in the Ritter Range.

A goal of this 1931 trip was to introduce the Sierra Club climbers to roped climbing techniques. Underhill joined the camp at Garnet Lake and organized a climbing school that practiced on the steep slopes of Mt. Ritter and Banner Peak. This important event, which later became known as the "Underhill Camp," led to increased safety during the Club's mountaineering activities and many difficult ascents.

Richard Leonard

Peakbagging on a Sierra Club High Camp

After the formal part of the camp was completed, some of the climbers moved on to the Palisades, where they made the first ascent of Thunderbolt Peak, the last 14,000-foot peak in the Sierra to be climbed. The highlight of Underhill's visit was undoubtedly the first ascent of the east face of Mt. Whitney by Underhill, Norman Clyde, Jules Eichorn and Glen Dawson. Eichorn recalls being roped with Clyde, because it was felt that he could deal best with Clyde's short temper. The two teams shared leads and moved quickly up the face. Their ascent was accomplished in a little over three hours and today is rated 5.6.

David Brower, one of the nation's foremost environmental activists and former Sierra Club executive director, was also very active in Sierra mountaineering. Brower remembers first meeting Norman Clyde for dinner at Glacier Lodge in 1933. After relating the story of his recent near-fatal fall on the Thumb in the Palisades, Clyde's advice to Brower was simple: "Always maintain three points of suspension on the rock." Although this was two years after the 1931 High Trip, it is curious that Clyde made no mention of the use of a rope, hardware or belays. Brower subsequently made an ascent of the U-Notch couloir on North Palisade, wearing basketball shoes and using a sliver of rock for an ice dagger. Above the notch is a crack that is rated 5.6. He later recalled, "Everything about the climb seemed reasonable after Norman's advice, but I do think people rope up for it now!"

Richard Leonard

David Brower on the Conness Glacier

In 1934, Brower and future Sierra guidebook author Hervey Voge went on a ten-week expedition from Kearsarge Pass to Tuolumne Meadows. The pair was joined by Norman Clyde for portions of the trip. Brower and Voge climbed 59 peaks in 69 days, including the first ascents of eight of the Devils Crags. These remain among Brower's most memorable climbs. Offering serious climbing on less than perfect rock, the Devils Crags are climbed infrequently. They did not climb Crag # 2 and in his journal, Hervey Voge wrote, "We saw that the ascent of #2 would have been quite severe and that there was already a cairn on top, probably Eichorn or Dawson."

Indeed, the year before, Jules Eichorn, Glen Dawson and Ted Waller had made the ascent during the Sierra Club's 1933 High Trip, with a rope commandeered from the camp kitchen and no hardware. During the descent, they were caught in an intense thunderstorm and were forced to seek refuge under a large chockstone. While huddled under this meager protection, rockfall destroyed their rope and opened an eight-inch gash on Eichorn's back.

Eichorn and Dawson were perhaps the most keen of the young Sierra Club climbers. Eichorn was introduced to Sierra Club outings by Ansel Adams, while Dawson's father, Ernest, had been President of the Sierra Club. They first climbed together on a Sierra Club outing in 1930, about which Will Colby wrote: "Some youthful enthusiasts, including Glen Dawson, Jules Eichorn, and John Olmstead, swarmed over everything that looked formidable in the way of a mountain peak." This trio made a number of first ascents that summer. The imperial style of the club's outings allowed Eichorn and Dawson to climb to their hearts' content.

During their long careers, Dawson and Eichorn made many notable ascents, including: Eichorn's Pinnacle, the Matthes Crest, Mt. Whitney, the Devils Crags, The Dragtooth, Middle Palisade, the Three Teeth, Mt. Ansel Adams, and Michael, Clyde, Eichorn and Dawson Minarets. Many of these routes are considered moderate fifth-class climbs today, and more often than not they were climbed unroped on the first ascents.

Richard Leonard joined the Sierra Club in the early 1930s. He was inspired to do so by reading summit registers during a ten-week trip in the Sierra. While attending law school, he took up rock climbing to "get some exercise." His climbing ability soon developed and along with other Bay Area climbers, he formed the Cragmont Climbing Club, which later became the Rock Climbing Section (RCS) of the Sierra Club. His wife Doris remembers "Grubby climbers with the seats blown out of their Levis" invading their home after practice sessions at Cragmont Rock, Pinnacle Rock and Indian Rock.

It was during this infancy of technical rock climbing that Leonard invented the "dynamic belay." The philosophy of the day had been "the leader must not fall," as decreed by the British Alpine Club. This philosophy maintained that anyone remiss in his duty as leader should have his rope severed from the rest of the team. Leonard found the idea of giving Jules Eichorn or Bestor Robinson "the chop" unthinkable, and so worked to develop a way to safeguard leader falls. Starting with six-inch practice falls, they eventually became comfortable holding up to 39-foot falls (measured) on their braided ropes!

After World War II, a new generation of climbers began to explore the range in pursuit of difficult free and aid climbs. Among this group were Yosemite climbers Allen Steck, Anton Nelson, Dick Long, Jerry Gallwas, Merle Alley and George Sessions, as well as Chuck Wilts, a Tahquitz climber who had invented the knifeblade piton. Their routes on the southeast buttress of Cathedral Peak, Castle Rock Spire, the south face of the Angel Wings and the southeast face of Clyde Minaret are still highly regarded today.

Introduction

Another energetic group of climbers, many of whom were members of the Sierra Club's Sierra Peak Section (SPS), made ascents of more remote peaks. Two of the most active of these were John Mendenhall and his wife Ruth Dyar Mendenhall. The Mendenhalls had a long and prolific climbing career in the Sierra. Although the 1931 High Trip is generally considered the introduction of formal roped climbing techniques in the Sierra, Mendenhall made a belayed climb on Laurel Mountain on September 7, 1930. He was 19 years old at the time. In 1975, at the age of 64, he climbed a new route on Middle Palisade, rated III 5.5.

Carl Heller (a research chemist and founder of the China Lake Search and Rescue Group) was also very active in seeking out unclimbed summits, as were A.J. Reymann, Chester Versteeg, Dr. Andrew Smatko, Tom Ross and Bill Schuller. After completing the SPS's "Peaks List," Barbara Lilley and Gordon MacLeod set a goal of climbing all of the marked elevations in the range. Their registers can be found on obscure summits throughout the Sierra.

The first true big wall ascents in the High Sierra were accomplished by Yosemite legend Warren Harding. Among his many visionary routes are the southwest face of Mt. Conness and the east face of Keeler Needle. Warren's able apprentice, Galen Rowell, was the most active Yosemite climber to explore

Richard Leonard

Bestor Robinson, Richard Leonard and Jules Eichorn on Higher Cathedral Spire

the range in search of unclimbed technical walls and arêtes. His impressive record includes first ascents on Bear Creek Spire, the west face of Mt. Russell, the south face of Charlotte Dome, the south arête of the Angel Wings and the north pillar of Mt. Chamberlin.

Other Yosemite-trained climbers of the 1960s who joined Rowell in the pursuit of backcountry routes were TM Herbert, Don Lauria, Gary Colliver, Chris

Vandiver, Chris Jones, Lito Tejada-Flores, Greg Donaldson, Ken Boche and Russ McLean. The skills they had acquired on Yosemite walls enabled them to make difficult climbs on The Citadel, Incredible Hulk, Mt. Russell, Mt. Brewer and others. The seemingly omnipresent Fred Beckey also spent a great deal of time in the range, searching out first ascents and enlisting young climbers to aid in his efforts.

The Palisades region of the High Sierra, recognized for its high concentration of quality alpine routes, was the site of the first climbing school and guide service in the range. The Mountaineering Guide Service was founded in 1959 by Larry Williams of Berkeley. In 1969, the guide service was bought by Allen Steck and Leo LeBon of Mountain Travel and the name was changed to the Palisade School of Mountaineering (PSOM). At that time, many of the top climbers in Yosemite Valley worked as guides for PSOM, including Chuck Pratt, Steve Roper, TM Herbert, Dennis Hennek and Kim Schmitz. Don Jensen and Frank Sarnquist were the most active of these guides in climbing new routes, and were often accompanied by young guides like Doug Robinson, John Sharsmith, Chuck Kroger and John Fischer.

After John Fischer and his wife Lois bought the school from Mountain Travel in 1976, a new generation of guides joined the school, including Gordon Wiltsie, Jay Jensen, Carl Dreisbach, Mike Farrell, Allan Pietrasanta, and Mike Graber. This group made a number of difficult technical climbs over the next few years, including Planeria (IV 5.10 A1) on Temple Crag and Larry's Pillar (III 5.10) on the east face of Mt. Sill. During this period, John Fischer guided Gerry Adams on the first traverse of the entire Palisade section of the Sierra crest. This lengthy and committing climb was accomplished over a period of seven days and to our knowledge has not been repeated.

Alpine ice climbing in the Sierra originated with Norman Clyde's ascents of the U-Notch and Clyde's Couloirs on North Palisade and the north face of Mt. Emerson during the 1920s. These climbs were accomplished early in the season when soft snow conditions allowed for easy step-cutting. By the 1950s, steep routes like the V-Notch in the Palisades and the Right Couloir on Mt. Mendel had been climbed, but these ascents were still made as early season snow climbs.

Doug Robinson and Yvon Chouinard were the pioneers of Sierra ice climbing in the '60s. After an epic late-season attempt on the Left Couloir on Mt. Mendel with Dennis Hennek in 1965, Chouinard set about designing tools specifically for steep ice. He spent the following summer in the Alps and designed a short axe with a curved pick, which was heralded as the most revolutionary development in modern ice climbing history. Chouinard described this pivotal era: "In 1967, Tom Frost and I not only designed a new 'alpine hammer' with a drooping pick, but also brought out an adjustable, rigid crampon made from chrome-molybdenum steel. Armed with these new tools (and with the reliable Salewa tube screws), we began approaching steep ice with a

Introduction

new attitude. The couloirs of the Sierra Nevada proved to have fantastic climbing in the autumn months, when the summer snows had matured into runnels of live water-ice. Doug Robinson and I took advantage of the lack of interest by others in climbing ice and scooped the first ascents of many fine Sierra gullies . . . The game soon evolved into doing these climbs in their 'worst' conditions: that is, solid blue ice."

The steep icefalls of Lee Vining Canyon provided the testing ground for these climbers, and by the early 1970s, they had become confident in tackling vertical and even overhanging ice. In 1976, Robinson paired up with Yosemite climber Dale Bard to climb the difficult "Ice-nine" couloir on the north face of Mt. Mendel. This is still considered the most difficult alpine ice climb in the range.

By the late 1970s and early '80s, the number of Yosemite climbers seeking difficult technical climbs in the High Sierra had grown. Many of these climbers spent their summers in Tuolumne Meadows, including Vern Clevenger, Dale Bard, Allan Bard, Claude Fiddler, Alan Bartlett, Allan Pietrasanta, Phil and Dave Bircheff, Bob Harrington and Rick Wheeler.

During this period, many high standard routes were done on remote peaks, including the Seven Gables, the East Pillar of Mt. Barnard, the Dumbbell Lakes wall, the Incredible Hulk and Cleaver Peak. Fiddler and Clevenger completed several noteworthy traverses of technical ridges, including traverses of the Sawtooth Ridge, the Rock Creek crest, the Minarets and the southwest ridge of Mt. Ritter.

After sixty years of technical climbing in the range, many fine lines still remain to be climbed. Galen Rowell and Claude Fiddler continue to seek out new routes, as do Dave Nettle, Scott Ayers, Jim Keating, Todd Vogel, Richard Leversee, Mike Strassman, Cameron Burns, Steve Porcella, Urmas Franosch, Peter Croft and others. Some examples of these "modern" routes are the Edge of Time Arête (IV 5.10) on the Citadel, the Bubbs Creek Wall (VI 5.11) in Bubbs Creek Canyon, the traverse of the Ericsson Crags (III 5.8), and the Southwest Buttress on North Palisade (IV 5.11). It is certain that the beauty of the High Sierra will continue to inspire climbers for generations to come.

"Of all the ranges in the United States there is probably none that offers such opportunity for strenuous but healthful mountain climbing as does the Sierra Nevada."

– Norman Clyde

Climbing

The single best word describing Sierra climbing is varied. The granite rocks of the range are generally solid, yet loose rock or loose blocks and flakes may be found on any given route. One may encounter perfect cracks, gritty slabs, overhanging offwidths and delicate face climbing on mediums as varied as solid granite, shattered metamorphic rock, alpine ice and more. In fact, it is not uncommon to encounter any or all of these on any individual climb.

Equipment

The equipment required for these routes will depend on the season, type of climb and your personal judgement. Due to seasonal differences in snow coverage, some of the approaches and descents may require an ice axe and crampons. A basic Sierra rack consists of a rope (two ropes are useful for longer routes, hauling and rappels), a selection of wired nuts and Friends, several runners and a number of carabiners. The longer technical routes may demand a larger rack. Ice routes require appropriate ice gear and protection.

Registers

Most Sierra peaks have a summit register of one form or another. These registers are of great historical interest. The tradition of placing summit registers in the Sierra started with the Whitney Survey Party in the 1860s. At present, the greatest threat to this tradition is theft and loss. Leave all registers in place.

In 1933, the Sierra Club formed the Mountain Records Committee to compile and preserve historical mountain information, specifically summit registers. This responsibility currently is handled by the Sierra Register Committee, with Robin

Introduction

Ingraham, Jr. serving as Director. This committee also serves as a repository for new route information. Any pertinent information should be addressed to: Sierra Register Committee, P.O. Box 3141, Merced, CA 95344-1141.

Ratings

This book uses the Class 1-5 rating system developed by the Sierra Club in 1937. These ratings begin with Class 1, which is easy walking. Class 2 denotes rougher terrain, where your hands may be needed for balance. Class 3 terrain is characterized by steeper terrain where hand and foot holds are used. The exposure may lead some climbers to feel more comfortable with a rope.

Class 4 routes involve more difficult climbing, and the exposure is such that a fall could be fatal. Ropes, belays and anchors may be used. Class 5 climbs require roped belays, placement of intermediate protection and specialized climbing techniques. Fifth-class climbs are further rated on a scale of difficulty based on the Yosemite Decimal System. This scale currently ranges from 5.0 (easiest) to 5.14 (most difficult). The ratings may be further defined as relatively easier or harder by a letter (a through d) or a symbol (–/+).

Aid climbs are rated from A0 (fixed protection) to A5 (pro is very difficult to place and extremely insecure). Although we have listed only a few aid climbs, it is not uncommon on alpine routes for a climber to use aid on a difficult section of an alpine book that they are unable to free climb. As an example, a climb we have rated 5.11 may turn out to be 5.9, A2 for a given climber. Likewise, a strong climber may be able to free climb a route that originally required aid.

The Roman numerals I through VI preceding a climb's rating describe the route's Grade or level of commitment. Allow a few hours for Grade I and II climbs. In this book, if a route does not have a grade listed, it is a Grade I or II climb. A Grade III climb may take the better part of a day, while a Grade IV takes a long day. A Grade V may require a bivouac and a Grade VI climb should take at least two days.

The ratings used in this guide are the consensus of the climbing community. These ratings are only as accurate as the information provided to us. It should be noted that the ratings determined by the climbers of the 1930s may seem underrated. Jules Eichorn described the simple method he and his peers used to rate climbs: "If we did not have a rope, it was Class 3; if we had a rope, but did not have the right pitons, it was Class 4; if we had a rope and pitons (and used them), it was Class 5."

"We abuse land because we regard it as a commodity belonging to us. When we see land as a community to which we belong, we may begin to use it with love and respect."

– Aldo Leopold

Wilderness impacts

A major concern in writing a guide book is the possibility of adverse impacts on the wilderness due to increased use. Gary Colliver, a climbing ranger in Yosemite National Park, pointed out that directing people to a limited number of backcountry climbs may diminish the wilderness value of those areas. The responsibility to use the wilderness with care and respect is shared by all.

The potential impacts to the wilderness are quite diverse. Litter, bolts, rappel slings and cairns are the most obvious signs of climber impact. There should be no reason to leave any sign of our passing. If a rappel sling must be left, use a rock-colored sling. Remove any existing slings. Any litter found in the wilderness should be picked up. We also should destroy fire rings, covering the old ashes with sand or duff.

Wilderness travel can also create less visible impacts to the fragile alpine ecosystem. Erosion, damage to vegetation, fouling of water sources and improper waste management are difficult to detect, yet create lasting damage. Beyond the ideal of "leaving no trace," wherever possible an area needs to be left cleaner than it was found.

Selecting a campsite is important. Camp at least 100 feet away from trails, water and open meadows, preferably on sandy soil. Water should be carried to camp for cooking and washing, and biodegradable soap should be used. Human waste should be disposed of at least 100 feet from water and buried at least 4 inches deep in sandy soil or duff. Most wilderness regulations would not be necessary if the mountains were treated with respect and common sense.

"We all share a responsibility to use the backcountry with care and respect; to be aware of how our travel in an area affects both the environment and other visitors there; and to determine ways that we can avoid or minimize those impacts."

– Gary Colliver

Wilderness Permits

Wilderness permits are required for overnight travel in all wilderness, primitive and national park backcountry areas, with quotas in effect for most of the popular overnight areas. Day use is not currently regulated. These permits are available on March 1 for the following summer's quota season. You may apply in advance for these permits at the addresses listed below. If the advance permits have already been issued, you will need to apply for your permit in person on the actual date you wish to enter the wilderness. These permits are available either at a trailhead kiosk or at the local ranger station. Contact the necessary agencies well in advance of your planned trip dates. Agency officials will advise you as to local regulations regarding daily quotas, wood fires, area closures and other limitations on wilderness travel.

Where to Obtain Information and Wilderness Permits

John Muir Wilderness: East Side

Inyo National Forest
Mt. Whitney Ranger District
P.O. Box 8 – S. Highway 395
Lone Pine, CA 93545
(619) 876-5542

Inyo National Forest
White Mountain Ranger District
798 N. Main St.
Bishop, CA 93514
(619) 873-4207

Inyo National Forest
Mammoth Ranger District
Highway 203 – P.O. Box 148
Mammoth Lakes, CA 93546
(619) 934-2505

Inyo National Forest
Mono Lake Ranger District
P.O. Box 10
Lee Vining, CA 93541
(619) 647-6525

Toiyabe National Forest
Bridgeport Ranger District
P.O. Box 595
Bridgeport, CA 93517
(619) 932-7070

Sequoia and Kings Canyon

Superintendent
Sequoia and Kings Canyon
Three Rivers, CA 93271
(209) 565-3306

Yosemite National Park

Superintendent
Yosemite National Park
P.O. Box 577
Yosemite, CA 95389
(209) 372-4232

"I have crossed the Range of Light, surely the brightest and best of the Lord has built, and rejoicing in its glory, gratefully, hopefully pray that I may see it again."

– John Muir

Mt. Whitney Area

The centerpiece of the southern Sierra is Mt. Whitney, the highest summit in the contiguous United States. There are many fine peaks in the area that offer excellent climbing on good quality granite. From Mt. Langley to Mt. Russell, the crest averages 14,000 feet and forms a dramatic backdrop for the small town of Lone Pine and Highway 395. Lone Pine offers restaurants, lodging, camping, showers and limited mountaineering supplies. Wilderness permits are available at the U.S. Forest Service office on the south end of town.

The prominent features of the area were named for two eminent scientific rivals of their day: John Muir and Josiah Whitney. Whitney, leader of the California Geological Survey (also known as the Whitney Survey), espoused the theory that a great cataclysm or earthquake had created Yosemite Valley. Meanwhile, Muir studied the area and determined that it was the slow work of glaciers, not a rapid movement of the earth, which had been the architect of the valley.

Whitney denounced the then unknown Muir, stating, "A more absurd theory was never advanced . . . This theory, based on entire ignorance of the whole subject, may be dropped without wasting any more time on it." With Professor Joseph LeConte's help, Muir's theory was ultimately substantiated, tarnishing Whitney's reputation.

Clarence King, a member of Whitney's Survey team, attempted to climb Mt. Whitney several times in the late 1860s and early '70s. One attempt led to the first ascent of Mt. Langley, where King, mistakenly thinking he had conquered Mt. Whitney, proclaimed his victory by leaving a dollar on the summit. Unfortunately for King, three fellow members of the survey later climbed Mt. Langley and made public King's mistake. By the time he finally made the summit of Mt. Whitney, King found he had been beaten to the top by a group of fisherman from nearby Lone Pine in the summer of 1873.

These climbers christened the mountain "Fishermen's Peak." The local paper heralded their ascent of the highest peak in the land, stating: "Some people are now trying to take the credit of their being the first there away from them, but they won't succeed. Professor Whitney's agent [Clarence King] has just returned from the mountain and finds fault with the people here for their lack of romance in calling it 'Fishermen's Peak.' Ain't it as romantic as Whitney? The fishermen who found it looked mighty romantic on their return to Soda Springs. Wonder who that old earthquake sharp thinks is running the country, anyhow?"

Later that year, John Muir made an ascent of the north side of the peak. His route, known as the Mountaineer's Route, climbs a steep east-facing gully and finishes up exposed ledges on the north face to the summit. Muir described his route: "A fine climb: strenuous, but not too difficult; but soft, succulent people should go the mule way (the Fishermen's Route)." Norman Clyde made the second ascent almost sixty years later, unaware of Muir's ascent. This route is now used as the descent for the climbs on Keeler Needle and the east face of Mt. Whitney.

Approaches

The Mt. Whitney Road travels west from Lone Pine to Whitney Portal. The Horseshoe Meadows road branches off the Mt. Whitney Road and leads to the trailhead for Cottonwood Lakes. This trail leads through the Cottonwood Lakes basin and over New Army Pass. A cross-country traverse from New Army Pass leads into the Rock Creek drainage and the Miter Basin.

The trailhead for the main group of peaks in this area is located at Whitney Portal. The Meysan Lakes trail begins from the summer cabins just south of the road end, and accesses Lone Pine Peak. The main Whitney trail heads over Trail Crest to join the John Muir Trail and reach the summit of Mt. Whitney, as well as providing access to Mt. McAdie and Mt. Chamberlin.

The climber's trail up the north fork of Lone Pine Creek encounters exposed ledges, slabs, talus and brush as it ascends to Upper Boy Scout Lake at the foot of Mt. Russell. The drainage to the south is followed to Iceberg Lake and East Face Lake (not marked on the map) at the base of Keeler Needle and the East Face of Whitney. The Russell-Carillon Col (Class 2-3), above Upper Boy Scout Lake, provides access to Mt. Carl Heller, as well as a number of other routes along the crest.

Karl Bird on the East Face of Mt. Whitney   Bela Vadasz

Mt. LeConte (13,960 ft.)
Southwest Ridge
II 5.6

F.A. Galen Rowell; August, 1970
Mt. Whitney Area Map: Page 22
USGS Quad Maps: Mt. Whitney, Mount Langley, Cirque Peak and Johnson Peak

Norman Clyde described Mt. LeConte: "If it is impressive when seen from the Owens Valley, it is much more so when seen from nearby peaks across deep cirques which greatly enhance the striking appearance of this giant pinnacle that rises sheer for hundreds of feet."

The summit of Mt. LeConte is the tallest spire on the ridge of striking Corcoran pinnacles. The peak is named for Joseph LeConte (1823-1901), a professor of geology at the University of California at Berkeley in the late 1800s. LeConte accompanied a number of his students on a University field excursion to Yosemite Valley in 1870, where he met John Muir. Impressed by Muir's geologic observations, LeConte published several articles in agreement with Muir's theories of Sierra glaciation.

In 1900, LeConte accompanied his son and his wife Helen Gompertz-LeConte on a long trip into the Kings Canyon backcountry. He wrote, "I enjoyed intensely every step of the journey, and in some parts, as we approached the summit [of Kearsarge Pass], the exhilaration of mind was such as I had not felt for ten years."

The following year LeConte and his family were participants on the Sierra Club's first Annual Outing. As the group prepared to leave Yosemite Valley for the hike up to Tuolumne Meadows, the elder LeConte suffered a heart attack and passed away. He was 78 at the time.

Route:
From Horseshoe Meadows, take the New Army Pass trail to the pass and then head cross country into the upper reaches of the Rock Creek drainage. From Iridescent Lake, take the main gully that leads to the crest, just north of the main summit tower of Mt. Corcoran. Follow the ridge crest north over towers, into notches and around gendarmes, to the final steep climb up the summit tower of Mt. LeConte.

Descent:
Work around the west side of the peak to the northwest ridge. This is followed down a short steep step into the broad gully leading back down to Iridescent Lake.

Mt. LeConte rising over Iridescent Lake   John Moynier

Mt. McAdie (13,760+ ft.)
East Ridge
Class 3

F.A. Norman Clyde, 1922
Mt. Whitney Area Map: Page 22
USGS Quad Maps: Mt. Whitney and Mt. Langley

Mt. McAdie is the prominent triple-summitted peak rising above Consultation Lake near the Mt. Whitney trail. It is named for Alexander McAdie, head of the U.S. Weather Bureau in San Francisco and a professor of meteorology at Harvard from 1913 to 1931. James Edward Church wrote to McAdie in 1905, informing him of the naming: "Our party had the honor of naming the peak directly south of Lone Pine Pass (now called Whitney Pass) 'Mt. McAdie,' to commemorate your services in advancing the science of climatology."

Church was a professor of the classics at the University of Nevada at Reno in the early part of this century. He was also an avid mountaineer, making ascents of many Sierra peaks, especially in winter. A lifelong adventurer, Church climbed peaks all over the world. He is perhaps best known as the "Father of the Snow Survey," for the invention of a simple snow-coring device that allowed snow surveyors to accurately measure the water content of the snowpack. His invention, and the system that correlated the data, are still in use today.

Most ascents of the peak are made from Arc Pass to the east. A gully leading to the notch between the main summits is the easiest route, but it is deceptively steep and greatly exposed above cliffs. To avoid this obstacle, most parties climb nearly to the summit of the middle peak before crossing to the base of the main summit.

Route:
Take the trail from Whitney Portal to Consultation Lake. The higher, north summit can seen from the lake, but the route is hidden. From the lake, scramble south up talus and sand to Arc Pass (Class 2). Climb west from the pass almost to the summit of the middle peak, passing through keyholes and over slabs, before climbing down into the notch between the two peaks. From the notch, Class-3 ledges lead to the exposed west ridge, which is followed over blocks to the summit.

Descent:
Retrace your steps.

Mt. McAdie from Arc Pass

Gary Guenther

Mt. Chamberlin (13,169 ft.)
North Face
V 5.10a A2

F.A. Claude Fiddler and Bob Harrington;
August, 1983
Mt. Whitney Area Map: Page 22
USGS Quad Maps: Mt. Whitney and Cirque Peak

This fine, glacially carved peak is named after Thomas Crowder Chamberlin (1843-1928), the prominent glacial geologist of his day. The impressive north face of this peak is one of the grand walls of the Sierra. Attractive pillars are found on both sides of this wall. In 1979, Mike Farrell and Galen Rowell climbed a chimney system (V 5.10) up the right-hand pillar.

Bob Harrington repeated this route, and was impressed by the wall to the left. Harrington returned to the wall with Claude Fiddler (who had first heard of the wall from Dave Bircheff years before) and climbed a route up the center of the north face.

Harrington had difficulty singling out which route is more classic: "Our route is undoubtedly more spectacular and harder, and takes a better line up the peak, but somehow the all-free nature of the Rowell-Farrell route has something in its favor; although a party of strong crack climbers should be able to free climb our route."

The pillar to the left of the north face had first been attempted by Dave Nettle. Andy deKlerk and Julie Brugger completed the route in the summer of 1992. They wrote, "The north face of Chamberlin is a real gem, and the rock is exceptional." The route offers consistently difficult climbing on very steep rock.

Route:
Take the Mt. Whitney Trail from Whitney Portal and follow it up the switchbacks to near Trail Crest. Discovery Pass is just southeast of Discovery Pinnacle, and provides access to the Crabtree Lakes basin. From the largest Crabtree Lake, the route can be seen as a series of prominent left-facing corners leading up the center of the wall, just left of the deep chimney separating the north pillar from the north face. A crack system (5.9) leads to a slab apron at about one-third height. The route continues into the huge, left-facing corner that splits the center of the wall. Five pitches up difficult cracks (some 5.10) lead into the corner. The wide cracks above require some aid (A1) through a series of roofs. Two hundred feet of easy ground leads to the summit ridge.

Alternative Routes:
The pillar to the left (East Pillar) is rated V 5.11a, with 13 pitches of interesting climbing on good rock (F.A. deKlerk and Brugger; Sept, 1992). The route begins with a left-leaning flake above a cairn and climbs through a difficult roof. Higher, follow a right-facing corner on the right side of the pillar, with a sustained 5.11a finger crack forming the crux on the tenth pitch (see topo).

The pillar to the right was climbed by Galen Rowell and Mike Farrell in July, 1979. It is rated V 5.10 and is a varied 13-pitch route up mostly moderate cracks, flakes and chimneys on the right side of the pillar.

Descent:
Head west down a loose gully (Class 2) toward Crabtree Meadow and Crabtree Creek.

The north face of Mt. Chamberlin

Peter Fisher

Mt. Chamberlin
left - East Pillar – V 5.11a
right - North Face – V 5.10a A2

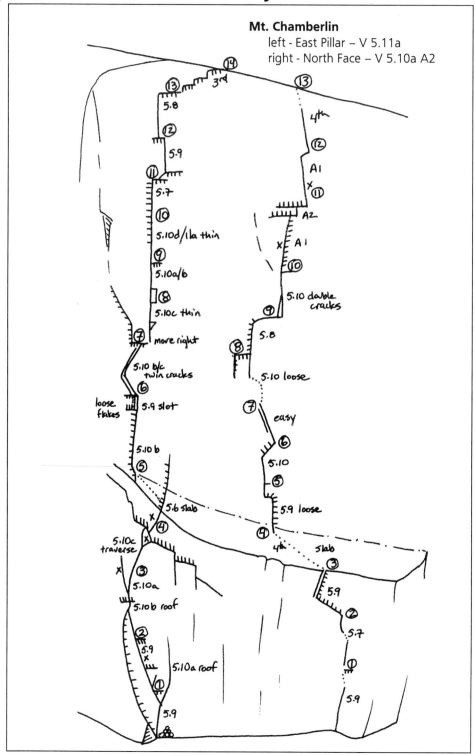

Climbing on Lone Pine Peak   Chris Keith

Mt. Whitney Area

Lone Pine Peak (12,944 ft.)
North Ridge
III 5.4

F.A. Ray Van Aken and Art Lembeck, September, 1952
Mt. Whitney Area Map: Page 22
USGS Quad Map: Mt. Langley

This spectacular granite peak possesses a number of fine climbs. The south side of the peak is a massive wall featuring long routes. On the east side of the peak, there are two prominent ridges that rise more than 4,500 ft. to the summit. The east ridge was first climbed by Dave Krueger, solo, in the early 1980s.

The north ridge is less difficult. Chris Keith described a recent ascent: "Finding easy ground again (high on the ridge), we unroped and followed the top of the ridge, at times straddling the blade of granite, at times hand-traversing the edge of the mountain. At the notch, the rope played out for four more pitches, generally staying to the right of the ridge. As soon as we stood on the summit, snow began to fall. The squall was minor, but it added a dramatic lighting to an already impressive alpine scene."

Route:
From Whitney Portal, take the Meysan Lakes trail to just below Lower Meysan Lake. The approach gully is hidden until you pass it on the trail. Follow the gully to the top of the ridge and scramble to a flat spot at the base of the steep upper portion of the ridge. The first part of the climb is mostly a Class 3 and 4 traverse along the crest to the base of the first step.

Three pitches of easy fifth-class climbing lead up (sometimes straddling) and along a spectacular fin to a deep notch on the level ridge crest. Moderate fifth-class climbing leads out of the notch and onto the massive second step. From there, four pitches of progressively easier climbing lead up the right side of the ridge to the summit.

Descent:
Walk out the west ridge toward the crest until you are even with the highest Meysan Lake. Class 2 and 3 talus slopes lead down into the basin and the trail.

Lone Pine Peak from the Alabama Hills

Keeler Needle (14,000+ ft.)
East Face
V 5.10+

F.A. Warren Harding, Glen Denny, Rob McKnight and Desert Frank; July, 1960
F.F.A. Galen Rowell, Chris Vandiver and Gordon Wiltsie; August, 1976
Mt. Whitney Area Map: Page 22
USGS Quad Maps: Mt. Whitney and Mt. Langley

Keeler Needle is a stunning satellite peak on the Mt. Whitney massif. Warren Harding made the first ascent two years after making the historic ascent of the Nose route on Yosemite's El Capitan. The Keeler route, along with his route on Mt. Conness, marked the introduction of difficult big wall climbing in the High Sierra.

The route begins just right of the couloir between Keeler and Day Needles, and follows a prominent crack system up the left side of the face. Although the route has been done in a long day, many climbers find the prospect of climbing 5.10 offwidths at 14,000 feet challenging enough, choosing instead to break up the ascent.

On an early attempt of the route, Rick Ridgway and Michael Graber made the mistake of camping too near the base of the tower. They were awakened very early in the morning by a large boulder, which fell from the Day-Keeler Couloir and smashed into the ice cone at the base of the couloir, showering their bivy with ice chunks.

Route:

From Whitney Portal, follow the north fork of Lone Pine Creek to East Face Lake and then scramble up to the base of the needle. A slabby area at the start leads to a roof (5.10) with a wide crack. Continue past a horn through a gritty overhang (5.9+) with parallel cracks, then traverse right to a left-facing corner. Another strenuous wide crack through a roof (5.10) leads to a comfortable stance on a ledge. Moderate climbing above leads to a small stance at the base of a right-facing reddish dihedral.

Fine climbing up the dihedral (5.9) finishes on a square-cut ledge. A short pitch up a corner leads to a sloping ledge at the base of the crux (5.10+) offwidth/chimney. Strenuous climbing leads past a few old bolts to a chockstone. Above, a chimney (5.7) eventually reaches a large ledge via a crack-and-flake system (loose 5.8) at the base of a steep headwall. Although it is possible to escape left here, the route makes a devious traverse up and right on steep flakes (5.7+) to a spectacular ledge on the prow. Finish up steep cracks (5.8) and fourth-class blocks.

Descent:

Continue to the summit of Mt. Whitney and take the Mountaineer's Route down ledges on the north face to the prominent east-facing gully that leads back to Iceberg Lake. Alternately you can follow the summit trail back to Whitney Portal.

Keeler Needle on the right   Chris Falkenstein

Mt. Whitney Area

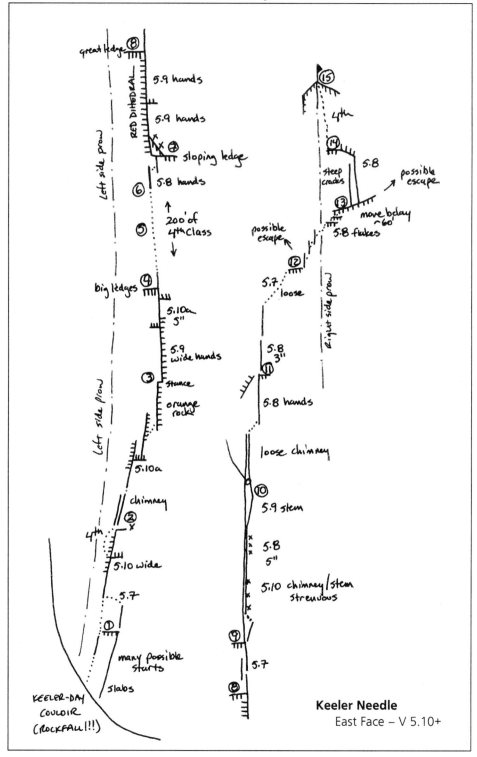

great ledge ⑧

5.9 hands

RED DIHEDRAL

5.9 hands

⑦ sloping ledge

⑥ 5.8 hands

↑
200' of
4th Class
↓

big ledges ④

5.10a
5"

5.9
wide hands

③ stance

orange
rock

5.10a

chimney

②
4th
5.10 wide

5.7

①
many possible
starts

slabs

KEELER-DAY
COULOIR
(ROCKFALL!!!)

Left side prow

Left side prow

⑤

⑮
4th

⑭ 5.8

steep
cracks
possible
escape

⑬ move belay
~60'
5.8 flakes

possible
escape

⑫ 5.7
loose

5.8
3"
⑪

5.8 hands

loose chimney

⑩
5.9 stem

5.8
5"

5.10 chimney/stem
strenuous

⑨
5.7

⑧

Right side prow

Keeler Needle
East Face – V 5.10+

Climbers on East Buttress of Mt. Whitney

Mt. Whitney (14,494 ft.)
East Face
III 5.6

F.A. Robert Underhill, Jules Eichorn, Glen Dawson and Norman Clyde; August, 1931
Mt. Whitney Area Map: Page 22
USGS Quad Maps: Mt. Whitney and Mt. Langley

Mt. Whitney has the distinction of being the highest peak in the contiguous United States. It was named by Clarence King in honor of the leader of the California Geological Survey: Josiah Dwight Whitney. Whitney was a professor of geology at Harvard from 1865 to 1896, and served as the state geologist of California from 1860 to 1874.

The first ascent of the east face was made during Dr. Robert Underhill's visit to the High Sierra in 1931. Underhill was an experienced climber who had made a number of impressive ascents in the Tetons and Canadian Rockies. Upon arriving at the Sierra Club camp in the Ritter Range, he instructed young climbers like Glen Dawson and Jules Eichorn in the use of proper roped belays. The culmination of the trip was an attempt on the east face of Mt. Whitney.

Underhill later described their climb: "At Francis Farquhar's invitation and under his expert arrangement of program, I was enjoying a first climbing season in the High Sierra. The unclimbed east face of Mt. Whitney had been in our minds from the start . . . As we contemplated our mountain, I felt that it would be a mighty hard nut to crack . . . We had rather grown into the feeling in the Palisades that every Sierra mountain wall could be climbed if only one tackled it properly, but I began to doubt this position . . . Suddenly I saw what seemed to be a just possible route and simultaneously (Glen) Dawson and (Jules) Eichorn exclaimed to the same effect. It turned out we all had exactly the same thing in mind.

"The route we followed was exactly that which we had mapped out originally . . . The rock work was not really difficult; there is, I should say, less than a thousand feet of it from the roping-up to the unroping place. The beauty of the climb in general lies chiefly in its unexpected possibility, up the apparent precipice, and in the intimate contact it affords with the features that lend Mt. Whitney its real impressiveness."

Route:
From Whitney Portal, follow the north fork of Lone Pine Creek to Iceberg Lake. From the lake, ascend to the notch behind the First Tower, high above the true east face. From the notch, make the delicate Tower Traverse across the south face of the Second Tower. A short chimney leads to moderate climbing up the Washboard. Climb the left wall, then traverse across to the start of the aptly named Fresh-Air Traverse (5.4). Fixed pitons protect this dramatically exposed step, which is followed by a scramble up a short chimney. Above this, the rubble-strewn ledges of the Giant Staircase end in a wide crack up the left side of an alcove. Easier ground above leads up and over blocks to the summit.

Descent:
Follow the Mountaineer's Route down ledges on the north face to the prominent east-facing gully that leads to Iceberg Lake.

The east face and east buttress of Mt. Whitney

John Moynier

Mt. Whitney (14,494 ft.)
East Buttress
III 5.8

F.A. Glen Dawson, Bob Brinton, Richard Jones, Howard Koster and Muir Dawson
– September, 1937

Mt. Whitney Area Map: Page 22
USGS Quad Maps: Mt. Whitney and Mt. Langley

On an ascent of the east face of Mt. Whitney, Glen Dawson admired a route on the east buttress. This route became Dawson's favorite climb in the High Sierra, and he was to repeat it many times. Many climbers prefer the east buttress route because it offers a more direct line, less rockfall and is less crowded.

There are a number of ways to go on the buttress. Dawson's team tried to find the line of least resistance. They called their climb the "Sunshine-PeeWee" route for the major features on the buttress. This is not to say he was incapable of climbing a more direct route up the buttress. In fact, he is credited with making the hardest climb in the country prior to World War II, the Mechanics Route (5.8) at Tahquitz Rock.

The year after the ascent, a group of Sierra Club climbers made the long trek up the Whitney trail to the base of the east face. Ruth Dyar Mendenhall was a member of the group. She recalled: "Over Labor Day that year, eleven RCS members, nine men and two women, made the strenuous backpack (largely cross-country) over Pinnacle Pass to camp at East Face Lake. The next day we all climbed Mt. Whitney's East Face by the "Sunshine-PeeWee" route (now more decorously referred to as the "East Buttress"). The difficulty of the pack-in made an even more lasting impresssion on my mind than the climb itself."

Route:
From Whitney Portal, follow the north fork of Lone Pine Creek to Iceberg Lake. From the lake, climb to the notch behind the First Tower. The direct route ascends a left-facing corner (5.8) for two pitches to the top of the Second Tower. From the notch, climb a beautiful but poorly protected pitch (5.7) up the crest of the arête. A right-facing corner (5.7) is followed by flakes and cracks (5.6). Easy climbing through a loose slabby area is followed by discontinuous cracks and flakes (5.5). Stay just right of the huge, detached Pee Wee pillar, finishing on its top. Face climbing leads to a right-facing corner (5.7) near the top of the buttress, where 300 feet of third-class climbing leads over blocks to the summit.

Descent:
Follow the Mountaineer's Route down ledges on the north face to the prominent east-facing gully that leads down to Iceberg Lake.

Mt. Whitney Area

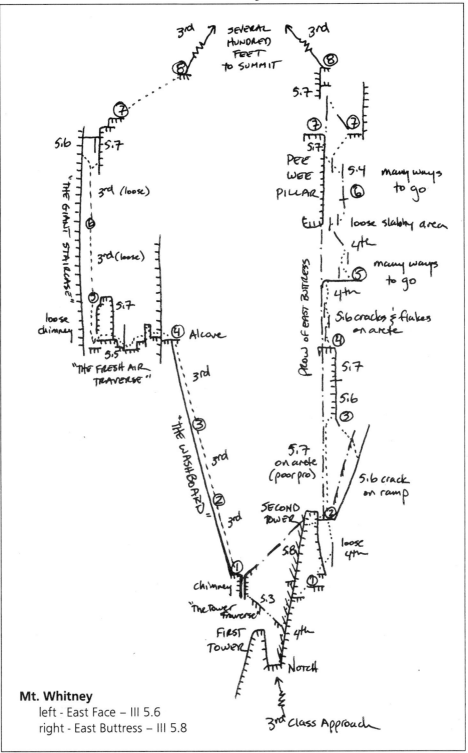

Mt. Whitney
left - East Face – III 5.6
right - East Buttress – III 5.8

Mt. Russell (14,086 ft.)
East Ridge
Class 3

F.A. Norman Clyde, June 1926
Mt. Whitney Area Map: Page 22
USGS Quad Maps: Mt. Whitney and Mt. Langley

Mount Russell is named for Israel Cook Russell (1852-1906), who was a geologist with the Wheeler Survey party and the USGS. In the summer of 1883, he made intensive studies of the glaciers on Mt. Lyell and Mt. Dana with Grove Karl Gilbert.

Norman Clyde made the first ascent of the peak (via the east ridge) 53 years after the first ascent of Mount Whitney. This fine ridge offers tremendous exposure on excellent granite. Clyde described his climb: "The route ahead looked formidable – at times impossible. To the south the wall dropped abruptly; to the north after descending at a steep angle for a few feet, it fell away sheer. Difficult as it seemed from a distance, nevertheless the way opened up as I progressed. There were always enough protuberances and crevices to afford secure handholds and footholds."

As a technical alternative, the southeast arête offers fine climbing in a spectacular setting. On the first ascent, Bob Harrington described one section of the climb as: "The most classic arête pitch I've ever done!"

Route:
From Whitney Portal follow the north fork of Lone Pine Creek to Upper Boy Scout Lake. Scree slopes lead to the Russell-Carillon Col. From the saddle, the knife-edged east arête is followed on top of its crest to the lower east summit. Any difficulties are passed on the north side of the arête. A short, exposed traverse along the ridge leads to the higher west summit.

Alternative Routes:
From the lake, ascend scree to the rightmost of two arêtes that merge with the southeast face (III 5.10; F.A. Bob Harrington, Vern Clevenger and Claude Fiddler; July, 1984). Follow flakes and cracks up the arête to a lieback and finger crack on the knife-edged crest. Wind around towers to a drop-off into a notch where the arête merges with the face. Easier climbing above leads to the east ridge.

Descent:
Retrace your steps down the east ridge.

The East Ridge of Mt. Russell

Gary Guenther

Mt. Russell (14,086 ft.)
Fishhook Arête
III 5.9

F.A. Gary Colliver and John Cleare, June 1974
Mt. Whitney Area Map: Page 22
USGS Quad Maps: Mt. Whitney and Mt. Langley

This peak would be a classic in any range, with a number of beautiful routes with excellent exposed climbing, topping out on a great summit. From the summit of Mt. Whitney, an obvious "J"-shaped, curving arête can be seen dropping from the west summit of Mt. Russell. This is the Fishhook Arête, perhaps the finest route on the peak.

John Cleare, a British climber and writer of mountaineering literature, had climbed with Yosemite local Gary Colliver on Mt. Everest in 1971. Colliver has been a guide and climbing ranger in Yosemite Park for nearly thirty years. After many trips in this area, Colliver recommended this route to Cleare as a fine chance for a first ascent. Colliver returned later that summer with TM Herbert and Don Lauria to climb the massive southwest buttress (III 5.8).

Route:
From Whitney Portal, follow the north fork of Lone Pine Creek to Iceberg Lake. From the lake, cross over the Whitney-Russell col and drop down to the small tarn near the base of the south face of Mt. Russell. Gain the toe of the arête and follow it (some 5.8) to the base of a steep headwall. Traverse left onto the northwest face of the arête for two pitches (5.8) to avoid the headwall, before returning to the arête at a prominent notch. The next pitch offers stimulating face climbing (5.8+) on the prow of the arête. Above, four moderate pitches lead to the top.

Descent:
Traverse to the east summit and drop down a loose chimney (Class 3-4) at the junction with the south ridge onto talus slopes on the south side of the peak.

The Fishhook Arête and south buttress of Mt. Russell Chris Falkenstein

Mt. Russell (14,086 ft.)
Mithral Dihedral
III 5.9

F.A. Alan Bartlett and Alan Roberts; July, 1976
Mt. Whitney Area Map: Page 22
USGS Quad Maps: Mt. Whitney and Mt. Langley

The steep walls of Mt. Russell's south face are cut by several corner-and-crack systems, all on excellent granite. The most striking line on the face follows a huge left-facing corner known as the Mithral Dihedral. The source of this route's name comes from J.R.R. Tolkein's classic Lord of the Rings trilogy.

Alan Bartlett recalled this as being his first introduction to backcountry climbing. "The route was Alan Robert's idea," he said. "I thought it was a lot of hiking to do for a climb, but the route really opened my eyes to the possibilities of the high country." Bartlett returned to Mt. Russell in September, 1979 with Allan Pietrasanta and climbed the steep face to right (Pilgrimage, III 5.9) and the slender corner to the left of the Mithral route (Bloody Corner, III 5.10).

Route:
From Whitney Portal, follow the north fork of Lone Pine Creek to Iceberg Lake and cross the Whitney-Russell Col. The Mithral Dihedral is the obvious, huge left-facing corner rising above the toe of the Fishhook Arête. Ascend a few hundred feet of broken ledges to the base of the corner. Two pitches of moderate climbing (5.6) lead up the lower corner, passing a sandy ledge. Parallel cracks split the clean face above and left, but the route stays in the corner itself (5.9) for two more fine pitches to the top of the southwest buttress. From here, the west arête (Class 4) is followed to the west summit.

Alternate Route:
To the left of the Mithral Dihedral is another shallow, left-facing corner system which is capped by a small roof. This is the Bloody Corner (III 5.10). This route offers excellent, moderately difficult climbing in a spectacular location.

Descent:
Traverse to the east summit and drop down a loose chimney (Class 3-4) that is at the junction with the south ridge, then head down talus slopes on the south side of the peak.

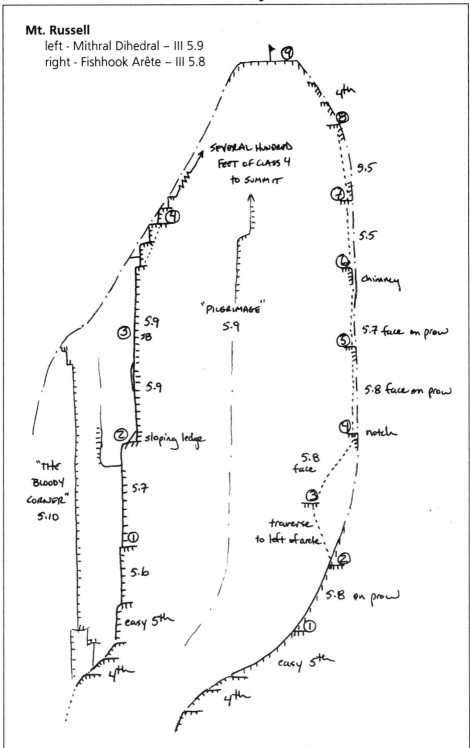

Mt. Russell
 left - Mithral Dihedral – III 5.9
 right - Fishhook Arête – III 5.8

⑨

4th

⑧

5.5

⑦

5.5

④

⑥

chimney

SEVERAL HUNDRED
FEET OF CLASS 4
to SUMMIT

5.7 face on prow

⑤

"PILGRIMAGE"
5.9

③ 5.9
JB

5.8 face on prow

5.9

④ notch

② sloping ledge

5.8
face

"THE
BLOODY
CORNER"
5.10

5.7

③

traverse
to left of arete

①

②

5.6

5.8 on prow

easy 5th

①

4th

easy 5th

4th

Mt. Carl Heller (13,211 ft.)
East Arête
Class 3

F.A. Carl Heller and Al Green; August, 1966
Mt. Whitney Area Map: Page 22
USGS Quad Maps: Mt. Langley, Mt. Whitney, Mt. Williamson, and Manzanar

This attractive arête offers fine climbing in a remote setting. Al Green and other members of the China Lake Mountain Rescue Group have unofficially named this peak (formerly known as Vacation Peak) in honor of Carl Heller, the founder of their search and rescue team. Green writes: "All of us feel that Mt. Heller's east ridge is one of the best Class 3 climbs in the range." Carl Heller had attempted this climb many times before succeeding in making the first ascent.

Heller and Al Green were members of the "Occasional Peaks Gang," a group making hundreds of ascents throughout the range, often in winter. Bob Rockwell (also a member of the Gang), related a story about a traverse he did in the Palisades with Carl and others from the group. As they made their way from Thunderbolt Peak to North Palisade, Rockwell found himself separated from the group. The climbing was not difficult, and he felt comfortable climbing unroped.

Rounding a corner, Rockwell was suddenly confronted with a short, serious section of rock. His feeling of security quickly gave way to fear. Loose rock added to his discomfort and Rockwell knew he was about to fall to his death. Desperate, he called out, "Carl?" Five feet above him and lowering a rope, Heller replied, "Yes, Bob?" Heller's mountaineer's "sixth sense" made him a universally admired partner and a very successful search and rescue leader.

On a winter attempt of Mt. Sill in 1983, Heller felt unusually weak and was forced to abandon the climb. He was diagnosed with terminal cancer and died a year later at the age of 62.

Route:
From Whitney Portal, follow the north fork of Lone Pine Creek to Upper Boy Scout Lake. Climb up steep scree to the Russell-Carillon Col (Class 2-3), and descend past Tulainyo Lake to Wallace Lake. From the lake, cross over Vacation Pass (Class 2-3), on the north side of the peak, and drop down to the lake on the northeastern end of the ridge. From here, the route follows the crest of the knife-edge ridge over steps (Class 3) to the summit.

Alternative Routes:
The west face of the peak has two distinct ribs dropping from the twin summits. Both have been climbed. Of the two, the right-hand rib is the more enjoyable climb (II 5.7). The first ascent was made by Claude Fiddler and Vern Clevenger in September, 1979.

Descent:
Descend the south ridge (Class 3-4) until easier terrain can be followed down the west face.

The East Arête of Mt. Carl Heller   John Moynier

Mt. Williamson Area

Mt. Williamson is the second tallest peak in the Sierra and is known for its massive size. Located a mile east of the crest, Mt. Williamson rises more than 9,000 feet from the Owens Valley floor. At the foot of Mt. Williamson lie the ruins of the Manzanar Relocation Camp, where many Japanese-American citizens were detained during World War II.

The ascent of Mt. Tyndall was first accomplished in 1864 by Clarence King and Richard Cotter. Mt. Williamson was first climbed in 1884 by W. L. Hunter and C. Mulholland. Ascending the brushy George Creek drainage, their climb involved a trailless gain of over 10,000 feet from the town of Independence to the summit. Bolton and Lucy Brown made the first ascent of the west face of the peak in 1896.

The Kings-Kern Divide, connecting the Sierra Crest with the Great Western Divide to the west, is a spectacular and rugged area. The divide runs east to west and forms the border between Kings Canyon and Sequoia National Parks. The John Muir Trail originally passed over Shepherd and Junction Passes to avoid this obstacle, until the trail over Forester Pass was completed in 1932.

The divide was first crossed by Clarence King and Richard Cotter in 1864 on their way to climb Mt. Tyndall. The story of this crossing is told in King's *Mountaineering in the Sierra Nevada*. At one point, the pair was forced to make a committing rappel. Upon retrieving the rope, they were cut off from retreat. King writes: "'We're in for it now King,' remarked my comrade, as he looked aloft and then down; but our blood was up, and danger added only an exhilarating thrill to the nerves."

Approaches

The small town of Independence marks the jump-off point for this area. Although basic amenities can be found here, there is not much in the way of mountaineering supplies. From the blinking yellow light in the center of town, follow the Onion Valley road west toward the crest. After about 5 miles, the dirt Foothill Road heads south to the Symmes Creek/Shepherd Pass trailhead. The main road continues to the road end at Onion Valley.

To reach the Symmes Creek trailhead, follow the signs to the newly relocated trailhead. The trail follows the creekbed, then heads south and crosses a saddle into the Shepherd Creek drainage. This area is home to one of the Sierra's bighorn sheep herds. As a result, access is limited for much of the year. Contact the Inyo National Forest offices for information on these closures.

Mt. Williamson Area

To reach the south side of the Kings-Kern Divide, continue west on the Shepherd Pass Trail to its junction with the John Muir Trail and the Lake South America Trail. The north side of the divide may be reached from the road end at Onion Valley. The Kearsarge Pass Trail leads past Bullfrog Lake into the Bubbs Creek drainage at Vidette Meadow. The John Muir Trail can be followed south to Center Basin and Center Peak, as well as to Forester Pass and Junction Peak. It is also possible to reach Center Basin and the John Muir Trail from Onion Valley via the cross-country route over University Col. This Class 2-3 pass is just south of University Peak and involves steep scree and talus. To reach East Lake, continue down Bubbs Creek to Junction Meadow, where a trail leads south to East Lake and Lake Reflection. From Lake Reflection, it is possible to climb over Lucy's Foot Pass (Class 3) to the south, or Harrison Pass (Class 3), to the southeast to access the upper Kern Basin.

Dean Hobbs on the north rib of Mt. Williamson   Andy Selter

Mt. Williamson (14,375 ft.)
North Arête
III 5.4

F.A. Claude Fiddler and Jim Keating; July, 1984
Mt. Williamson Area Map: Page 52
USGS Quad Maps: Mt. Williamson and Manzanar

Mt. Williamson is the second highest peak in California. It was named after Major R.S. Williamson (1824-1882), a topographer with the U.S. Corps of Engineers. In 1853, Williamson was given the task of finding a potential rail route through the southern Sierra. After exploring the Walker Pass area, he reported it unsuitable and the federal government dropped the project.

The north side of Mt. Williamson is a dramatic wall dominating the view for travelers heading south from Big Pine to Independence on Highway 395. The north arête can be seen dropping over 3,000 feet from Williamson's West Horn into Williamson Creek. The first-ascent team was inspired by Steve Roper's 1976 guidebook description of the neighboring North Rib climb, which was described as being to the right of a long, twisting ridge.

Claude Fiddler and Jim Keating had viewed this "long, twisting ridge" on previous trips into the area and were intrigued. Their route proved an interesting climb on excellent rock. Midway up the ridge is a steep tower; above this, the ridge narrows and ends on the summit of the West Horn.

Route:
From the Symmes Creek Trailhead, follow the trail over Shepherd Pass into Williamson Bowl. The Williamson Creek drainage is followed down to the base of the north face. The lower portion of the rib is accessed from the west side. Wander up the moderate ridge, aiming for a prominent tower high on the route. Pass the tower on the left side and continue up the narrow ridge as it steepens to the summit of the West Horn.

Alternative Routes:
The north rib (IV 5.7, F.A. Lito Tejada-Flores and Edgar Boyles; July, 1972) offers slightly more technical climbing, and ends on the summit plateau.

Descent:
From the summit of the West Horn, downclimb or rappel onto the summit plateau. A short Class 3 headwall at the top of the west face leads down a gully to the lakes in Williamson Bowl.

Vern Clevenger

The north face of Mt. Williamson

Mt. Tyndall (14,018 ft.)
North Rib
Class 3

F.A. Clarence King and Richard Cotter; July, 1864
Mt. Williamson Area Map: Page 52
USGS Quad Maps: Mt. Williamson and Manzanar

Clarence King and Dick Cotter made the first ascent of this peak in the summer of 1864 while working on the Whitney Survey. They named the peak for John Tyndall, a noted British scientist and alpine explorer. In his book, Mountaineering in the Sierra Nevada, *King presented an epic account of their ascent: "If Nature had intended to secure the summit from all assailants, she could not have planned her defenses better; for the smooth, granite wall which rose above the snow slope continued, apparently quite round the peak and we looked in great anxiety to see if there was not one place where it might be climbed . . .*

"At last I reached the top and with the greatest of caution, wormed my body over the brink, and rolling out upon the smooth surface of the granite, looked over and watched Cotter make his climb.. We now had an easy slope to the summit, and hurried over rocks and ice, reaching the crest at exactly twelve o'clock. I rang my hammer upon the topmost rock; we grasped hands, and I reverently named the peak Mount Tyndall."

King's romanticized account may have been an exaggeration. In his official report he stated, "The summit was reached, without serious difficulty, after some risky climbing." Chris Keith recently climbed the peak and said, "The route is so obvious from Shepherd's Pass that it hardly needs any description other than get on the rib and follow it to the ridge, turn left and head for the top."

Route:
From the Symmes Creek trailhead, follow the trail over Shepherd Pass to the base of the north face. A shallow rib splits the face. Climb this to the top of the face, and then follow the knife-edge ridge (Class 3) to the summit.

Descent:
Retrace your steps.

Mt. Tyndall and the Great Western Divide

Junction Peak (13,888 ft.)
South Ridge
Class 3

F.A. E.B. Copeland and E.N. Anderson; August, 1899
Mt. Williamson Area Map: Page 52
USGS Quad Maps: Mt. Williamson and Manzanar

In 1896, Joseph N. LeConte named this Junction Peak due to its prominent location at the junction of the Sierra Crest and the Kings-Kern Divide. E.B. Copeland and E.N. Anderson visited the Kings-Kern Divide and made the first ascent of the peak in August 8, 1899, placing Sierra Club Cylinder No. 36 on the summit.

The first-ascent party approached Junction Peak from their camp at East Lake. After crossing the Kings-Kern Divide at Harrison Pass, they headed east and climbed the south summit of Mt. Stanford (Gregory's Monument). They then descended to the southeast and climbed to the summit of Diamond Mesa. An exposed section of knife-edged ridge led to the top of Junction Peak.

Copeland wrote: "The peak itself, like Stanford and Ericsson, is a high and less comfortable knife-edge. The view cannot be rivalled by that from any neighboring mountain, including as it does the basins of the Kings and Kern, with the Inyo Valley, the picture of depth . . . "

Route:
From the trailhead at Symmes Creek, follow the trail over Shepherd Pass to the southern end of the Diamond Mesa. Climb onto the mesa and cross it to the south ridge of the peak. The final hundred yards climb the crest of the knife-edged ridge (Class 3) to a point just below the summit. Traverse around the west side and climb to the top.

Descent:
Retrace the route.

John Moynier

Junction Peak and the Diamond Mesa

Mt. Stanford (13,963 ft.)
South Ridge
Class 3

F.A. Bolton C. Brown; August, 1896
Mt. Williamson Area Map: Page 52
USGS Quad Maps: Mt. Williamson and Manzanar

Bolton Coit Brown was a professor of fine arts at Stanford University. In the summer of 1896, he and his wife Lucy made a long trip exploring the headwaters of the Kings River. After crossing Harrison Pass into the Kern drainage, the pair made an ascent of the west face of Mt. Williamson. The next day, they made the first ascent of Mt. Ericsson and then climbed to the southern summit of a prominent peak to the east.

Lucy Brown waited at the south summit of Mt. Stanford (known as Gregory's Monument for the cairn placed by Warren Gregory there in 1894), while her husband traversed the exposed knife-edge to the higher north summit. Brown named the peak Mt. Stanford and later commented: "For some time, Lucy and I had wished to capture a desirable mountain and name it after Stanford University; and so, when somebody left a Sierra Club cylinder down at the Stanford camp, I brought it up and we proposed to plant it."

On the top of the peak, Brown built a monument and "left Club register No. 14, with the name Stanford on it." Three years later, the president of Stanford University, David Starr Jordan stood on the summit and exclaimed, "I have never seen a more magnificent mountain panorama!"

Norman Clyde wrote, "Along the Kings-Kern Divide, slightly to the south of Mt. Brewer, are numbers of lofty peaks, the finest of which is Mt. Stanford. It has twin peaks of almost equal height, the northern one being perhaps a few feet the higher. The most southerly of these can be readily scaled from the upper Kern, but few care to traverse the ragged knife-edge that connects it to the more northerly one."

Route:
From the Symmes Creek trailhead, follow the trail over Shepherd Pass to its junction with the John Muir Trail. Follow the John Muir Trail north, then take the trail to Lake South America. From Lake South America, ascend talus slopes almost to the saddle of Harrison Pass, then continue up to the ridge crest to Gregory's Monument. An exposed knife-edged ridge (Class 3) leads to the north summit. The traverse stays mostly on the eastern side, about 100 feet below the top of the arête.

Descent:
Retrace your steps.

Mt. Stanford above Harrison Pass

John Moynier

Mt. Ericsson (13,608 ft.)
South Ridge
Class 3-4

F.A. Lewis Clark and Carl Jensen; 1936
Mt. Williamson Area Map: Page 52
USGS Quad Maps: Mt. Williamson, Manzanar and Mt. Brewer

The first ascent of Mt. Ericsson was made by Bolton and Lucy Brown in 1896. Bolton Brown later described their experience, "Facing now southeast, we scrambled on, up among the wild pinnacles and at noon gained the summit crag. The view, especially to the south down the long and peculiarly straight canyon of the Kern, and to the southeast to the Williamson-Tyndall group and southwest to the beautiful, snowy Kaweahs, was extremely interesting and wonderfully beautiful. As it seemed we were the first to make this ascent, we built a monument and left a record, naming it in honor of Capt. John Ericsson." Capt. Ericsson was an engineer best known for designing the ironclad ship Monitor, which fought the Merrimac in a famous Civil War naval battle.

Three years later, the Browns returned to the Kings River region with their daughter Eleanor, who traveled mostly by burro and seemed to thoroughly enjoy the trip. For two months, she lived on malted milk, chocolate and trout: "I verily believe she injured the fishing by her consumption of the last," wrote Brown.

The first ascent of the jagged south ridge of Mt. Ericsson was made by Lewis Clark and Carl Jensen, active Sierra Club climbers of the 1930s. The day before climbing Mt. Ericsson, Clark (chairman of the Sierra Club's Mountaineering Committee) and Jensen made the first ascent of nearby Mt. Jordan via its exposed east side. Both ascents were made during the Sierra Club's 1936 Annual Outing to the Upper Kern Basin.

Route:
From the Symmes Creek trailhead, follow the trail over Shepherd Pass to its junction with the John Muir Trail. Follow the John Muir Trail north, then take the trail to Lake South America. The south ridge of Mt. Ericsson extends dramatically into the headwaters of the Kern River. Gain the toe of the jagged south ridge from the east and negotiate gendarmes along the top of the nearly level ridge to the summit tower.

Descent:
Descend from the summit tower over ledges along the east ridge towards Harrison Pass, then head down talus slopes and back to Lake South America.

The South Ridge of Mt. Ericsson

Center Peak (12,760 ft.)
Northwest Arête
II 5.7

F.A. Claude Fiddler and Vern Clevenger; June, 1983
Mt. Williamson Area Map: Page 52
USGS Quad Maps: Kearsarge Peak and Mt. Williamson

Center Peak is at the head of Bubbs Creek, at the western edge of Center Basin. This striking peak was first climbed by C.G. Bradley, who ascended the east face in July, 1898. David Brower and Hervey Voge made the first ascent of the north face in May, 1934, as part of their "Knapsack Survey of Sierra Routes and Records" trip. Beginning with a scramble over University Col on May 20, the pair made ascents of 59 peaks during the course of their ten-week trip. At various points, Norman Clyde met up with Voge and Brower for combined ascents.

Voge and Brower's adventure ended in Matterhorn Canyon where the annual Sierra Club outing took place. Brower remembered climbing Matterhorn Peak by moonlight to "avoid the crowds." He would later lead these "crowds" as Executive Director of the Sierra Club. Brower and Voge last climbed together on the 1939 Sierra Club Knapsack Trip, as Voge never warmed up to the imperial nature of the outings, while Brower was to become the leader of them.

Fifty years later, Claude Fiddler and Vern Clevenger made similarly productive ventures into the range in search of technical climbing challenges. Their route up the northwest arête forms the prominent western skyline of Center Peak when seen from Golden Bear Lake in Center Basin, and offers excellent climbing on relatively sound rock.

Route:
From the roadend at Onion Valley, follow Robinson Creek south past Robinson Lake. Trail-less scrambling over University Col (Class 2-3) leads into Center Basin and Golden Bear Lake. From the lake, head west to the toe of the arête. Fine, moderate crack climbing (5.7) on the arête leads to easier ground as the ridge reaches the summit.

Descent:
Drop down Class-2 talus on the southeast slopes and hike back to the lake.

Center Peak from Center Basin

Claude Fiddler

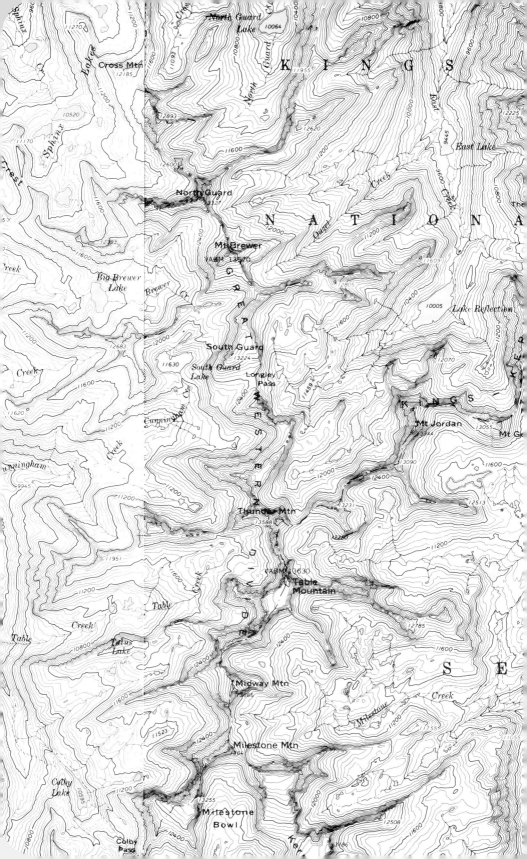

Mt. Brewer Area

From the west, the Great Western Divide appears to be the main crest of the Sierra. In fact, this was the main divide of the range before subsequent uplifting raised the main crest to the east. In the early summer of 1776, Pedro Font viewed these snowy peaks from the Coast Range and described them as "una gran sierra nevada," or a great snowy range.

The Great Western Divide extends from the Kings River Canyon in the north to Florence Peak near Mineral King Valley in the south. This high range forms the divide between the Kern River to the east and the Kings and Kaweah Rivers to the west. The Kings-Kern Divide branches east from Thunder Mountain to meet the main crest at Junction Peak. The Kaweah-Kings Divide joins the Great Western Divide at Triple Divide Peak.

The California Geological Survey, under the field leadership of William Brewer, spent most of the summer of 1864 exploring this region. They, too, believed the divide was the main crest. During their efforts to study and map the area, they climbed a number of peaks, including Mt. Brewer. From the summit of Mt. Brewer, they thought they would look down into the Owens Valley. Clarence King later wrote about their experience: "These snowy crests bounding our view at the eastward we had all along taken to be the summits of the Sierra, and Brewer had supposed himself to be climbing a dominant peak, from which he might look eastward over the Owens Valley and out upon leagues of desert. Instead of this, a vast wall of mountains, lifted still higher than his peak, rose beyond a tremendous canyon which lay like a trough between the two parallel ranks of peaks."

Approaches

To reach the peaks on the Great Western Divide south of the Kings-Kern Divide, take the trail from the Symmes Creek trailhead over Shepherd Pass to the Kern River. This is the same approach used for the Mt. Williamson and Mt. Stanford areas. From the Kern River, follow Milestone Creek into Milestone Basin.

Thunder Mountain, Mt. Brewer and North Guard can be reached by following the trail from Onion Valley over Kearsarge Pass to Junction Meadow in the Bubbs Creek canyon. After crossing Bubbs Creek (difficult in years of high runoff), follow the trail to East Lake. All of these peaks can also be reached by long approaches from west-side trailheads.

Milestone Mountain (13,641 ft.)
West Ridge from the East
Class 3

F.A. Norman Clyde; July, 1927
Mt. Brewer Area Map: Page 68
USGS Quad Maps: Manzanar, Mt. Williamson and Mt. Brewer

The slender summit pinnacle of this appropriately named mountain is a landmark feature on the Great Western Divide. During the Sierra Club's 1912 High Trip, three prominent members of the club (Francis Farquhar, William Colby and Robert Price), made the first ascent of Milestone Mountain via the southwest ridge of the peak.

Francis Farquhar served on the Sierra Club's Board of Directors from 1924 to 1951 and was editor of the Sierra Club Bulletin for most of that time. He also served two terms as President of the club. He is perhaps best known as the author of the excellent book, The History of the Sierra Nevada.

William Colby made his first venture into the High Sierra in 1894, climbing Mt. Dana and Mt. Conness. Colby started the Sierra Club's Annual Outings in 1901 with the support of John Muir, stating: "Without his support, I would not have dared to embark on such an enterprise, with its multiplicity of new and untried problems." Colby led these trips until 1929, and served on the club's Board of Directors for 49 years.

On Colby's first trip to the Sierra, he and two friends made plans to descend the Grand Canyon of the Tuolumne River. They had heard of this trip from John Muir and Robert Price. As they were about to enter the canyon, Price appeared and joined them on the trip to Hetch Hetchy. Price was a charter member of the Sierra Club and also served as President of the club. Colby later wrote of Price: "He was a friend of John Muir and his heart was in the mountains."

Route:
From the Symmes Creek trailhead follow the trail over Shepherd Pass to the Kern River. Cross the river and follow Milestone Creek into Milestone Basin. Steep talus slopes lead to a notch just north of the summit pinnacle. Pass through the notch and contour around the west side of the peak to the west ridge. This is followed to the summit.

Descent:
Retrace your steps.

Robin Ingraham, Jr.

Milestone Mountain from Milestone Basin

Table Mountain (13,630 ft.)
South Face
Class 3-4

F.A. Norman Clyde; July, 1927
Mt. Brewer Area Map: Page 68
USGS Quad Maps: Manzanar, Mt. Williamson and
Mt. Brewer

The nearly level summit of Table Mountain is an amazing place and stretches for acres. This is one of the best examples of the pre-glacial Sierra topography. The plateau drops off in sheer walls in all directions, with no false summits or endless talus walks to the top of this peak.

"It is a great, flat-topped mountain," wrote Norman Clyde, "whose sides in most places seem almost vertical. Although comparatively easy of ascent from the south along narrow shelves and up a rocky chimney, it has been climbed but few times. It can also be surmounted by forcing one's way up a precipitous chimney on its northern face and over several hundred feet of broken, steeply sloping wall above it, but this route is likely to entail a good deal of snow and perhaps some ice-climbing."

Route:
From the Symmes Creek trailhead, take the trail over Shepherd Pass to the Kern River. Follow Milestone Creek into Milestone Basin and scramble to the base of the southern escarpment of the peak. A large brown ledge diagonals up across the face. Wander up the left side of the face and drop onto this ledge to a chute leading to the summit plateau. The top is on the northern side of the plateau.

Descent:
Retrace your steps.

John Moynier

Table Mountain

Thunder Mountain (13,588 ft.)
East Ridge
Class 4

F.A. George Davis; August, 1905
Mt. Brewer Area Map: Page 68
USGS Quad Maps: Manzanar, Mt. Williamson and Mt. Brewer

Thunder Mountain is the pyramid-shaped peak standing at the junction of the Great Western Divide and the Kings-Kern Divide. There are three summit towers connected by a narrow ridge. The northern summit is the highest.

The first ascent of Thunder Mountain was made by cartographer George Davis, who carried his heavy surveyor's equipment to the summit. Davis was an important figure in the history of Sierra mountaineering, and made a number of fine first ascents during his early career as a cartographer for the United States Geological Survey. In addition, his Mt. Whitney and Mt. Goddard quadrangle maps set a new standard for alpine map-making.

In 1912, Davis was promoted to the position of topographic engineer in charge of the Pacific Survey, a position he held until his death in 1922. During this time, he produced detailed maps of Yosemite and Mt. Rainier National Parks, the Kings Canyon region and the Territory of Hawaii. He was eulogized as an "expert topographic engineer . . . In his death, geographic science has sustained a distinct loss."

Route:

From Onion Valley, take the trail over Kearsarge Pass to its junction with the John Muir Trail. Follow this to Vidette Meadow, then take the Bubbs Creek trail to Junction Meadow. Take the East Lake trail to its end at Lake Reflection, then follow the drainage up to Thunder Col on the east ridge of Thunder Mountain. Scramble up the east ridge to the southern-most of the three summit towers. An airy traverse leads around the east and north sides of the middle tower to the notch at the base of the highest, northern tower. A crack (Class 4) on the south side leads to the top.

Descent:

Retrace your steps.

John Moynier

Thunder Mountain from the northeast

Mt. Brewer Area

Mt. Brewer (13,570 ft.)
Northeast Face
III 5.7

F.A. Russ McLean and Ken Boche; September, 1963
Mt. Brewer Area Map: Page 68
USGS Quad Maps: Kearsarge Peak, Mt. Clarence King and Mt. Brewer

After making the first ascent of Mt. Brewer in 1864, William Brewer described the view from the summit: "(It is) wilder than we have ever seen before . . . such a landscape! A hundred peaks in sight over thirteen thousand feet – many very sharp – deep canyons, cliffs in every direction almost rivaling Yosemite, sharp ridges almost inaccessible to man, on which human foot has never trod."

Brewer, field leader of the Whitney Survey Party, made the ascent with Charles Hoffmann, the survey's topographer. Apparently, they had a great glissade down one of the wide gullies on the southwest face: "We slid down a great snow slope. We were less than two minutes coming down what it had taken us over three hours to surmount." The pair climbed the peak again the next day, and left a bottle with their signatures on the summit. In 1896, this record was found and taken to the Sierra Club's archives in San Francisco. Unfortunately, this room and all of its contents were destroyed in the 1906 San Francisco earthquake.

The beautiful northeast face of Mt. Brewer is split by a prominent rib. To the authors' knowledge, a direct route up this rib has not been climbed. The first ascent followed a line to the right of the rib, and was made by two figures from Yosemite's bohemian Camp Four of the 1960s: Russ McLean and Ken Boche.

Route:
From Onion Valley, take the trail over Kearsarge Pass to its junction with the John Muir Trail. Follow this to Vidette Meadow, then take the Bubbs Creek trail to Junction Meadow. Take the East Lake trail to the north fork of Ouzel Creek and scramble up to the small glacier at the base of the face. The route begins by ascending a chimney on the right side of the prominent rib. The middle part of the route follows cracks up slabs before taking the chimney splitting the headwall above. The climb tops out just north of the summit.

Descent:
Head south down the summit ridge to a short headwall (Class 3) that drops onto the east ridge. Follow this down to Ouzel Creek.

Robin Ingraham, Jr.

The Northeast Face of Mt. Brewer

North Guard (13,327 ft.)
Southwest Face
Class 4

F.A. Norman Clyde; July, 1925
Mt. Brewer Area Map: Page 68
USGS Quad Maps: Kearsarge Peak, Mt. Clarence King and Mt. Brewer

Norman Clyde made the first ascent of North Guard in 1925. He described the summit tower as: "A fine rock climb . . . a granite monolith some twenty feet in height may be the highest point and which, without hand-holds or foot-holds, leans in an embarrassing way over a five-hundred foot precipice." Even after the long climb, many parties forego the exposed summit pillar.

There are two options leading to the summit. Both start in the central talus gully in the middle of the face. At a point below the top, you must choose whether to go right to the south ridge or left to the west ridge. Either way, the crux is making the exposed moves onto the final tower.

Knowing one's limits is an important part of mountaineering. Clyde said: "Mountaineers differ considerably in their ability to find a ready means of reaching a summit. This is partly a matter of experience, partly one of a certain innate skill that some seem to possess in greater degree than others. Although one may seek mountaineering challenges in order to have the satisfaction of overcoming them, skill in mountain climbing consists as much in being capable of avoiding them as surmounting them."

Route:
From Onion Valley, take the trail over Kearsarge Pass to its junction with the John Muir Trail. Follow the John Muir Trail to Vidette Meadow, then take the Bubbs Creek trail to Junction Meadow. Take the East Lake trail to East Lake, then follow the north fork of Ouzel Creek to the small glacier at the base of Mt. Brewer. A steep chute, which may be icy in the heavy snow years, climbs to the crest between Mt. Brewer and North Guard. Cross the crest and traverse north across talus and slabs to the base of the peak. Follow a broad talus-filled gully in the center of the southwest face. A traverse left leads to a saddle on the west ridge. Follow the ridge up steep steps to the exposed summit pinnacle.

Alternative Routes:
The south ridge also can be followed. At the top of the broad gully, head right and make a steep climb onto the ridge.

Descent:
Retrace your steps.

North Guard from Mt. Brewer

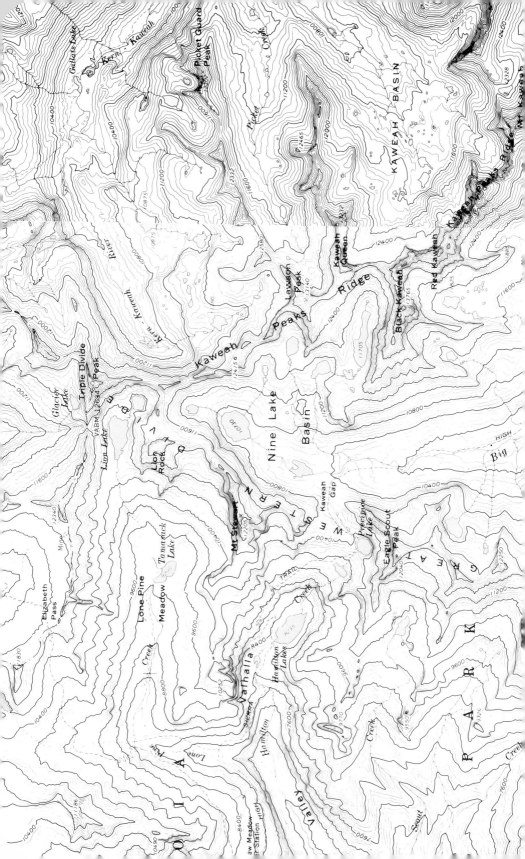

Kaweah Area

The Kaweah area is an excellent example of the diversity of Sequoia National Park. Scattered throughout the dense forests of the western slope are beautiful groves of Giant Sequoias. Granite spires and domes rise above the deep canyons of the forks of the Kaweah River. The beauty of this area made it the perfect choice to become one of America's first national parks. Originally, this designation, which was made in 1890, protected only the main groves of Sequoias and the immediate area surrounding them.

Eventually, the park was increased to include the Kaweah and Kern River drainages, because of their scenic attractions and the need to protect these important watersheds. Stephen Mather, Assistant to the Secretary of the Interior, led the propaganda efforts by enlisting the aid of such notable public figures as Gilbert Grosvenor, President of the National Geographic Society. Many members of the Sierra Club lobbied intensively for enlargement of the park to include the Kings River area. Walter L. Huber was especially active, first as a Forest Service engineering supervisor who stalled development of a hydro-electric project in the proposed park area, and second as a member of the club's Board of Directors. He was serving as President of the Sierra Club in 1926 when the bill was passed enlarging Sequoia Park to nearly its present size. The Kings River area had to wait until 1940 to receive national park status.

The High Sierra Trail travels through the heart of Sequoia National Park, linking Giant Forest with the summit of Mt. Whitney. The route passes through the beautiful subalpine cirque known as Valhalla. This basin is bordered by the spectacular granite towers of the Angel Wings and Hamilton Dome, and embraces the Hamilton Lakes.

The northern boundary of this region is marked by Triple Divide Peak, which is at the apex of the three major drainages of the area: the Kings, Kern and Kaweah Rivers. To the east, the metamorphic Kaweah Range stands in striking contrast to the granite peaks of the southern Great Western Divide. Towering above the Kern river drainage, the Kaweahs form a rugged line of peaks between the main Kern River canyon and the glacial valley of the Big Arroyo.

Approach

Take Highway 198 into Sequoia National Park and the small resort of Giant Forest. Wilderness permits and general supplies are available a few miles further up the road at Lodgepole. From the trailhead at Crescent Meadow (near Giant Forest), the High Sierra Trail traverses the deep canyon of the Middle Fork of the Kaweah to Bearpaw Meadows.

The trail contours around the canyon, past the trail to Elizabeth Pass, and crosses Lone Pine Creek. To reach the north face of Mt. Stewart, follow the trail up Lone Pine Creek to Tamarack Lake. The main trail contours below the immense granite face of the Angel Wings into the Hamilton Lakes cirque. Hamilton Dome is the impressive fin of granite to the south. There is a fine seven-pitch climb ascending the north arête (II 5.7), which was first climbed by TM Herbert and Don Lauria in 1971. The High Sierra Trail continues over Kaweah Gap to the Big Arroyo and the Kaweahs.

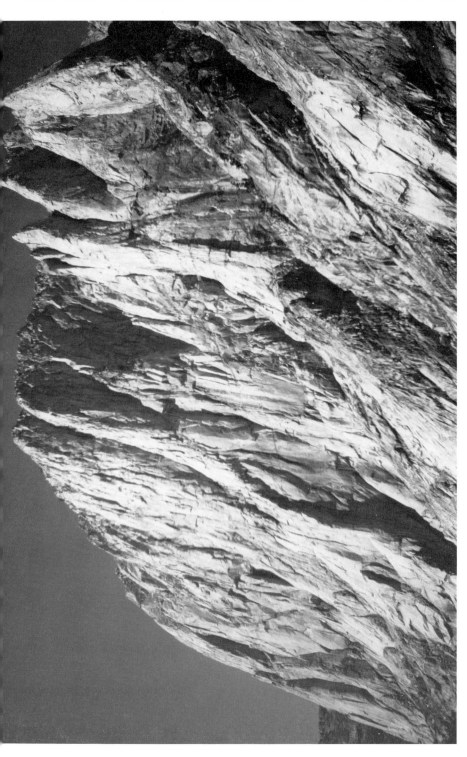

Richard Leversee

Angel Wings

Black Kaweah (13,765 ft.)
Southwest Face
Class 4

F.A. Philip Smith, Marian Simpson, and Irene Smith; July, 1921
Kaweah Area Map: Page 80
USGS Quad Maps: Lodgepole and Triple Divide Peak

Norman Clyde called Black Kaweah: "One of the most difficult and dangerous peaks of the High Sierra." The first ascent was made by James Hutchinson, Onis Imus Brown and Duncan McDuffie in August, 1920 by way of the long west ridge. Hutchinson, a charter member of the Sierra Club, was 53 at the time of the ascent. He described the less than perfect rock: "The peak was seamed, cracked, scarred and broken by weathering like no peak we have ever climbed; the whole ridge appeared to be disintegrating rapidly."

The route up the southwest face has become the most popular on the peak. Although it looks intimidating from below, the gully has many ledges, creating a loose staircase that spirals to the summit. For climbers looking for a more challenging climb, the east ridge can be followed from the saddle to the south of the summit. This Class-4 ridge was first climbed by John and Ruth Mendenhall in August, 1968.

Route:
Take the High Sierra Trail over Kaweah Gap and down into the Big Arroyo. Follow the drainage to the lake on the southwest side of the peak. From the lake, two chutes drop from the summit. Climb the short cliff between the two chutes, then enter the right chute. Follow this until blocked by a steep step. Skirt this to the left and pass through a "V"-shaped slot on the arête between the chutes. Climb the left-hand chute to the summit ridge.

Alternative Route:
From the lakes south of the peak, climb a steep chute to the saddle on the east ridge between Black Kaweah and Pyramidal Pinnacle. Follow the exposed knife-edge ridge around gendarmes and up chimneys to the top.

Descent:
Retrace your steps, looking for the "V"-shaped slot on the arête.

The Southwest Face of Black Kaweah   John Moynier

Eagle Scout Peak (12,040 ft.)
North Face
III 5.7

F.A. Dave and Cindy Nettle; 1984
Kaweah Area Map: Page 80
USGS Quad Maps: Lodgepole and Triple Divide Peak

The first ascent of Eagle Scout Peak was made in July, 1926 by Francis Farquhar and three Boy Scouts from the San Joaquin Valley. A newspaper report of their ascent stated: "This first expedition of Boy Scouts from the San Joaquin Valley into the High Sierra was commemorated by giving the name Eagle Scout to a prominent point . . . Three scouts, Frederic Armstrong, Eugene Howell, and Coe Swift, led by Francis Farquhar of the Sierra Club, ascended this peak on July 15, 1926, and finding no sign of a prior ascent, erected a monument and declared the name."

Dave Nettle wrote of his climb on the north face: "At the time, my wife Cindy and I were working at Bearpaw Meadows. We climbed this face via six pitches that never seemed to be harder than 5.6/5.7. It turned out to be a very nice route." On their ascent, the Nettles watched a deer frolic on the snowslope below them, inspiring them to name the route Dancing Deer Direct.

Route:
Follow the High Sierra Trail to Precipice Lake, located below the north face of Eagle Scout Peak. A non-descript ridge leads to the base of the route. Ascend a gully just right of the prominent north rib, then climb up and right on moderate rock, reaching the ridge about 100 feet left of the teetering summit block.

Descent:
Descend Class-2 slopes to the east and return to Kaweah Gap.

Eagle Scout Peak from the High Sierra Trail

Kaweah Area

Mount Stewart (12,205 ft.)
North Face, West Pillar
III 5.9+

F.A. Dave and Cindy Nettle; 1984
Kaweah Area Map: Page 80
USGS Quad Maps: Lodgepole and Triple Divide Peak

Mt. Stewart features an impressive north-facing wall with many possibilities for fine routes. The peak honors George W. Stewart, who has been called "the father of Sequoia Park." His efforts as editor of the Visalia Delta *helped promote creation of the park.*

Dave and Cindy Nettle described their route on the north face of Mt. Stewart: "(It is) the striking line that takes the wall to the west of the original route and ends on a point west of the true summit." The first pitch follows a corner system through the slightly undercut and overhanging lower wall, and is the crux of the climb.

The original route on the face was climbed by Mike Graber, Jack Roberts and Hooman Aprin in August, 1973. They ascended the left-most of the two prominent buttresses on the north face (III 5.6). Graber returned with David Wilson in 1986 and climbed a route on the right-hand buttress, which may have been the Nettles' west pillar route. There are at least two other routes on the broad face.

Route:
Follow the High Sierra Trail to Bearpaw Meadows, then take the Lone Pine Creek Trail to Tamarack Lake. From Tamarack Lake, ascend slabs and talus to the permanent snowfield at the base of the face. The route begins at a large stacked block that leans against the right side of the face. Climb the left-facing corner (5.9+) above and move left at an overhang to the top of the first pitch. A series of ledges is reached at the top of the second pitch (5.9). Follow corner systems for six more pitches to the top of the west buttress. A tricky traverse leads east along the shattered ridge to the summit.

Descent:
To return to Tamarack Lake, head east down slabs to Nine Lakes Basin, then cross over Lion Rock Pass to the Lone Pine Creek drainage.

The north face of Mt. Stewart   Dave Nettle

Kaweah Area

Angel Wings (10,252 ft.)
South Arête Direct
V 5.9 A3 or 5.11

F.A. Galen Rowell and Chris Jones; June, 1971
F.F.A. Dave Nettle and Jim Nowak; October, 1991
Kaweah Area Map: Page 80
USGS Quad Maps: Lodgepole and Triple Divide Peak

The Angel Wings is the beautiful granite wall standing as the northern sentinel to the Valhalla cirque. The sheer south face is the largest rock wall in Sequoia National Park and is host to a number of dramatic climbs. To the right of the main wall is a spectacular arête, which merges with the south buttress near a prominent black band at mid-height.

The first ascent of the arête was made by two prolific backcountry climbers, Galen Rowell and Chris Jones. Their route escaped the arête above the crux "black roof" and followed the central gully to the top. On the first free ascent, the striking arête was followed directly to the summit. This provided six more pitches of excellent, exposed climbing on the very edge of the arête. Richard Leversee says, "These last pitches really make the climb. The upper arête offers some of the best climbing on the route."

Route:
Follow the High Sierra Trail, leaving it just before it traverses above Lower Hamilton Lake. Scramble through talus and brush to the big gully that separates the west wall from the south arête. Follow the gully a short way, then angle up and right across exposed ledges and slabs to the highest ledge at the base of the arête. The main crack system is followed through four black bands, and skirts a prominent headwall on its right. The crux of the route involves climbing the strenuous "black roof" (5.11) in the highest black band. This is followed by a 5.9 face traverse into the central gully. The original route followed this gully to the top. The direct route leaves the gully above the second chockstone and traverses right (5.10–) to cracks on the edge of the arête. Six more pitches of moderate face and crack climbing lead to the top of the tower. From here, it is a short scramble to the summit.

Descent:
Head west down talus (Class 3-4) on the back side of the peak (do not stray too far north) and take the second gully leading back to the base of the west wall. Scramble down this and ledges back to the trail.

Alternative Route:
The prominent dome to the east of the Angel Wings is known as "Cherubim Dome." The clean south buttress of this attractive dome is an excellent eight pitch climb on superb granite, and is considered an "unknown classic" of the Sierra. This route (IV 5.10+, AO) was first climbed by E.C. Joe and Richard Leversee in October, 1985. From upper Hamilton Lake, the High Sierra Trail switchbacks below the dome before turning east toward Kaweah Gap. Scramble up steep slabs and manzanita slopes to the apron at the base of the south buttress, aiming for the south buttress. Thin cracks and face climbing lead into "The Harp," a prominent left-trending arch. Scary face climbing (5.10) leads out of the arch and into a thin flake system above (one pendulum). The crux is a horizontal traverse (5.10c) above a prominent tiered roof to the prow of the buttress. Thin cracks (5.9) connect steep face climbing up the smooth prow. Near the top of the prow the rock becomes more featured and knobby face climbing leads to the summit.

Descent:
Head east on the summit ridge toward Mt. Stewart until it is possible to descend slabs to the High Sierra Trail.

The Angel Wings and Cherubim Dome

Kaweah Area

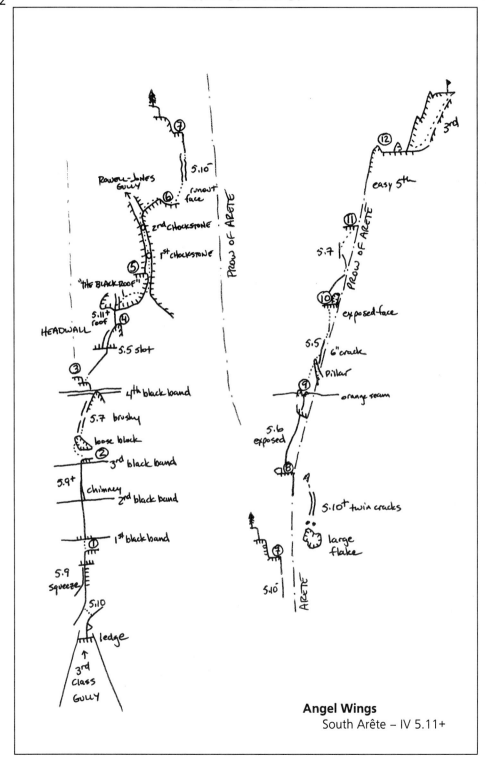

Angel Wings
South Arête – IV 5.11+

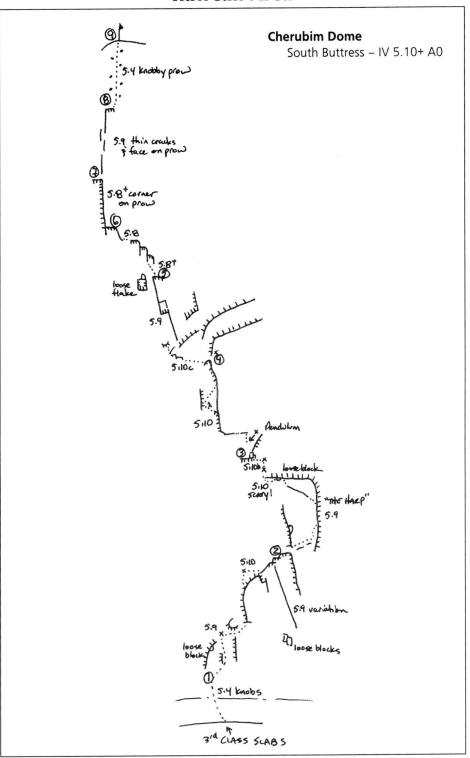

Cherubim Dome
South Buttress – IV 5.10+ A0

Mt. Clarence King Area

This area lies at the head of the south fork of the Kings River. Bolton Brown was entranced by its beauty and made three trips into the area in the 1890s. He wrote with enthousiasm: "I put it down as distinctly the finest and completest epitome of Sierra scenery I had seen. Whatever makes the charm and the peculiar character of the High Sierra is here in typical perfection – peaks, walls, precipices, snow-fields, table-lands, gorges, ice-smoothed rocks, willow-bowered cascades, mountain pines, columbine and many other blossoms, perfect and extensive meadows, and lakes – ah, the lakes! – in every variety, form and position – fifty of them if there is one."

Rising above Gardiner Basin are three exceptionally fine peaks named for members of the Whitney Survey Party: Clarence King, Dick Cotter and James Gardiner. The first ascent of Mt. Clarence King was made by Bolton Brown in 1896. His solo ascent was one of the most difficult climbs done before the turn of the century. It remains a challenging climb by today's standards.

Approaches

From the west, take Highway 180 from Fresno into Kings Canyon National Park. Continue past Cedar Grove to the trailhead at Roads End, and follow the Bubbs Creek Trail to Charlotte Creek. The Bubbs Creek Wall is the prominent cliff seen just ahead. Wander up slabs and manzanita slopes along side of the creek to the base of the dome.

To reach the main part of the region, continue up the Bubbs Creek trail past Junction Meadows to the John Muir Trail. Follow the Muir Trail over Glen Pass into Rae Lakes Basin. A trail leads over the ridge into Sixty Lakes Basin. The Gardiner Lakes are accessed by way of the broad saddle just south of Mt. Cotter.

To reach this area from the east, take the road from Independence to Onion Valley. Follow the trail over Kearsarge Pass to its junction with the John Muir Trail and head over Glen Pass into the Rae Lakes Basin. To reach Charlotte Dome from the Kearsarge Trail, cross the Muir Trail and continue down Charlotte Creek on a faint trail past Charlotte Lake to the base of the dome.

Charlotte Dome (10,690 ft.)
South Face
III 5.7

F.A. Galen Rowell, Chris Jones and Fred Beckey; October, 1970
Mt. Clarence King Area Map: Page 94
USGS Quad Maps: Mt. Clarence King, The Sphinx and Kearsarge Peak

The Whitney Survey Party noted the impressive granite face of Charlotte Dome in 1864. The first ascent of the south face featured the combined talents of three of America's finest alpinists: Galen Rowell, Chris Jones and Fred Beckey, all of whom have enviable records of first ascents in the Sierra and throughout the world.

When Rowell, Jones and Beckey reached the base of the wall, they were dismayed to find a lack of obvious crack systems directly up the south buttress. Beckey felt they should try a more moderate route on the side of the face, but as Jones later wrote, both he and Rowell believed it would be "better to fail on a great route than succeed on an indifferent one."

The route looked intimidating from the ground, so to save time they compromised and scrambled up a deep alcove to the left of the buttress, following Class-4 ledges as high as they could onto the face. Once they were on the route, the climbers were ecstatic to find numerous knobs and "chickenheads," which allowed for wonderful free-climbing at a moderate level of difficulty.

Bob Harrington ventured that although the original route is undeniably a classic, the route Charlotte's Web is even better. "Anywhere you go on the dome," he said, "You're going to find good rock, so that's not the issue. I'm sure many parties that 'repeat' the classic route actually go a number of different ways. Charlotte's Web takes the most striking line on the face, starting at the very toe and leading straight up the great south buttress. It's also the longest route on the peak and was most likely the line Galen and Chris wanted to climb."

Route:
From Onion Valley, follow the Kearsarge Pass trail past Charlotte Lake and continue down the creek until you can scramble up steep brushy slabs to the base of the dome. The route begins near the toe of the rounded south face. The first three pitches follow Class-4 slabs and shallow grooves to a belay on the right side of a huge bowl. A short headwall above the belay is split by numerous cracks. A steep slot (5.7) leads up to a prominent white dike at the base of a right-leaning dihedral (5.7). An ambiguous, runout face pitch (5.7) leads up and right to the base of the Furrows, a series of steep grooves cut in a headwall. Face climbing on knobs and chickenheads leads to the summit ridge.

Alternative Routes:
There are a number of possibilities, all about the same degree of difficulty, on the face. Charlotte's Web (IV 5.8; F.A. Bart O'Brien and Dave Harden; August 1976) takes a direct line up the south buttress. E.B. White (IV 5.9+; F.A. Alan Bartlett and Allan Pietrasanta; August, 1979) follows a bolt-protected line up the right side to the base of the Furrow Pitch.

Descent:
Head north along the summit ridge (Class 3), before dropping down brushy slabs to the north fork of Charlotte Creek.

The south buttress of Charlotte Dome

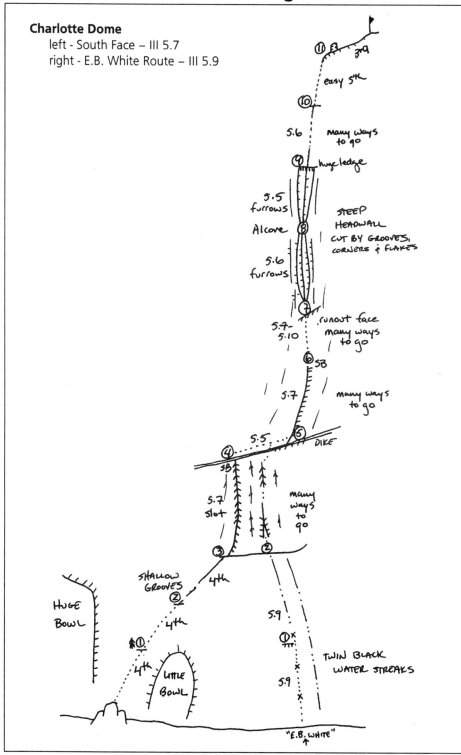

Charlotte Dome
left - South Face – III 5.7
right - E.B. White Route – III 5.9

⑪ B 3rd

easy 5th

⑩

5.6   Many ways to go

⑨ huge ledge

5.5 furrows

Alcove   ⑧   STEEP HEADWALL CUT BY GROOVES, CORNERS & FLAKES

5.6 furrows

⑦

5.7-5.10   runout face many ways to go

⑥ SB

5.7   many ways to go

⑤   5.5   DIKE

④   5.5

SB

5.7 slot   many ways to go

③   ②

SHALLOW GROOVES   4th

②

HUGE BOWL   4th   5.9

⑪ x

4th   LITTLE BOWL   TWIN BLACK WATER STREAKS

5.9   x

"E.B. WHITE"

Alan Bartlett on Charlotte Dome

Mt. Clarence King Area

Mt. Gardiner (12,907 ft.)
East Ridge
Class 4

F.A. Bolton Brown, Joseph N. LeConte and others; July, 1896
Mt. Clarence King Area Map: Page 94
USGS Quad Maps: Mt. Clarence King and Kearsarge Peak

Mt. Gardiner was named for James Gardiner by his fellow members of the California Geological Survey. Their leader, Josiah Whitney, wrote: "Two peaks lying in front of the crest are especially fine, the northern one being a little the highest. This we named Mt. King, and the southern one Mt. Gardiner." Mt. Gardiner sits like a mountain island above the deep canyons of Bubbs Creek, Woods Creek and the South Fork of the Kings River. The top is a sharp, U-shaped crest with the higher summit on the north end. The exposed traverse along this knife-edge ridge leads to one of the most thrilling summits in the Sierra.

The first ascent of the peak was made by two eminent mountaineers of the day: Bolton Brown and Joseph N. LeConte. Throughout their careers, the pair had been competitive with one another in their quest for first ascents. Meeting by chance in Bubbs Creek Canyon, they discovered they both had plans to climb Mt. Gardiner. They combined forces and made their only joint first ascent.

The two rival climbers also happened to be professors at rival universities and each had a strong sense of school pride. A few weeks prior to the ascent of Mt. Gardiner, LeConte had climbed University Peak, naming it in honor of the University of California at Berkeley, where he and his father were faculty members. Brown had just come from the Kings-Kern Divide, where he had climbed a prominent peak and christened it Mt. Stanford after his university.

Route:
From the Onion Valley Trailhead, take the Kearsarge Pass trail to its junction with the John Muir Trail. Follow the Muir trail over Glen Pass to Rae Lakes Basin. Take the trail into Sixty Lakes Basin, then head over Sixty Lakes Col into the Gardiner Lakes. From the largest lake, follow the east ridge (Class 2) to the south summit of Mt. Gardiner. Scramble north over blocks to the knife-edge north ridge. An exposed traverse leads along a narrow shelf on the south side before crossing over to the north side of the ridge. A large block is passed on the north side to reach the summit.

Descent:
Retrace your steps.

Mt. Gardiner above Gardiner Lakes   John Moynier

Mt. Clarence King (12,905 ft.)
South Face
5.4

F.A. Bolton Brown; August, 1896
Mt. Clarence King Area Map: Page 94
USGS Quad Maps: Mt. Clarence King and Kearsarge Peak

Clarence King, a prominent member of the Whitney Survey party, described the survey's travels in his book Mountaineering in the Sierra Nevada. *Although these accounts were greatly romanticized, King's scientific observations did much to advance knowledge of the range. After his work with the Whitney Survey, he took over the Geological Exploration of the Fortieth Parallel as Geologist-in-Charge. Following this work, King organized the United States Geological Survey and became its first director. His later life was influenced by a broad of range of interests, including literary and business pursuits.*

Bolton Brown's solo ascent of this difficult peak was considered the hardest climb of the time. Brown had tried the route the year before. " But it was all in vain," he wrote. "Presently there loomed above me a vertical cliff 50 ft. high and smooth as the side of a house. Only wings could go up there." A year later, he "began to hanker for another try at Mt. King." This time, he was able to surmount the final obstacle by lassoing the summit, standing in a makeshift sling and hauling himself onto the top. After a glorious summer in the Sierra, Brown wrote in his journal: "That ended our mountaineering for the summer. The grass plumes held ripened seeds, and in the swamps, tiger lilies and columbine had given place to golden rod. And so we headed west with sincere regret, and many pledges to return . . . "

Route:

From Onion Valley, take the Kearsarge Pass trail to the John Muir Trail and follow the Muir trail over Glen Pass to the Rae Lakes Basin. Gain the King Spur about a mile north of Mt. Cotter at a low saddle, and proceed up talus slopes until steep rock forces you onto the edge of the precipitous southeast face. A narrow shelf is followed diagonally up to just below the summit blocks. Here, a fifteen-foot "pitch" leads to the summit boulder, where a difficult and exposed move is required to gain the top.

Descent:

Most climbers choose to rappel off the summit boulder back to the ledge. From there, retrace your steps.

John Moynier

Mt. Clarence King above Sixty Lakes Basin

Mt. Clarence King (12,905 ft.)
Southeast Face
III 5.8+

F.A. Galen Rowell and Greg Henzie; August, 1970
Mt. Clarence King Area Map: Page 94
USGS Quad Maps: Mt. Clarence King and Kearsarge Peak

This route up the attractive southeast face of Mt. Clarence King was the focus of one of Galen Rowell's many weekend climbing trips. His route followed obvious ramps to the left of a prominent chimney system in the center of the face.

Rowell lives in Berkeley, California, which for most people is a seven-hour drive from the eastern Sierra. Originally an auto mechanic and ex-hot rodder, Rowell discovered that the driving time to Sierra trailheads could be considerably shortened with proper driving techniques. Vern Clevenger remembered accompanying Galen as a teenager on many of these adventures: "Since I was just learning, I figured he knew how to drive better than I did. I would just close my eyes and hope we'd get there in one piece. We must have averaged close to 80 miles per hour, counting stops. Once we'd reach the trailhead, I'd have to run to keep up with him."

As a youth, Rowell had been greatly influenced by David Brower and other Sierra Club climbers. He had grown up in the neighborhood where Brower and Richard Leonard lived, and his family was active with the Sierra Club's annual outings. Rowell's mother had participated in the first ascent of the Hermit on the 1924 High Trip. Brower remembered Rowell as "the neighborhood juvenile delinquent." Doris Leonard fondly recalled that her daughter thought that Galen was a "real nerd," as he always walked around with a knapsack.

Route:
From Onion Valley, take the Kearsarge Pass trail to the John Muir Trail and follow the Muir trail over Glen Pass to the Rae Lakes Basin. A prominent dihedral and chimney system drops directly down the southeast face of Mt. Clarence King. Midway up the wall is a large, right-trending ramp. The route follows the ramp for three pitches of fine crack climbing (5.8) before ascending a broken grey face, with short difficult sections interspersed with easier terrain. The last few pitches ascend a prominent corner system (5.8+) to the right of a blank white face. The corner system ends at a notch on the summit ridge just east of the airy 5.4 summit block.

Alternative Route:
The prominent dihedral and chimney system can also be followed. Begin in a left-facing corner (awkward 5.9) to a ledge. Follow cracks and ledges to the left of the chimney for two pitches. A wide crack (5.9) leads to the top of the ramp system, then a 5.7 crack finishes on a ledge. Loose cracks (5.8) lead to the large sandy ledge above the grey area of the preceding route. The route finishes in the same corner system as the ramp route.

Descent:
Rappel off the summit to a ledge that diagonals to the south face. Descend talus to the saddle between Mt. King and Mt. Cotter, then to the lakes below.

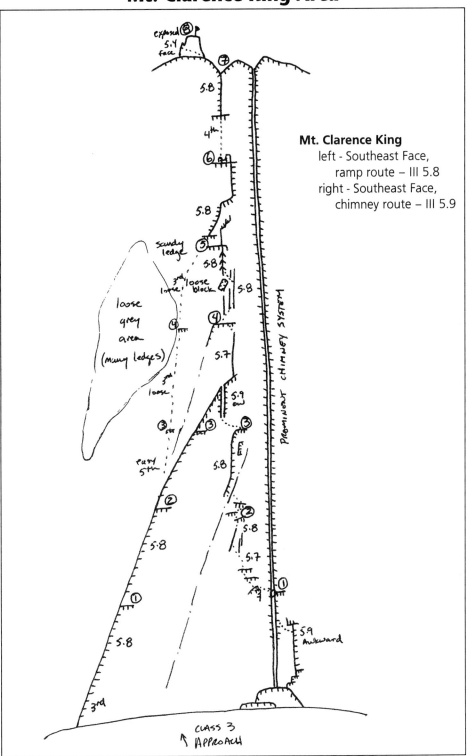

exposed ⑧
5.4
face

⑦

5.8

4th

⑥

5.8

sandy
ledge

⑤

5.8

3rd   loose
lnse   block ⑧   5.8

loose
grey
area
(many ledges)

⑤   ④

5.7

loose

5.9
ow

③   ③   ③

E

easy
5th

5.8

②

②

5.8

5.8

5.7

①   ①

5.8

4
5.9
Awkward

PROMINENT CHIMNEY SYSTEM

Mt. Clarence King
left - Southeast Face,
    ramp route – III 5.8
right - Southeast Face,
    chimney route – III 5.9

3rd

CLASS 3
↑ APPROACH

Dragon Peak (12,955 ft.)
Northwest Arête
II 5.8

F.A. Vern Clevenger and Claude Fiddler; June, 1984
Mt. Clarence King Area Map: Page 94
USGS Quad Maps: Mt. Clarence King and Kearsarge Peak

Dragon Peak is an attractive peak with no easy way to its summit. The south face was first climbed by Norman Clyde in 1920. Clyde described the peak: "One of the most fantastically banded of the mountains along the crest is Dragon Peak. It terminates in a sharp pinnacle, which offers an interesting scramble, and overlooks an extremely ragged and broken portion of the eastern escarpment of the Sierra."

The route up the northwest arête is a thrilling climb and was made by two longtime Yosemite climbers. As teenagers, Clevenger and Fiddler began climbing new routes in Yosemite Valley and Tuolumne Meadows in the 1970s. Galen Rowell was known to accompany the pair, acting as a "chaperone" and elder statesman of the team. The inspiration for Fiddler and Clevenger's backcountry routes often came while looking at photographs from a backpacking trip. Such was the case with Dragon Peak.

Route:
From Onion Valley, take the trail toward Golden Trout Lake. Just below the lake, the trail branches, with one branch heading toward the lakes at the base of Dragon Peak. Climb over steep, loose talus and scree to North Dragon Pass (Class 3) and descend more of the same to the moraine above Dragon Lake, at the base of the northwest arête. Gain the steep arête and follow it to the north ridge and the top.

Descent:
An exposed ledge (Class 3-4) leads around the south side of the summit to a col on the south ridge. Continue along the south ridge until it is possible to drop down ledges on the east side back to the trail. The south ridge also can be followed over Mt. Gould to Kearsarge Pass.

Vern Clevenger

Dragon Peak from Dragon Lake

Arrow Peak Area

Arrow Peak is the prominent, solitary peak standing above the 5,000 ft. deep canyon of the upper South Fork of the Kings River. The western ramparts of the peak form a great wall above the river which is known as the Muro Blanco. This rugged canyon is one of the least visited areas in the High Sierra, due to its lack of trails and distance from popular trailheads. Arrow Peak is best viewed from Bench Lake to the east, where the symmetrical lines of its converging ridges are beautifully reflected in the morning light.

Bolton Coit Brown named the peak during his first ascent in 1895. He wrote of reaching the summit: "About midday I clambered up the last and summit rock...and swept my eyes around. It was perfect.... A sense of profound peace came over me. It was so still I heard only the ringing in my ears." Due to its remote location, Arrow Peak receives few ascents, but for those willing to make the long journey in over Taboose Pass or as a side trip from the John Muir Trail, Arrow Peak is a rewarding summit.

Approach

Although Arrow Peak lies to the west of crest, the best approach to the peak is from the east side and the traditional Indian trading route over Taboose Pass. To reach the trailhead, leave Highway 395 at the Taboose Creek road, midway between the towns of Big Pine and Independence. Take the paved road past the Taboose Campground to the dirt road leading to the trailhead at Taboose Creek.

The trail climbs steeply alongside the creek, with a gain of over 6,000 ft. from the trailhead to the broad saddle of Taboose Pass. From the pass, the trail descends toward the South Fork of the Kings River to the junction with the John Muir Trail. Follow the Muir Trail south to the junction with the Bench Lake trail and then take this trail to Bench Lake at the foot of Arrow Peak.

Arrow Peak (12,958 ft.)
Northeast Ridge
Class 3

F.A. Bolton C. Brown; August, 1895
Arrow Peak Area Map: Page 108
USGS Quad Maps: Mt. Pinchot and Aberdeen

Arrow Peak is a beautiful, symmetrical mountain, especially when viewed from nearby Bench Lake. Camping along these shores nearly 100 years ago, Bolton Brown was impressed by the peak. "Of course I wanted to climb it, " he wrote, "But my feet were literally on the ground, rations were low and the future unknown. It worried me a great deal, but just before falling asleep I decided it would be foolish to attempt it, and that I would not.

"In the night I awoke and saw its snowy slopes gleaming serenely in the moonlight. At daybreak it was still there – it called to me at breakfast, its rocky pinnacles beckoned me, its soaring summit challenged me. I could stand it no longer and hurriedly swallowing the last of my coffee, I threw prudence to the winds . . . almost on the run for the sheer joy of that mountain and the delight of climbing up it."

On the way up, the professor engaged in the mountaineering tradition of trundling. He described pushing off a huge boulder balanced on the knife-edge: "Crunch! Crash! Boom! – the awful thunderous roaring down the horrid throat of the crevice – a far, growling rattle and a smell of brimstone – it was a huge success!"

Route:

From the trailhead at Taboose Creek, take the trail over Taboose Pass and down to the Kings River. Follow the Muir Trail south, then take the trail to Bench Lake. From the lake, ascend talus on the ever-narrowing ridge to its junction with the southeast ridge, which is followed to the summit.

Descent:

Retrace your steps.

Vern Clevenger

Arrow Peak from Bench Lake

Split Mountain Area

Split Mountain was formerly known as the South Palisade, as it is the southernmost 14,000-foot peak in the Palisade region. But its geology and position a few miles to the south of the Palisades on the crest warrant consideration of this peak as a separate area.

From the west, the dark mass of Split Mountain rises above the broad expanses of Upper Basin at the headwaters of the South Fork of the Kings River. On the east, a series of convoluted arêtes and narrow gullies drop from the summit of Split Mountain into the sagebrush of the Owens Valley, 10,000 feet below.

To the south of Split Mountain and its neighboring peak Cardinal Mountain, is the broad saddle of Taboose Pass, one of the historic trade routes for the Piute Indians. The mountains in this region are very colorful, with the ancient metamorphic cap rocks visibly overlying the granitic core of the Sierra batholith. These rocks also are heavily fractured, as in other regions where the remnant cap rocks are exposed, and present potentially serious objective hazards.

The first traverse of the Sierra Crest in this region was made by Jules Eichorn and Glen Dawson in 1932, when they traversed from Cardinal Peak to Split Mountain. All that Eichorn could remember of this traverse was that " It was long." In June, 1989 Dick Beach and his longtime friend and climbing partner Bob Good attempted to repeat this traverse. The pair spent a fine evening on the summit of Cardinal Mountain and Good remarked, "This is as close to heaven as we can get."

The next day Beach and Good were off to an early start, and had reached a sharp notch on the crest. Beach described the next few moments: "In the notch, there was a twenty-foot section of brick-like rocks standing on end. I went across without a moment's hesitation." Then, "The noise every climber fears, loose rock falling, immediately broke the silence behind me. I turned instantly, only to see my dear companion being pushed out and down the eastern escarpment . . . Horrifying was the silence that returned to fill the morning air."

Beach descended to Good, recalling, "All I could do was focus on the fact that he would have done the same for me." Beach reached the body in an hour and a half, gathered Bob's gear and bid farewell to his friend, " ...with tears in my eyes and a prayer on my lips, I hugged him and said a last good-bye."

Dick Beach's experience is a poignant reminder that mountaineering is a serious and sometimes tragic pursuit. As Beach reflected on his lonely hike out of the mountains, "I could not help remembering the reality that all who climb in the mountains face: we all hope the odds are with us each time we visit these peaks."

Approaches

To reach the eastern base of Split Mountain, leave Highway 395 at the blinking light in Big Pine and drive west on the Glacier Lodge Road to McMurry Meadows Road. Follow this rough dirt road past McMurry Meadows to Red Mountain Creek, driving as far west on the road as possible before parking and continuing on the unmaintained trail to Red Lake.

An alternate approach leaves Highway 395 at the Fish Springs/Tinemaha Creek Road, passing the Tunemaha Campground and continuing to the locked gate near Red Mountain. Follow the rough trail/road along Red Mountain Creek to the aforementioned road and Red Lake.

Jim Howe – Sierra gully climbing   Dave Nettle

Split Mountain (14,058 ft.)
Northeast Couloir
Class 4 ice and snow

F.A. Bob Harrington, December 1981
Split Mountain Area Map: Page 112
USGS Quad Maps: Split Mtn. and Fish Springs

The great eastern escarpment of Split Mountain is a series of sharp arêtes radiating from its twin summits. Hidden in the deep recess between the two central arêtes is a narrow couloir that holds the longest snow and ice climb in the Sierra. Galen Rowell climbed the northeast arête of the south summit (IV 5.9) in February, 1976. The climbing was so satisfying that he made the steep journey to Red Lake again in October of the same year and soloed the northeast arête of the north summit (III 5.8).

Bob Harrington also made repeated visits to the peak: "A lot of the climbing we did in the high country was motivated by Galen Rowell. He would do a route, write it up, and we would go in, do his route and scout around for other stuff to do. Rowell's reports of his routes on Split Mountain were intriguing, because the face was so big and the peak was so high. Dean Hobbs and I climbed the left-hand arête and felt that it was a classic – like a Temple Crag route, but longer, on a higher summit, and in a more remote location."

Harrington recounted his ascent of the central ice gully: "I went back to climb the gully that goes up between the arêtes in December, 1981. The start of this long gully (which may be the longest in the Sierra) is amazing. Instead of the usual bergschrund, it necks down to a 20-foot-high, three foot wide strip of 65 degree ice that you have to climb to gain access to the easier gully above. After a few hundred feet, I came to a cliff band in the gully. On the right was a 70-foot pitch of very steep water ice (climbed later by Yvon Chouinard, Richard Leversee and James Wilson) and on the left was a snow-choked chimney.

"The water ice wasn't solo material for me, so I started up the chimney, but after a few feet I realized it was too hard. I took off my crampons and traversed out left on the rocks and went up until I could get back into the gully above the cliff. The rest of the climb was great, low-angled water ice leading to a long section of perfect névé, ending right at the notch between the summits."

Route:
From Big Pine, take the Glacier Lodge Road to the McMurry Meadows Road and follow it to the start of the Red lake Trail. Alternately, leave Highway 395 and take the Tinemaha Creek road past the Tinemaha Campground to the end of the road. Climb onto the ridge just south of the creek and follow the creek to Red Lake. Gain the couloir at the base of the two central arêtes and climb a steep pitch into the gully. The crux ice pitch is higher up at a short headwall. (It also is possible to climb around the headwall (5.4) on the left.) Moderate climbing above leads to the notch between the two summits. A short Class-4 pitch leads to the higher north summit.

Alternative Routes:
The left-hand arête (IV 5.9) attains the south summit and was climbed by Galen Rowell and David Belden during drought conditions in February, 1976. The right-hand arête (III 5.8) was climbed solo by Rowell in October, 1976 and gains the north summit.

Descent:
The north talus slopes are Class 2. Follow the ridgeline north toward Point 12,627, where a Class-3 headwall and gully leads back to Red Lake.

The northeast face of Split Mountain   John Moynier

Palisade
Area

The Palisade region offers the highest concentration of alpine climbs in the Sierra. The area is host to many significant (by Sierra standards) glaciers, including the Palisade Glacier, which is the largest in the range. The peaks in this area are primarily composed of compact meta-granitic rocks that have weathered into spectacular arêtes and gendarmes. Geographically, the Palisades region extends from the fractured summits of the Inconsolable Range in the north to Taboose Pass in the south. Half of the 14,000-foot peaks in the Sierra are found here, including Split Mountain, Middle Palisade, Mt. Sill, North Palisade and Thunderbolt Peak.

The basic orientation of the Palisade crest runs southeast to northwest. A significant ridge branches northeast from Mt. Sill to Mt. Gayley, Temple Crag and Mt. Alice, and forms the divide between the north and south forks of Big Pine Creek. The southwest side of the Sierra crest is a convoluted escarpment cut by deep gullies and airy ridges, making for interesting route-finding. Some very beautiful lakes lie west of the crest in Dusy, Palisade and Upper Basins. From these lake basins, it is hard to distinguish individual peaks, as the crest rises as an almost continuous vertical wall. In 1895, Bolton Brown sketched these peaks from the summit of Mt. Woodworth and described this side of the Palisades: "This region is undoubtedly the wildest and roughest part of the whole Sierra Nevada range."

There is a great history of climbing in the Palisade area. The Whitney Survey Party named the area in 1864: ". . . Along the main crest of the Sierra is a range of peaks, from 13,500-feet to 14,000-feet high, which we called 'the Palisades'. . . They were very grand and fantastic in shape." J.N. LeConte, James Hutchinson and James K. Moffitt made the first ascent of North Palisade from Palisade Basin in July, 1903. Norman Clyde was particularly active in this area, having served for many years as the caretaker of Glacier Lodge, the rustic resort at the road's end. This area was also home to the first guide service in the High Sierra, which was formed in the late 1950s.

Approaches

The Palisade region is approached from the town of Big Pine, where groceries, showers and gas can be found. Wilderness permits and mountaineering supplies are available in Bishop, 15 miles to the north. From Big Pine, take the road west from the center of town to Glacier Lodge. Overnight wilderness users must park in the lot one mile east of the roadend. A short distance from the road the trail splits, with the South Fork trail heading left and the North Fork going right.

Palisade Area

The South Fork approach accesses the peaks along the crest from The Thumb to Mt. Sill, as well as the route over Southfork Pass. The long Firebird Ridge, which extends northeast from Norman Clyde Peak to Firebird Peak, divides the south fork of Big Pine Creek. As a result of this divide, the trail splits in the vicinity of Willow Lake. The route to Elinore Lake serves the climbs north of the Firebird Ridge, while the trail to Brainard and Finger Lakes accesses the routes south of the Firebird Ridge. The North Fork trail provides access to the popular routes near Palisade Glacier. The marked trail to the glacier leaves the main trail between Third and Fourth Lakes, and climbs past Sam Mack Meadow to the Palisade Glacier.

The Bishop Pass trail provides access to the west side of the crest. From Bishop, head west on Highway 168 to the road end at South Lake (limited overnight parking). Take the trail over Bishop Pass into Dusy Basin. Thunderbolt Col provides a high crossing (Class 2-3) of the west ridge of Thunderbolt Peak into the Palisade Basin.

The main passes crossing the Sierra crest in this region are Southfork Pass (between The Thumb and Disappointment Peak), Scimitar Pass (on the north ridge of Mt. Jepson), Agassiz Col (between Mt. Winchell and Mt. Agassiz) and Jigsaw Pass (just north of Mt. Agassiz). Glacier Notch, the saddle between Mt. Gayley and Mt. Sill, provides a high link between the north and south forks of Big Pine Creek. This pass requires some glacier travel and steep, loose rock. It is primarily recommended as an approach to the Swiss Arête of Mt. Sill. Contact Pass (between Mt. Alice and Temple Crag) offers a safer crossing between the north and south fork drainages, and is the main access to the Celestial Arêtes on Temple Crag.

Rosie Andrews on the Sun Ribbon Arête   Michael Graber

The Palisade Traverse
Southfork Pass to Jigsaw Pass
VI 5.9

F.A. John Fischer and Gerry Adams; July, 1979
Palisade Area Map: Page 118
USGS Quad Maps: Split Mtn., North Palisade and Coyote Flat

The Sierra Crest in the Palisade region is the highest continuous ridge in the range, averaging almost 14,000 feet for nearly nine miles. The first traverse of this jagged section of the crest was highly coveted and was attempted many times over the years. In 1938, Ken Davis and Jack Riegelhuth made the traverse from Mt. Winchell to North Palisade. Carl Heller and others from the China Lake group pushed the route between Thunderbolt Peak and Mt. Sill. This section is now popular, and is best done from north to south.

Doug Robinson tried the complete traverse at least four times, but never quite made it. Vern Clevenger and Claude Fiddler were making an attempt when they were surprised by an intense lightning storm. Pinned by the storm on the exposed ridge, they were horrified to see a lightning bolt make a direct strike on their camp, two thousand feet below! Neither has returned to attempt the traverse.

John Fischer and his client Gerry Adams managed the traverse in a seven-day push, having previously cached their food along the crest. Fischer described their effort: "The traverse we did is several miles longer than any other technical traverse yet done in the Sierra. The complete Palisade traverse would be from Taboose Pass to Bishop Creek, although I can't imagine anyone sustaining that level of energy for that long."

Route:
This traverse climbs nine major peaks (six over 14,000 feet) and many lesser summits between Southfork and Jigsaw Pass. Depending on which direction you make the traverse, the access for Jigsaw Pass is via Fifth Lake and the north fork of Big Pine Creek; the access for Southfork Pass is via the south fork of Big Pine Creek and the trail to Brainard Lake.

John Moynier

The Palisade crest from Mt. Sill to Mt. Winchell

Middle Palisade (14,040 ft.)
Northeast Face
Class 3-4

F.A. Norman Clyde; June 1930
Palisade Area Map: Page 118
USGS Quad Map: Split Mtn.

In 1919, a team consisting of J.M. Davies, A.L. Jordan and H.H. Bliss made the first recorded attempt of an ascent of Middle Palisade. The trio climbed a gully to the top of a subsidiary peak. Finding no reasonable way to traverse to the main peak, they christened their summit Disappointment Peak. Two years later, Francis Farquhar and Ansel Hall made the same mistake. However, they rectified this by dropping back down and climbing another gully to the top of Middle Palisade.

Lewis Clark, Chairman of the Sierra Club's Mountaineering Committee in the 1930s, wrote: "There is no easy approach to Middle Palisade, either from the ends or the sides; rather it is generally considered the most inaccessible and the most difficult of the state's 14,000-ft. peaks." Norman Clyde climbed the peak from the east, ascending a series of steep gullies from the glacier to the summit. Although this route looks intimidating from below, stair-step ledges in the gullies allow for relatively safe and moderate climbing.

Route:
From Glacier Lodge, take the South Fork trail to Finger Lake. From Finger Lake, scramble up the moraine ridge that divides the Middle Palisade Glacier. At the top of the moraine, climb onto the glacier. Near the top of the glacier, a ledge system traverses right across the headwall into a chute. Climb this past a prominent pinnacle to where it merges with a wider chute. Continue up this broad gully to where it splits, then follow the left-hand chute to the crest. Steep blocks lead left to the summit.

Descent:
Retrace your steps, heading right at the prominent pinnacle and watching for the exit ledge to the glacier below.

Middle Palisade and Norman Clyde Peak

Norman Clyde Peak (13,920 ft.)
Twilight Pillar
III 5.8+

F.A. Don Jensen and Frank Sarnquist; July, 1966
Palisade Area Map: Page 118
USGS Quad Map: Split Mountain

Norman Clyde made the first ascent of this striking peak by way of the north face (Class 4) in June, 1930. On this ascent, Clyde climbed the steep snow couloir leading to the col between Norman Clyde Peak and the peak to the north (Mt. Williams). Clyde described the peak: "(It is) the second in the group in scenic beauty and possibly the first in mountaineering difficulty. From the south, it [Norman Clyde Peak] presents an impressive array of crags and pinnacles; from the north it is even more impressive as it rises in sheer cliffs above a steep glacier at the head of a deep canyon. There is an especially fine view of it looking up the south fork of Big Pine Creek about a half-mile west of Glacier Lodge."

Clyde made more than 160 first ascents in the High Sierra between 1914 and 1946. The summer of 1925 was typical for Clyde; he climbed 48 peaks, half of which were first ascents and all but six solo. The following year, at age 40, he climbed 60 peaks. Clyde made his last first ascent in 1946, at the age of 61, with his longtime friend Jules Eichorn. He made his last trip into the Sierra in 1970 at age 85. Two years later, he died.

Smoke Blanchard and Eichorn climbed Norman Clyde Peak in 1972 and scattered Clyde's ashes from the summit. Eichorn recalled, "Norman in his prime was a superb climber, whose strength and endurance have hardly been equaled by any other in the Sierra."

The two prominent features on the eastern face of Norman Clyde Peak are Firebird Ridge (which splits the south fork drainage), and the stunning Twilight Pillar. Allan Pietrasanta commented, "This climb is an overlooked classic and a fine memorial to a great climber . . . "

Route:
From Glacier Lodge, follow the South Fork trail to Finger Lake. From Finger Lake, climb onto the glacier at the eastern base of the peak and cross the glacier to a point down and left of the prominent snowfield on the right side of the pillar. Climb one pitch (5.7) on the headwall above the glacier, then scramble up to a ramp that gains the base of the steep upper part of the buttress. A long pitch up a right-facing dihedral leads to a belay ledge. Continue up the corner until it is possible to make the crux (5.8) traverse on small face holds to the right side of the buttress. Four more pitches on the crest of the pillar lead to the summit.

Alternative Routes:
The Thunderbird Wall (III 5.7; F.A. Hank Abrons and Pete Carmen; July, 1965), to the left of the pillar, is also recommended. A snow-covered ledge bearing a resemblance to a Kachina Thunderbird lies about halfway up the wall. The direct Firebird Ridge (IV 5.9; F.A. Fred Beckey, Mike Graber and Dave Black; July, 1975) also has been climbed. A more circuitous route up the Firebird Ridge (Class 3-4) was climbed in July, 1922 by Arkel Erb and Mike McNicholas. This route is the most popular descent.

Descent:
Follow the summit ridge west to the point where it joins Firebird Ridge. Drop down the north side of this ridge and either rappel or downclimb a steep chimney. From the base of the chimney, a series of cairns marks the easiest way down ledges on the ridge. At the saddle between the main peak and Firebird Peak to the north, drop down to the glacier.

Todd Vogel

The Twilight Pillar of Norman Clyde Peak

Temple Crag (12,999 ft.)
Moon Goddess Arête
IV 5.7

F.A. Carl Dreisbach and Pat Armstrong; September, 1969
Palisade Area Map: Page 118
USGS Quad Map: Split Mtn.

Norman Clyde wrote of Temple Crag: "It is doubtful that there is a more beautiful and striking 'crag-mountain' in the Sierra. Its northern and north-eastern faces are sheer precipices varied by numbers of spirey, turret-like pinnacles, beautifully placed." The pinnacles and arêtes radiate from the summit and are accentuated by early morning light and dreamily illuminated by moonlight. Known as the "Celestial Arêtes," these features were named the Sun Ribbon, Moon Goddess and Venutian Blind Arêtes by Don Jensen and his wife Joan. The names for the latter two arêtes were inspired one summer night when the moon and Venus shone particularly bright on these features.

In July of 1969, Jensen and J. Connors made a reconnaissance of the Moon Goddess Arête. Jensen and Connors progressed to a notch at the base of a prominent gendarme, which they named the Ibrium Tower. Finding the route above the tower difficult, they escaped left into a gully. Later that summer, Carl Dreisbach and Pat Armstrong repeated the route to this point, traversed around the north side of the Ibrium Tower and continued up the long arête to the summit.

Route:
From Glacier Lodge, follow the North Fork trail to the outlet of Third Lake. Scree and snow slopes lead to the gully between the Moon Goddess and Sun Ribbon Arêtes. Follow a large ledge left to the low-angled toe of the arête. Several moderate pitches up the arête lead to the base of a large gendarme, which is passed on its right by way of an exposed traverse (5.4) to a notch. From this notch, continue up to the base of the prominent Ibrium Tower. From this tower, it is possible to escape into the gully to the left and either rappel the gully (using fixed anchors) or scramble up to the southwest ridge (Class 4) and the summit. Otherwise, the climb traverses up and right to cracks leading to the top of the Ibrium Tower (5.6). Continue up the arête for many pitches (some 5.7), passing most of the difficulties on the right. There are at least two other possibilities for escape on the upper part of the arête.

Descent:
Head east down talus and ledges to a point just above Contact Pass. At this point, downclimb a corner (Class 4) or make a short rappel to the pass.

Michael Graber

Temple Crag from Second Lake; with the Moon Goddess and Sun Ribbon Arêtes on the left and the north buttress on the right

Temple Crag (12,999 ft.)
Sun Ribbon Arête
IV 5.9

F.A. Don Jensen and John Fischer; September, 1969
Palisade Area Map: Page 118
USGS Quad Map: Split Mtn.

As the northeastern face of Temple Crag catches the first oblique rays of sunrise, a narrow ridge in the center stands as a ribbon of sunlight against the dark face. This lead Don Jensen to name it the Sun Ribbon Arête. A complete ascent of the arête involves about 20 pitches of fifth-class climbing. Most of the lower part of the route is moderate face climbing on the crest of the arête. Two-thirds of the way up, the arête levels off at a prominent gash. The traditional means of crossing this gap is by a tyrolean traverse. Above this, the route becomes more complicated, weaving around gendarmes and into deep notches.

George Lowe and Brock Wagstaff made a direct ascent of this arête under winter conditions in February, 1982. The daily air temperatures were extremely cold and the climbers faced heavy snow and ice-covered rock. The ascent took all of the pair's alpine experience to survive, and Wagstaff ended up suffering frostbite on both of his feet.

In May of 1990, Gordon Wiltsie and Andy Selters made an ascent of the arête, join-ing John Moynier (who had ascended another route) for a stormy bivouac near the summit. In the morning, they climbed to the top, placing Tibetan prayer flags on the summit as a memorial to long-time Palisade climber and guide, Smoke Blanchard. Blanchard spent his final years dividing his time between Bishop and guiding in the Japanese Alps, chronicling his life's adventures in his book Walking Up and Down in the World.

Route:
From Glacier Lodge, take the North Fork trail to the outlet of Third Lake. Scree and snow slopes lead to the gully between the Moon Goddess and Sun Ribbon Arêtes. At the mouth of the gully, a huge ledge leads to the right, below a steep face. Climb the large left-facing corner system at the end of the ledge and scramble up broken ground above to a notch behind a small gendarme, which is visible from Third Lake. Five pitches of moderate climbing lead up the prow of the arête to the tower with the gash. Either lasso a block on the far side of the gash and make a tyrolean traverse, or rappel into the notch and climb up the right side of the ridge. Continue out the flat arête to another notch at the base of a steep step. From here, you can escape left into the gully and gain the southwest ridge. Continuing, the next pitch involves difficult, intricate climbing (5.9) on the crest of the arête. Several more pitches of moderate climbing around towers and into notches leads to the top. There are a number of escapes off the upper arête into the gully to the left (Class 4), which also leads to the summit area.

Descent:
Head east down talus and ledges to a point just above Contact Pass. At this point, downclimb a corner (Class 4) or make a short rappel to the pass.

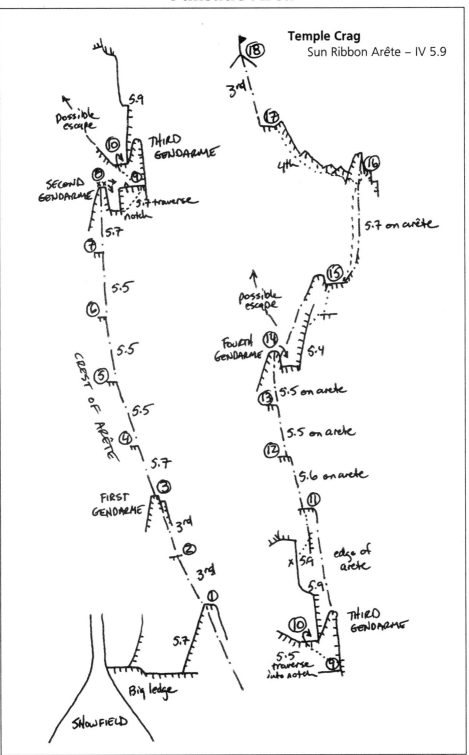

Temple Crag
Sun Ribbon Arête – IV 5.9

Temple Crag (12,999 ft.)
Dark Star
V 5.10 A0

F.A. Don Jensen and John Fischer; Sept. 1970 – Lower Buttress
Jensen, Fischer and Keith Brueckner; July, 1971 – Upper Arête
Palisade Area Map: Page 118
USGS Quad Map: Split Mtn

*The great north buttress of Temple Crag, which is characterized by two obvious fea-
tures – the massive lower buttress and the steep upper arête leading to the summit –
is to the right of the Celestial Arêtes. The parallel routes Dark Star and Barefoot
Bynum climb the face of the lower buttress. Doug Robinson, a longtime guide in the
Palisade area, considers Dark Star to be the most classic route of the High Sierra. He
cited the spectacular location, excellent climbing and stunning exposure of this route.*

*Robinson recently wrote, "The character of the climbing changes abruptly at the bivy
(the top of the lower buttress). Up to there, the rock is reminiscent of Middle
Cathedral Rock in Yosemite: fine face and crack climbing on dark granite. After the
ledge, it is a pure alpine ridge – long, intricate and full of surprises."*

*The first ascent of Dark Star was done in two parts. Don Jensen and John Fischer climbed
the steep lower buttress, then escaped into the north couloir. That same day, Robinson
and Chuck Kroger were making the first ascent of Barefoot Bynum and reached the top
of the buttress first. Fischer said, "We knew Doug and Chuck would be celebrating back
at camp, so we decided to join them and come back later to finish the route. It wasn't
until the next year that we were able to return and finish the upper arête."*

*The first ascent of the entire north buttress was made in August, 1975 by Robinson,
Fischer, Gordon Wiltsie and Jay Jensen. Fischer said, "Depending on your routefinding
and where you place your belays, the buttress involves 25-30 pitches of fifth class
climbing, making it the longest technical climb in the High Sierra."*

Route:
From Glacier Lodge, take the North Fork trail to the outlet of Third Lake. From
Third Lake, ascend ledges to the base of the north buttress. There are two right-
facing corners (Dark Star and Barefoot Bynum) at the base of the buttress. Climb
the left-most corner (5.10) to a ledge. Traverse left (5.8) past a fixed pin into a
clean corner (5.9). Climb past a white tooth of rock to a wide chimney (exposed
5.8) on the edge of the arête. Obvious cracks and moderate face climbing lead to
the top of the lower buttress. It is possible to traverse down and right from here
into the north couloir.

From the top of the buttress, traverse up and left by way of moderate face climbing to a wide crack (5.7) on the edge of the arête. This crack leads to a sandy gap.
From here, it is possible to escape left, and make a third-class scramble to the top
of the ridge. The route continues up a difficult crack (5.10) ten feet right of the
arête, followed by many moderate pitches on the narrow crest to the top.

Alternative Routes:
To the right of Dark Star are two climbs worth mentioning: Barefoot Bynum (IV 5.10,
A2; F.A. Doug Robinson and Chuck Kroger; September, 1970) starts in the next dihedral right of Dark Star and climbs cracks to a roof (A1). Above this roof, a chimney-
and-crack system is followed to the top of the lower buttress. Planeria (IV 5.10, A2;
F.A. Gordon Wiltsie and Jay Jensen; September, 1977) climbs the steep face to the
right of Barefoot Bynum into the prominent dihedral on the right side of the buttress.

Descent:
Gain the summit and head east down talus and ledges to a point just above Contact
Pass. At this point, downclimb a corner (Class 4), or make a short rappel to the pass.

John Moynier

The northwest side of Temple Crag

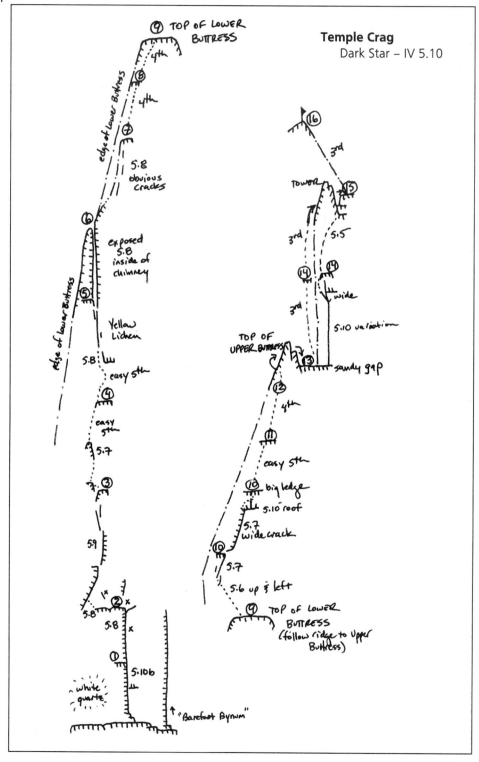

Temple Crag
Dark Star – IV 5.10

⑨ TOP OF LOWER BUTTRESS
4th
⑧
4th
⑦
5.8 obvious cracks
edge of Lower Buttress
⑥
exposed 5.8 inside of chimney
⑤
Yellow Lichen
edge of Lower Buttress
5.8
easy 5th
④
easy 5th
5.7
⑦ 5.7
③
5.9
1x
② x
5.8
5.8 x
①
5.10b
white quartz
↑ "Barefoot Bynum"

⑯
3rd
Tower
⑮
3rd
5.5
⑭ ⑬
wide
3rd
5.10 variation
TOP OF UPPER BUTTRESS
⑬ sandy gap
⑫
4th
⑪
easy 5th
⑩ big ledge
5.10 roof
5.7 wide crack
⑩ 5.7
5.6 up & left
⑨ TOP OF LOWER BUTTRESS (follow ridge to Upper Buttress)

Gordon Wiltsie on the Sun Ribbon Arête   Andy Selters

Mt. Sill (14,162 ft.)
Swiss Arête
III 5.6

F.A. Spencer Austin, Ruth Dyar, Ray Ingwersen,
Richard Jones and Joe Momyer; July, 1938
Palisade Area Map: Page 118
USGS Quad Maps: North Palisade and Coyote Flat

*Mt. Sill is known to the local Piute Indians as Ninamishi or "Guardian of the valley."
Joseph N. LeConte renamed the peak after Edward Sill, one of his professors at the
University of California, on the first ascent in 1903. Walter A. Starr, Jr. described Mt.
Sill as: "The peer of all Sierra peaks in the extent and quality of its views." Starr's
1931 route on the north face is now used as the standard descent to the Palisade
Glacier.*

*The north ridge of this peak forms an impressive prow when viewed from the
Palisade Glacier, and is known as the Swiss Arête. The first ascent team included
Spencer Austin and Richard Jones, active members of the Sierra Club in the 1930s
and '40s. Austin is perhaps best known for his ascents of the southeast buttress of
Cathedral Peak and Echo Peak #9 with Chuck Wilts. Jones, a skilled rock climber, had
accompanied Glen Dawson on the first ascent of the east buttress of Mt. Whitney in
1937.*

*This was the first season of a long mountaineering career for Ruth Dyar (Menden-
hall). She later wrote: " I was one of two ropes that made a new route up the north
buttress (now called the Swiss Arête in climbing guides). We had two experienced
rope leaders. The rest of us were in our first season of climbing. The other two men,
whose bent was not really rock climbing, didn't seem to appreciate the exposure. I
was so exhilarated by making a first ascent of a real mountain, by the elevation and
difficult moves and by the lovely surroundings that, though I kept my cool, I was running over with sheer joy."*

Route:
From Glacier Lodge, take the North Fork trail to above Third Lake, then follow the
glacier trail to the Palisade Glacier. Cross the bergschrund and climb loose ledges
to Glacier Notch. There is an L-shaped snowfield between Mt. Sill and the subsidiary Apex Peak to the north. Cross the snowfield to a Class-4 ramp leading onto
the arête. The first part of the arête is low-angled, with short steep steps. As the
ridge gets gradually steeper and narrower, the climbing becomes more interesting.
After five pitches, an impasse is reached. An exposed step around to the right
leads to a short difficult corner (5.6). Soon, the angle decreases and easier climbing
leads to a short chimney and the summit.

Descent:
From the summit, descend the northwest ridge toward North Palisade. Cross over
the ridge to the north side at a prominent spike of rock on the ridge, and head
down to a large flake of rock. A steep pitch descends to a ledge leading across the
north face to the notch between Mt. Sill and Apex Peak. From here, descend the L-
shaped snowfield or the rocks on the left to Glacier Notch.

Andy Selters

Mt. Sill from the east

Polemonium Peak (14,000+ ft.)
V-Notch Couloir
Class 5 ice

F.A. John Mathias and John Ohrenschall; September, 1957
Palisade Area Map: Page 118
USGS Quad Maps: North Palisade and Coyote Flat

Polemonium, or "Sky Pilot," is a lovely purple flower that often is found on the highest summits. Its beauty and sweet, musky fragrance have made it a favorite of mountaineers. Dana Morgensen, longtime Yosemite Park photographer and author of Yosemite Wildflower Trails, described this unique flower: "Not the least remarkable characteristic of the polemonium is its ability to flourish in crevices of the summit rocks, which appear to offer almost nothing in the way of viable soil. Yet flourish it does in its sky garden, a glorious reward for weary climbers as they stand at last on the mountain top. Polemonium is appropriate to its setting; it is a creature of the sky, drifting clouds and the summit wind."

The status of Polemonium Peak as a separate 14,000-foot peak is open to debate. It would not receive much interest at all, if not for the wonderful V-Notch ice couloir that graces its north face. Rising above the Palisade Glacier, this steep couloir ends at a V-shaped notch on the crest.

By mid-summer, this 50-degree couloir is prime alpine ice. James Wilson described it as: "Perhaps the best gully ice climb in the Sierra for most climbers." Climbing a short vertical pitch on the wall of the bergschrund is often necessary to gain access to the couloir, and is the crux of the climb. Once in the gully, it is best to keep to the right side to avoid rockfall.

Route:
From Glacier Lodge, take the North Fork trail to above Third Lake, then follow the glacier trail to Palisade Glacier. Cross the glacier (be aware of crevasses) to the bergschrund at the base of the couloir. Negotiate the bergschrund and head up the couloir, staying to the right side of the gully to avoid rockfall. At the notch, contour around the south side to the summit.

Descent:
Head east along the ridge toward Mt. Sill. As the ridge steepens, cross over to the north side at a prominent spike of rock on the ridge and head down steep talus to a large flake of rock. A steep pitch descends to a ledge leading across the north face to the notch between Mt. Sill and Apex Peak, the small summit to the north. From here, either glissade down the L-shaped couloir or downclimb rocks on the left to Glacier Notch.

North Palisade, with the V-Notch Couloir on the left, U-Notch Couloir in the middle and Clyde Couloir on the right

John Moynier

North Palisade (14,242 ft.)
U-Notch Couloir
Class 4 ice, 5.6 rock

F.A. Norman Clyde; June, 1928
Palisade Area Map: Page 118
USGS Quad Maps: North Palisade and Coyote Flat

North Palisade is the third tallest peak in the range. There is no easy way to its summit. J.N. LeConte, James Hutchinson and James K. Moffitt made the first ascent of North Palisade in July, 1903 from the lakes southwest. An attempt to reach the summit from the south was halted at the deep gash of the U-Notch, so they made the first ascent of Mt. Sill as a consolation. Disappointed, the trio returned to their camp having seen no feasible way to the top of North Palisade.

The next day, the climbers made a renewed effort to climb North Palisade, following the gully leading straight to the U-Notch. Already aware that the wall above the notch would be too difficult, they found a ledge system that enabled them to climb into the next gully and eventually reach the summit. LeConte described their final steps: "We worked up toward the knife-edge just to the south, and instantly the stupendous panorama of precipice, glacier, and desert burst upon us . . . " This Class-3/4 route is the easiest way to the top.

From the Palisade Glacier, the U-Notch couloir is the broad ice gully leading to the deep col left of the summit of North Palisade. As with the neighboring V-Notch, the crux of the U-Notch couloir is crossing the bergschrund. Above the U-Notch, two pitches of moderate crack climbing lead to the summit area. As an alternative, the gully on the southwest side can be descended and LeConte's route can be followed to the top.

Norman Clyde made the first ascent of the couloir as an early season snow climb. Although Clyde was a skilled snow and ice climber, his solo adventures were not without incident. On a climb of another couloir in the Palisades, Clyde fell while cutting steps, losing his axe in the process. Self arrest was out of the question and Clyde decided to meet the fast-approaching bergschrund with as much aplomb as he could muster in his dire predicament. At the lip of the gaping abyss, he leapt into the air, shouting, "Here I go to Hell!" He landed with a badly injured ankle and spent the rest of the summer recuperating at Fourth Lake.

Route:
From Glacier Lodge, follow the North Fork trail to Third Lake. At the top of the switchbacks above Third Lake, take the signed Glacier trail past Sam Mack Meadow and ascend the ridge to the Palisade Glacier. Continue along the moraine toward North Palisade before dropping onto the glacier. Cross the bergschrund and ascend the gully to the notch, staying to either side to avoid rockfall. From the U-Notch, climb the crack/chimney on the headwall above for two pitches before crossing to the west side of the ridge, then follow ledges to the summit.

Descent:
Make a long rappel back into the notch and either downclimb or rappel the couloir.

Bela Vadasz

Mimi Vadasz on the U-Notch Couloir

Thunderbolt Peak (14,000+ ft.)
West Chute
Class 4-5

F.A. Oscar Cook, Sylvia Kershaw, Mildred Jentsch, Hunter and Isabella Morrison (Descended); September, 1949
Palisade Area Map: Page 118
USGS Quad Maps: North Palisade and Mt. Thompson

Thunderbolt Peak was the last 14,000-foot peak in the Sierra to be climbed. The first ascent was made during the Sierra Club's "Underhill" camp of 1931, with a team that included Robert Underhill, Norman Clyde, Francis Farquhar, Bestor Robinson, Lewis Clark, Glen Dawson and Jules Eichorn. Their route up the "Underhill Couloirs" from the Palisade Glacier is now a popular late season ice climb.

An intense thunderstorm almost ended the first ascent in tragedy, and was responsible for the naming of the peak. Jules Eichorn later recalled, "At the summit, I may have climbed the monolith first or it might have been Glen (Dawson). Anything I could climb, Dawson could, too. We climbed it free, which the others weren't agile enough to do.

"Within five minutes, it seemed, the storm moved north and suddenly enveloped the whole peak. Norman (Clyde), being much more aware and experienced, didn't think it could happen so soon. There were sparks coming off my fingers and ice axe. I had never experienced this before and Norman felt we should get off the damn thing immediately.

"I was the last man down. It seemed that there was an unbelievable force of electrical energy around the area. I was about 25 yards from the pinnacle when suddenly there was a tremendous explosion right in my face. The electrical blast immobilized me for a moment. I felt paralyzed. Then almost as quickly, I got back my facilities and strength. It was a very uncomfortable feeling, to say the least. I felt very lucky I wasn't directly struck by the lightning."

From the west, Thunderbolt Peak is an impressive wall cut by a number of gullies, many of which end in cliffs. The west chute route begins at Thunderbolt Col and follows steep gullies to the top of the peak. Faced with surmounting the final monolith, most climbers throw a rope over the top, rather than "free" it as the first-ascent party did. This exposed summit boulder problem is rated 5.8.

Route:
From South Lake, follow the trail over Bishop Pass to Dusy Basin. Cross the top of the basin to Thunderbolt Col, located high on the ridge between Thunderbolt and Isosceles Peaks. Climb the first gully south of the pass to an alcove. A ledge and short headwall leads up and right into the next gully. Further up the gully, where it branches, always take the right-hand option. Near the notch between the twin summit pinnacles, a chimney-and-crack system leads up the northeast face of the summit tower. From here, a ledge leads around the east side to the final monolith. This is surmounted by either tossing a rope over the top or a difficult bouldering move.

Alternative Routes:
From the Palisade Glacier, both the Underhill couloirs and the north couloir provide fine snow-and-ice climbs to the summit.

Descent:
Retrace your steps, taking care near the bottom to find the ledge system leading back to the starting gully.

Thunderbolt peak above the Palisade Basin   John Moynier

Mt. Winchell (13,768 ft.)
Southeast Face
to East Ridge
Class 3

F.A. W.B. Putnam, J.N. Newell and H.C. Mansfield; June, 1923
North Face to East Ridge – Class 4
F.A: Robert Stebbins, Bill Rogers and G. Stebbins; August 1955
Palisade Area Map: Page 118
USGS Quad Maps: North Palisade and Coyote Flat

Mt. Winchell was named by Elisha Winchell for his cousin Alexander Winchell, a professor of Geology at the University of Michigan in the late 1870s. Elisha was a judge and one of the pioneers of Fresno County. His son, Lil A. Winchell, accompanied Frank Dusy on his extensive explorations of the Kings River drainage, and made the first ascent of Mt. Goddard in 1879 with L.W. Davis.

There are two routes gaining the classic knife-edged east ridge. Both offer some of the best climbing at their grade in the range. The southeast face approach is the most popular route on the peak, featuring challenging climbing and thrilling exposure. The north face provides a fine mixed climb; from the small glacier, climb slabs and moderately steep ice.

Route:
From Glacier Lodge, take the North Fork trail to Third Lake. At the top of the switchbacks above Third Lake, follow the signed Glacier trail to Sam Mack Meadows and scramble up the drainage to Sam Mack Lake.

Continue up the drainage until you can climb a talus slope on the southeast shoulder of the peak. There are two obvious chutes: ascend the right-most one to a headwall, then traverse left near a prominent dike into the left-hand chute. Climb this to the knife-edged east arête and follow it to the summit.

Alternate Route:
As a more difficult alternative, the north face can be climbed to the east ridge (F.A.: Robert Stebbins, Bill Rogers, and G. Stebbins; August, 1955). To reach the north side of the peak from Sam Mack Lake, follow the drainage past a small lake at the base of the east ridge and continue over talus to the Winchell Glacier. From the top of the glacier, climb slabs to an ice gully, which is followed to the east arête and the summit.

Descent:
Follow the southeast face route back down to Sam Mack Lake.

Mt. Winchell from the Thunderbolt Glacier   Gary Guenther

Mt. Winchell (13,768 ft.)
Southwest Arête
Class 4-5

F.A. Jules Eichorn, Glen Dawson and John Olmstead; July, 1930
Palisade Area Map: Page 118
USGS Quad Maps: North Palisade and Coyote Flat

The southwest arête of Mt. Winchell is an excellent and airy climb. In places, the arête is only eight to ten feet wide and very exposed. Chris Keith described this as "the best climb of its type in the Sierra."

On July 6, 1930, Glen Dawson and Jules Eichorn made their first climb together, ascending the north ridge of Red and White Mountain. They spent the rest of the month moving south (accompanied by John Olmstead), climbing roughly one peak a day. During the first week, the trio climbed Mt. Abbot, Mt. Dade and Bear Creek Spire. The next week, they headed on to Mt. Darwin, Mt. Mendel, the Hermit and Mt. McGee. Mt. Goddard was added on July 20th, and a few days later, they made ascents of Devils Crag #1 and Mt. Woodworth.

Eichorn, Dawson and Olmstead climbed Middle Palisade on July 26, then traversed from Mt. Sill to North Palisade the following day. On July 29, the climbers tackled the impressive southwest face of Mt. Winchell. After reaching the summit, the team continued on to climb Mt. Agassiz before returning to their camp in Dusy Basin.

Route:
From South Lake, follow the trail over Bishop Pass to Dusy Basin. Climb the broken wall to the left of the two main gullies on the west face of Mt. Winchell, then traverse into the left-hand gully. Climb the gully until it narrows and exit via a steep, yellowish gully on the right wall, which leads onto the crest of the arête. Four pitches of exposed climbing on the arête lead to the northwest ridge and the summit.

Alternative Routes:
The next ridge to the north is the West Arête (III 5.8; F.A. Galen Rowell and Warren Harding; May, 1976). Begin by climbing the broken face (as for the Southwest Arête), then proceed up and right onto the crest of the west arête. The steep lower section is the crux; higher up, the climbing eases until you reach the northwest ridge and the summit.

Descent:
Retrace your steps or downclimb the southeast face (Class 4) and traverse over Agassiz Col into Dusy Basin.

The west face of Mt. Winchell   John Moynier

Mt. Darwin
Area

The section of the Sierra Crest from Bishop Pass to Piute Pass offers many fine snow and ice climbs, including routes on Mts. Gilbert, Thompson, Haeckel, Darwin, Mendel and Lamarck. The north faces of Mt. Goode, Mt. Powell, Mt. Haeckel and the Clyde Spires, as well as the east faces of Picture Peak and Mt. Darwin, present a number of spectacular rock climbs.

Theodore Solomons visited the area in the summer of 1895, naming Evolution Valley and the peaks surrounding it. "As I photographed and sketched," he later wrote, "I felt that here was a fraternity of Titans that in their naming should bear in common an august significance. And I could think of none more fitting to confer upon it than the great evolutionists, so at one in their devotion to the sublime in nature."

Approaches

The Mt. Darwin area encompasses the headwaters of Bishop Creek. The bustling town of Bishop serves the area and is complete with cowboy bars, supermarkets, campgrounds and camera shops. Backpacking and climbing supplies are available at Wilson's Eastside Sports, as well as up-to-date route condition information. Wilderness permits are available at the forest service ranger station on Main Street at the north end of town.

To get to the Bishop Creek trailheads of South Lake, Lake Sabrina and North Lake, take Highway 168 west from the center of town. The Bishop Pass trail and Mt. Goode are accessed from the South Fork of Bishop Creek at South Lake. A spur trail leads to Treasure Lakes and Mts. Gilbert and Thompson. Lake Sabrina serves as the trailhead for the middle fork of Bishop Creek, and provides access to Mt. Haeckel and Picture Peak. At the head of this cirque is Echo Col, offering a Class 3 route to the John Muir Trail near Muir Pass.

The trail over Piute Pass leaves the road end at North Lake, as does the route over Lamarck Col to Mts. Darwin and Mendel. An unmaintained trail leads to Lamarck Col from the east. When heading back over the pass from the west, aim for the higher saddle on the south ridge of Mt. Lamarck.

Mt. Goode (13,092 ft.)
North Buttress
III 5.9+ (direct start 5.10)

F.A. TM Herbert, Jay Jensen, Dennis Hennek and John Fischer; September, 1974
Mt. Darwin Area Map: Page 148
USGS Quad Maps: Mt. Thompson and North Palisade

Mt. Goode is named for Richard Goode, a topographer with the USGS during the late 1800s. The north face of the peak is an impressive sight to the hundreds of backpackers who make the trek over Bishop Pass every year, and it is somewhat surprising that the first ascent of this feature did not occur until the mid-seventies. After the somewhat loose first pitch, the rock and climbing improves with each pitch. The crux involves passing a roof high on the spectacularly exposed crest of the buttress.

The first ascent team included John Fischer and Jay Jensen, who were working as guides in the nearby Palisades. TM Herbert was a pioneer of many difficult climbs in Yosemite in the sixties and early seventies, including the first ascent of the Muir Wall on El Capitan with Yvon Chouinard in June, 1965. This marked the first time a Yosemite "Big Wall" was climbed by a two-man team without using siege tactics. Dennis Hennek had participated in the first "clean" ascent of the northwest face of Half Dome with Doug Robinson and Galen Rowell in 1973.

Route:
From South Lake, follow the Bishop Pass trail to Saddlerock Lake. From Saddlerock Lake, scramble up to the small glacier at the base of the wall. Two large open books are at the base of the prow; begin climbing in the right-hand one (the left one is a chimney). Climb two pitches (5.8) of somewhat loose rock in the book, finishing with an exposed traverse left below a steep and clean wall. The traverse continues with poor protection on small holds into the left chimney (5.8), which is climbed to a notch on top of the north pillar. A direct route follows the left-hand chimney/crack system to the notch (5.10). The next pitch is the crux, involving a difficult move around a small roof. Above the roof, a variety of cracks lead to the crest of the buttress. Near the top, an exposed hand traverse (5.8) is followed by the final mantel onto the summit blocks.

Descent:
Head south down sand and talus slopes to the Bishop Pass trail.

The north face of Mt. Goode

Allan Pietrasanta

Mt. Darwin Area

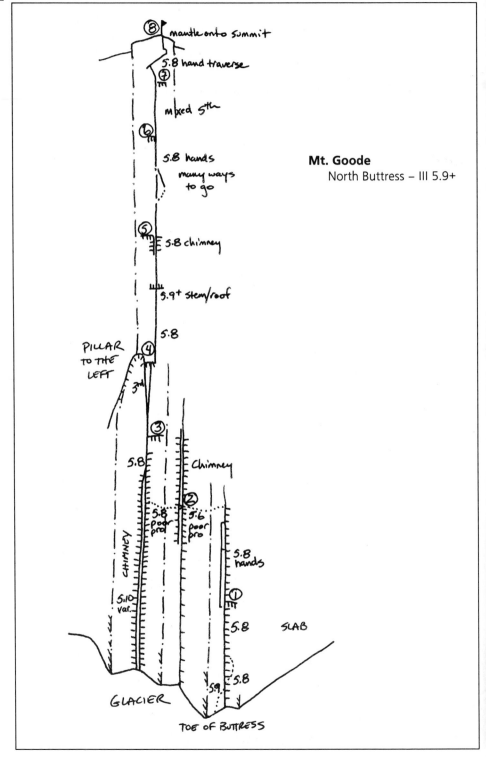

⑧ mantle onto summit

5.8 hand traverse

⑦

mixed 5th

⑥

5.8 hands

many ways to go

Mt. Goode
North Buttress – III 5.9+

⑤ 5.8 chimney

5.9+ stem/roof

5.8

PILLAR TO THE LEFT

④

3rd

③

5.8

Chimney

5.8 poor pro

②

5.6 poor pro

5.8 hands

CHIMNEY

①

5.8

SLAB

5.10 var.

5.8

5.8

5.9

GLACIER

TOE OF BUTTRESS

Andy Selters

Darla Heil on Mt. Goode's North Buttress

Mt. Gilbert (13,103 ft.)
Northwest Couloir
Class 4-5 ice

F.A. Al Fowler, Dan Eaton and Ron Cale;
September, 1972
Mt. Darwin Area Map: Page 148
USGS Quad Map: Mt. Thompson

Grove Karl Gilbert was a geologist with the Wheeler and Powell surveys in the late 1800s and later a frequent contributor to the Sierra Club Bulletin. Along with Willard Johnson and Israel Russell, Gilbert carried out an extensive survey of the Lyell and Dana Glaciers, as well as the Mono Lake area, during the summer of 1883.

The spectacular cirque on the north sides of Mt. Gilbert and Mt. Thompson is home to two large glaciers (by Sierra standards), and a number of fine ice couloirs. Allan Pietrasanta recalls the northwest couloir on Mt. Gilbert as perhaps the most attractive couloir he climbed during a summer spent soloing the main ice gullies in the Sierra. The couloirs in this area offer an excellent introduction to Sierra gully climbing and each can be accomplished in a day from South Lake.

Route:
From South Lake, follow the Bishop Pass trail to the Treasure Lakes trail. Follow this to just below the first Treasure Lake, then climb slabs over a ridge into the hidden cirque at the base of Mt. Gilbert. Cross the glacier to the bergschrund and climb the couloir, which ends at a notch below the summit. Climb a short headwall (Class 4) to the broad summit plateau.

Descent:
Head east along the crest to a steep gully leading into the next cirque east, and descend to the Treasure Lakes.

Allan Pietrasanta

The northwest side of Mt. Gilbert

Mt. Thompson (13,440 ft.)
North Couloir
Class 4-5 ice

F.A. Possibly Norman Clyde; 1930s
Mt. Darwin Area Map: Page 148
USGS Quad Map: Mt. Thompson

Mt. Thompson is named for Almon Harris Thompson, who accompanied John Wesley Powell on his explorations of the Colorado River and plateau in the late 1800s. Thompson later became a geographer with the USGS. The next peak to the west on the crest is named for Major Powell.

Norman Clyde made four of the first seven ascents of this peak. Unfortunately, he did not leave a good record of which routes he had climbed. On the left side of the northeast face are a trio of fine moderate ice gullies. Bob Harrington climbed the right-most of these in the early 1980s, and did not believe Clyde had climbed it. Hidden in the middle of the face to the right is a narrow ice couloir. The crux is passing a large chockstone two thirds of the way up. The upper part of the couloir offers excellent climbing on steep water ice.

John Moynier made perhaps the first ascent of this gully in August, 1986. Near the top is a narrow, ice-filled chimney. Moynier was so engrossed in the climbing that he did not notice a thunderstorm building up. As a blanket of dark clouds rolled over the slot at the top of the chimney, his ice axe began humming. The mounting flux of static electricity soon had the rocks of the chimney humming, and sparks leaping from his axe. Moynier waited until the humming subsided, then he made a dash across the summit plateau and scrambled down the north ridge, reaching the glacier as lightning began striking the summit.

Route:
From South Lake, follow the Bishop Pass trail to the Treasure Lakes trail. Follow this to just below the first Treasure Lake, then climb slabs over the ridge into the cirque between Mts. Gilbert and Thompson. Cross the glacier to the base of the north face of Thompson; the central ice gully is hidden until you almost reach the Thompson Ridge. Six pitches of moderately steep ice lie in the narrow couloir leading to the summit plateau. The crux is passing a chockstone two-thirds of the way up.

Descent:
Cross the plateau to the summit, where a short gully drops onto the north ridge (Class 3). Follow the ridge down sandy slopes onto the east glacier.

Mt. Thompson and the Thompson Glacier

John Moynier

Mt. Darwin Area

Picture Peak (13,120 ft.)
Northeast Face
IV 5.9

F.A. Gary Colliver and Steve Thompson; July, 1967
Mt. Darwin Area Map: Page 148
USGS Quad Maps: Mt. Thompson and Mt. Darwin

Viewed from Hungry Packer Lake, you can see that Picture Peak is aptly named. The first ascent of this peak was made via the southwest face by Norman Clyde in 1931. Two years later, Clyde returned with a Sierra Club party that included Jules Eichorn and Ted Waller, and climbed the stunning Clyde Spires across the cirque to the south.

The first ascent of the east face of Picture Peak was made by Gary Colliver and Steve Thompson, two Yosemite climbers who were working with a Sierra Club outing based at Dingleberry Lake. Gary Colliver was very active putting up first ascents throughout the Sierra in the 1960s and '70s. He is now a climbing ranger for Yosemite National Park, and is working on a climbing management plan for the park. The need for this plan has resulted from increased use of the area and a regrettable lack of responsibility practiced by climbers in the park.

Colliver voiced concerns about the increased impacts to the fragile alpine environment that a guidebook might cause. He feels that unless climbers exercise a greater degree of responsibility toward the environment, the park service will have to impose greater controls to protect the resources. He emphasized that climbers have to do more than practice "minimum impact" travel; we must leave no sign of our passing.

Route:
From Lake Sabrina, follow the trail past Blue Lake to Hungry Packer Lake, located at the base of the peak. From this lake, scramble up to the base of the east face. Moderate cracks and chimneys lead to a smooth face capped by twin flakes. Climb the face and continue between the flakes (5.7). The crux is a steep corner (5.9), followed by a difficult move onto a buttress. Steep ramps lead to easier climbing and eventually the top.

Descent:
Drop down the middle chute (Class 3) on the southwest side of the peak to a small lake, then continue down to Echo Lake.

The northeast side of Picture Peak

John Moynier

Mt. Haeckel (13,435 ft.)
Northwest Arête
Class 4

F.A. Jack Riegelhuth; 1933
Mt. Darwin Area Map: Page 148
USGS Quad Maps: Mt. Darwin and Mt. Thompson

Mt. Haeckel was named by Theodore Solomons for Ernst Haeckel, a professor of zoology at the University of Jena in the late 1800s. Haeckel was the first German biologist to express his support for the theory of evolution, thus the peak's geographical position between Mt. Darwin and Mt. Wallace. Solomons had named Mt. Darwin and Mt. Wallace for the British biologists who helped develop that theory.

"Mt. Haeckel is a very beautiful peak tapering to a narrow point," wrote Norman Clyde, "A fine example of what might be termed a Gothic type of peak, whose ascent is a fairly difficult climb." When viewed from the north, Mt. Haeckel features two jagged arêtes leading straight to the twin summit spires. The narrow ice gully between these arêtes was climbed by Yvon Chouinard and Choong-Ok Sunwoo in November 1971.

The northwest arête is the right-most of these two ridges. It was first climbed by Jack Riegelhuth, a skilled rock climber and a member of the Cragmont Climbing Club. Although his exploits have been somewhat overshadowed by his peers, Glen Dawson and Jules Eichorn, Riegelhuth made many difficult first ascents throughout his career. These included a daring traverse from Devils Crag #1 to #2, which involved descending the loose and tremendously exposed south face of Crag #1.

Route:
From Lake Sabrina, follow the trail past Blue Lake to Hungry Packer Lake. From Hungry Packer Lake, skirt the western headwall on the right, and enter the cirque directly below Mt. Haeckel's north face. Cross the small glacier and climb a steep gully to the prominent notch on the crest. The terrifically exposed arête above involves traversing knife-edges and gendarmes on excellent rock.

Descent:
Descend ledges on the southeast side of the peak into the basin below, then cross through the obvious col on the east ridge to the cirque leading to Hungry Packer Lake.

John Moynier

Mt. Haeckel from Mt. Lamarck

Mt. Darwin Area

Mt. Darwin (13,830 ft.)
North Glacier
Class 4 snow and ice

F.A. Jules Eichorn, John Olmstead and Glen Dawson; July, 1930 (Descended)
Mt. Darwin Area Map: Page 148
USGS Quad Maps: Mt. Darwin and Mt. Thompson

The massive hulk of Mt. Darwin dominates the Evolution region. There is no easy way to the high point, a small spire to the east of the broad summit plateau. Mt. Darwin was named by Theodore Solomons during his explorations of what was to become the John Muir Trail. E.C. Andrews and Willard Johnson of the USGS made the first recorded ascent of the peak in 1908 for surveying purposes.

Returning from the tiny summit, Jules Eichorn, Glen Dawson and John Olmstead descended the north face of Mt. Darwin during their peakbagging expedition of 1930. Dave Brower and Hervey Voge first climbed the north face in July of 1934, during their ten-week "Knapsack Survey of Sierra Routes and Records" tour of the range. Brower was wearing basketball shoes, so the pair kept to the rock rib splitting the glacier rather than tackling the steep snow of the north face.

As they descended towards Mt. Mendel, Voge recalls that he "stepped on a large flat plate of rock that started to slide. Not far ahead the ridge narrowed and dropped to the north. I cannot say exactly what happened, but I did not want to stay on the sliding plate and suddenly found my right ankle jammed between the plate and the wall to the north." Brower was able to lift the plate enough for Voge to extricate himself and continue the descent.

Route:
From the North Lake trailhead, follow the unmaintained trail over Lamarck Col to the lakes at the head of Darwin Canyon. From here, ascend the Darwin Glacier to where it narrows near the top. Take the left-hand branch to the summit plateau. At the eastern edge of the plateau, descend into the notch between the plateau and the summit pinnacle. A crack on the west side of the exposed pinnacle leads to the top (Class 3).

Descent:
Retrace your steps.

The north glaciers of Mt. Darwin and Mt. Mendel, with the twin Mendel couloirs on its north face Bob Harrington

Mt. Darwin Area

Mt. Mendel (13,691 ft.)
Right Mendel Couloir
Class 5 ice

F.A. Felix Knauth and John Whitmer; June, 1958
Mt. Darwin Area Map: Page 148
USGS Quad Maps: Mt. Darwin and Mt. Thompson

The Sierra Club proposed the name Mt. Mendel for this peak so that Johan Gregor Mendel could take his place among the other scientists and philosophers involved in developing the theory of evolution. Mendel was an Austrian geneticist whose study of gene characteristics laid the foundation for later evolutionary theories. The peak was first ascended by Jules Eichorn, John Olmstead and Glen Dawson during their peakbagging expedition of July, 1930.

The most distinctive features on the peak are the twin ice gullies on the steep north face. At the time of the first ascent, the right-hand couloir was considered the hardest ice climb in the Sierra. A steep bulge in the middle of the gully has been measured at more than 60 degrees. Yvon Chouinard and Dennis Hennek attempted the gully in full-on ice conditions in December 1965, but their equipment and techniques were not up to the sustained steepness of the route and they abandoned their attempt. Chouinard described reaching the crux bulge in his book Climbing Ice: *"The ice axe seemed to be holding okay, but the ice piton I was using for a dagger was just worthless; I was standing on my front-points about 20 meters out where the gully steepens to over 60 degrees. The pick of my axe was barely in because I couldn't get a good swing. It was so steep and I couldn't trust that wretched dagger to hold me in balance . . . There was one point when you could have knocked me over with a straw."*

Route:
From the trailhead at North Lake, follow the unmaintained trail over Lamarck Col to Darwin Canyon. Scramble up to the glacier at the base of the north face of Mt. Mendel. Cross the bergschrund and climb the ice apron to where the couloir splits. Climb the right-hand branch, negotiating a steep (60+ degree) bulge, and continue to the top of the couloir. A rock pitch (Class 4-5) gains the crest and the summit.

Descent:
From the summit, downclimb steep ledges on the east ridge (Class 3) to the glacier between Mt. Mendel and Mt. Darwin.

Micael Graber

Rick Ridgway on the Right Mendel Couloir

Mt. Mendel (13,691 ft.)
Left Mendel Couloir
Class 5+ ice

F.A. Mike Cohen and Roy Bishop; July, 1967
Mt. Darwin Area Map: Page 148
USGS Quad Maps: Mt. Darwin and Mt. Thompson

The left-hand couloir on the north face of Mt. Mendel is perhaps the most difficult alpine ice climb in the Sierra. This ephemeral route requires just the right combination of melting snow on the summit and cold temperatures for ice to form in the gully. In July, 1967, Yosemite climbers Mike Cohen and Roy Bishop completed the first ascent of the gully. Finding that the ice had melted in the steepest section, they were forced to climb the rock wall to the side of the couloir.

Doug Robinson, Dale Bard and Bob Locke approached Mt. Mendel in 1976, intent on making a direct start to the left-hand couloir. Locke took one look at their proposed route and realized he was in over his head.

Bard and Robinson began the climb with a direct start up a rarely formed ice smear leading into the gully. Although Bard was not as experienced at climbing ice as Robinson, he was one of the most skilled rock climbers in the country and ended up leading every pitch. They called their variation "Ice-nine." This name stuck in climbers' minds and now the entire left couloir is known as Ice-nine.

Dave Nettle recently lamented this confusion: "Ice-nine had always been one of those routes shrouded by an aura of mystery. Was it a separate climb? We found that it was not. Due to the ephemeral nature of ice, a climb like Ice-nine is never out of shape; it just slides along an ever-thinning scale until it becomes a rock climb."

Route:
From the North Lake trailhead, follow the unmaintained trail over Lamarck Col to Darwin Canyon. Scramble up to the glacier at the base of the north face. Cross the bergschrund and climb up the ice apron to where the couloir splits. Ascend moderate ice to an alcove with a chockstone. The crux is surmounting the chockstone and gaining the narrow runnel of ice above, which leads to the summit.

Descent:
From the summit, downclimb steep ledges on the east ridge (Class 3) to the glacier between Mt. Mendel and Mt. Darwin.

Todd Vogel on Ice-nine, Mt. Mendel   Richard Leversee

Mt. Goddard
Area

The Mt. Goddard area is a remote region of the range, requiring an approach of at least two days. The Goddard Divide lies at the heart of the High Sierra and separates the watersheds of the Kings and San Joaquin Rivers. Theodore Solomons visited the area in 1895 in attempt to find a high route along the Sierra Crest. After attempting Mt. Darwin, Solomons and partner Ernest C. Bonner made an ascent of Mt. Goddard. Unable to find a suitable route for their pack animals over the Goddard Divide, they abandoned their animals, shouldered their loads and headed down the Enchanted Gorge, eventually reaching the south fork of the Kings River "hungry and tattered."

Beginning in 1898, J.N. LeConte spent many summers following Solomons' route south from Yosemite, trying to find a "High Mountain Route" along the crest. His efforts were frustrated by the rugged terrain at the head of the middle fork of the Kings River. In 1907, George Davis managed to lead his pack animals over a snow-covered Muir Pass. A year later, LeConte, James Hutchinson and Duncan McDuffie once again faced the daunting prospect of crossing the Goddard Divide. LeConte wrote: "The Goddard Divide was now before us, the key to the whole situation. If we failed in our crossing it, our plan of a High Mountain Route failed, for the great spurs and canyons between Mt. Goddard and Mt. Woodworth formed an impassable barrier to the west of the Middle Fork . . . " After much effort, they found a route down into what is now known as LeConte Canyon, thus helping pioneer the route of the present-day John Muir Trail.

Approaches

The most direct approach to the Mt. Goddard area is from the east side via Echo Col (although it is also possible to use Lamarck Col and the John Muir Trail). Drive west on Highway 168 from Bishop to Lake Sabrina, then take the trail past Blue Lake and Hungry Packer Lake to Echo Lake. From the top of the small glacier, climb Class-3 rock to a notch to the right of a black tower. Steep talus slopes lead down the south side to the John Muir Trail. Follow the John Muir Trail to Helen Lake, then head south over the broad saddle of Black Giant Pass and into the Ionian Basin. Charybdis is the dark, jagged peak directly to the south. To reach Mt. Goddard, continue on the Muir Trail over Muir Pass to Wanda Lake, then cross the low saddle to Davis Lake. The north ridge of Goddard lies to the south.

To reach the Devils Crags and the Citadel, follow the Bishop Pass trail from South Lake into Dusy Basin and down to the Muir Trail in LeConte Canyon. Head south on the John Muir Trail. To reach the base of the Citadel, cross the Kings River wherever possible (impossible in years of heavy runoff). Cross-country travel follows Ladder Creek to Ladder Lake. The Devils Crags are most easily reached from the junction of Palisade Creek and the south fork of the Kings River. A trailless slog up scree and brush leads to the upper reaches of Rambaud Creek.

Vern Clevenger

Mt. Goddard

Devils Crag #1 (12,560+ ft.)
Northwest Arête
Class 5

F.A. Jules Eichorn, Helen LeConte and Alfred Weiler;
July 25, 1933
Mt. Goddard Area Map: Page 168
USGS Quad Maps: Mt. Thompson, North Palisade
and Mt. Goddard

Devils Crag #1 is the highest and most massive of the jagged line of peaks known as the Devils Crags. Charles Michael, one of the leading climbers of the day, made the first ascent of Crag #1 in July, 1913. His exceptional solo route involved difficult, exposed climbing on extremely loose rock. Jules Eichorn, Glen Dawson and John Olmstead repeated his route in July, 1930.

Eichorn returned to the Devils Crags in 1933 and made the first ascent of the northwest arête of Crag #1 with Alfred Weiler and Helen LeConte (daughter of Joseph N. and Helen Gompertz-LeConte). This route shares the same exposure and final pitches with Michael's route. Eichorn first met Michael in Yosemite Valley (where Michael was postmaster), and remembers him as a "delightful person." Michael, who was known for difficult first ascents in Yosemite Valley, the Minarets and the Kaweahs, once told Eichorn that he considered Yosemite's Cathedral Spires "unclimbable." Although he respected Michael's judgement, the youthful Eichorn was intrigued, and along with Richard Leonard and Bestor Robinson, made the historic first ascents of both of these spires in 1934.

Route:
From the trailhead at South Lake, take the Bishop Pass trail into Dusy Basin. From Dusy Basin, descend into LeConte Canyon. At the trail junction in LeConte Canyon, follow the John Muir Trail south to Rambaud Creek and climb up arduous brush slopes alongside the creek to the cirque just north of the peak. Gain the pass to the southwest and head east along the ridge to the white-capped peak at the northwestern terminus of the Devils Crag. Rope up and traverse the narrow ridge for many rope lengths, passing two prominent notches and finishing by way of the dramatically exposed knife-edge to the summit. This is a loose and dangerous route.

Descent:
Retrace your steps.

Claude Fiddler

Devil's Crag #1 from the southwest

The Citadel (11,744 ft.)
Northeast Arête of East Summit
IV 5.10+

F.A. Dave Nettle and Jim Howle; August, 1991
Mt. Goddard Area Map: Page 168
USGS Quad Maps: Mt. Thompson, North Palisade and Mt. Goddard

The impressive north wall of the Citadel looms high above the John Muir Trail in LeConte Canyon. The granite walls of Languille Peak and the Citadel rise more than 3,000 feet above the middle fork of the Kings River, making LeConte Canyon one of the more dramatic sights in the Sierra backcountry. Joseph N. LeConte described the view down the canyon bearing his name: "The other side, as I feared, broke down in the savage black gorges of the Middle Fork region, which were choked with snow and frozen lakes far down below."

Yosemite climbers TM Herbert, Don Lauria and Dennis Hennek made the first ascent of the steep north face of the Citadel in 1968. Their route (IV, 5.7, A3) followed a prominent dihedral capped with overhangs on the peak's main buttress. TM recalled: "The route was Gordy Webster's idea. He talked me into hiking in there to do it with him, but a storm came in and we ended up walking back out over Bishop pass in a foot of new snow. I went back in later and climbed it with Don and Dennis Hennek. I was disappointed that we had used so much aid and never really recommended the route to anyone."

Dave Nettle and Jim Howle made the first ascent of the arête to the left of the original route in a marathon push: "We left Tahoe one evening after work," Nettle said, "and got to the trailhead at about 2 a.m. We did most of the hike in the dark, and got our first view of the peak at sunrise. We had originally planned to free the '68 route, but this arête was so striking we couldn't resist. We reached the summit late in the afternoon and made it back to the car after midnight. We drove back to Tahoe in time to go to work the next day. The crux of the trip may well have been the ten hours of driving and the 32 or so miles we hiked that day." They called their striking line the Edge of Time Arête.

Route:
From the trailhead at South Lake, take the Bishop Pass trail into Dusy Basin. From Dusy Basin, descend into the LeConte Canyon. At the trail junction in LeConte Canyon, follow the John Muir Trail south to Ladder Creek; cross the stream and follow its north side. Steep scree leads to a pillar at the base of the arête. Begin by climbing an obvious right-trending corner on the left side of the pillar. Face climbing leads up and left to a ledge system with trees. Follow the arête for five pitches, passing the first roof on the right and the second on the left to a big ledge at an obvious notch. Above the notch, either climb a steep face (5.9) on the left or a strenuous thin corner (5.10). The last three pitches (Class 4-5) follow the right side of the arête, ending on the east ridge. This leads to the summit.

Descent:
From the summit, follow the west ridge (Class 2) to the east end of Ladder Lake.

Dave Nettle

The North Face of The Citadel

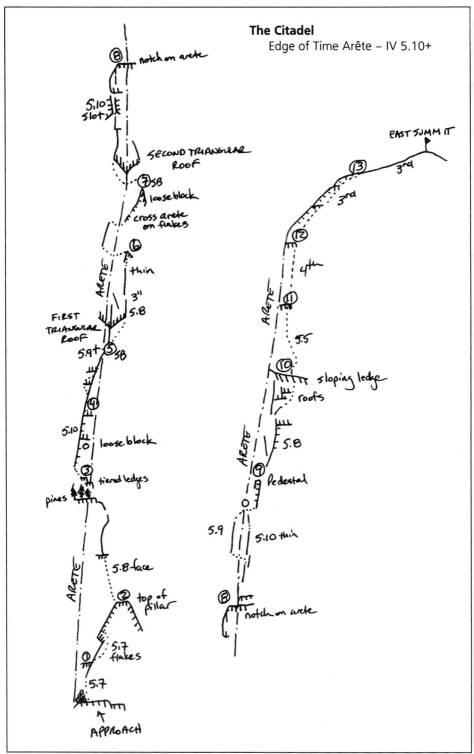

The Citadel
Edge of Time Arête – IV 5.10+

⑧ notch on arete

5.10 slot +

SECOND TRIANGULAR ROOF

⑦ 5.8
loose block

cross arete on flakes

⑥ thin

ARETE

3" 5.8

FIRST TRIANGULAR ROOF

5.9+ ⑤ 5.8

④

5.10 0 loose block

③ tiered ledges

pines

5.8 face

② top of pillar

① 5.7 flakes

5.7

APPROACH

EAST SUMMIT

⑬ 3rd

3rd

⑫ 4th

ARETE

⑪ TOP

5.5

⑩ sloping ledge

roofs

ARETE

5.8

⑨ Pedestal

0

5.9 5.10 thin

⑧ notch on arete

John Moynier

The Devil's Crags

Charybdis (13,091 ft.)
Northeast Shoulder
Class 3

F.A. Anna Dempster and John Dempster; July, 1931
Mt. Goddard Area Map: Page 168
USGS Quad Maps: Mt. Thompson and Mt. Goddard

Charybdis was named by Theodore Solomons during his trip down the Enchanted Gorge with Ernest Bonner in 1895. The metamorphic towers of Charybdis and the Scylla form a dark gate to the Enchanted Gorge, recalling Greek mythology. In Homer's Odyssey, *the Charybdis was a deadly whirlpool located opposite the cave of Scylla, guarding the Strait of Messina. Solomons wrote: "At half past one this gorge lay before us, and in an hour we had descended to its head, which we found was guarded by a nearly frozen lake, whose sheer, ice-smoothed walls arose on either side, up and up, seemingly into the very sky, their crowns two sharp black peaks of most majestic form. A Scylla and a Charybdis they seemed to us, as we stood at the margin of the lake and wondered how we might pass the dangerous portal."*

Route:

From the trailhead at Lake Sabrina, take the trail to Echo Lake and cross Echo Col (Class 3) to the John Muir Trail. Just beyond Helen Lake, travel cross-country south over Black Giant Pass to the base of the northeast ridge of Charybdis. Climb the south side of the ridge to the summit.

Descent:

Retrace your steps.

The northwest side of Charybdis. The Northeast Shoulder route is approached from the opposite side of the mountain, and roughly follows the left skyline shown here.

Vern Clevenger

Mt. Goddard (13,568 ft.)
East Ridge
Class 3

F.A. Walter A. Starr, Jr; August, 1928
Mt. Goddard Area Map: Page 168
USGS Quad Maps: Mt. Thompson and Mt. Goddard

Mt. Goddard is one of the dominant peaks of the High Sierra. This solitary giant's position west of the crest makes it visible from many points in the Sierra. Goddard's rock is very loose, however, and the peak is best climbed on skis in late spring. Mt. Goddard was named by the California Geological Survey in 1864 for George Henry Goddard, a civil engineer for the state of California in the 1850s.

The first ascent of the peak was made via the southwest ridge from Martha Lake by Lil A. Winchell and Louis Davis in 1879. Fifty years later, Walter A. Starr, Jr. chose the more interesting east ridge from Evolution Basin for his ascent. Both Starr and his father were active mountaineers and members of the Sierra Club. Francis Farquhar described his young friend: "He usually traveled alone, for few could keep up with him on the trails and few equaled him in the agility with which he climbed."

Starr, Jr. was the author of the definitive trail guide to the range, Starr's Guide to the John Muir Trail and the High Sierra Region. *This book was published posthumously by his father after Starr's tragic death while attempting a solo climb of Michael Minaret in 1933. The elder Starr dedicated the book to his son, stating: "May the traveler feel the companionship of that eager, joyous and generous youth who loved the beauty of the mountains and wanted others to share his love."*

Route:
From the trailhead at Lake Sabrina, take the trail to Echo Lake and cross Echo Col (Class 3) to the John Muir Trail. Continue over Muir Pass to Wanda Lake. As an alternative, the trail over Lamarck Col can be used to reach the John Muir Trail near Evolution Lake. Cross a low saddle west of Wanda Lake to the lakes at the base of the north side of Mt. Goddard. Climb the north ridge of the smaller peak just east of the summit, and ascend talus slopes on the east ridge to the summit of Mt. Goddard.

Descent:
Retrace your steps.

Mt. Goddard over Mt. Darwin

John Moynier

Mt. Humphreys Area

Viewed across the open expanses of Humphreys Basin, Mt. Humphreys rises well above its neighboring peaks, and is just fourteen feet shy of being the northernmost 14,000-foot peak in the Sierra. On a clear day, this landmark can be seen from the coast range and some spots in the central valley. Mt. Humphreys is an even more spectacular sight when viewed from Bishop, ten thousand feet below to the east.

Mt. Humphreys attracted the attention of early mountaineers, and was possibly first climbed by John Muir in 1873. Muir's notes mention climbing the highest peak at the head of the San Joaquin, " . . . either Mt. Humphreys or the next peak south." The first recorded ascent was made by James and Edward Hutchinson in 1904.

There are a number of fine ice gullies on the surrounding peaks, including the north faces of Mt. Lamarck, Mt. Emerson, the Glacier Divide and the Checkered Demon on Peak 13,112. An outlying peak of Peak 13,112 is known as Mt. Locke, home to the "Wahoo Gullies," some of the Sierra's finest spring ski descents. This peak commemorates Bob Locke, a popular Yosemite climber of the 1970s, who died in a fall on the south face of Mt. Watkins. "Bob O" (as he was known), was a keen skier who traveled the range in search of steep ski descents.

Approaches

The two best approaches to this area are both from the east side. To reach the Humphreys Basin area, head west from Bishop on Highway 168 to North Lake. From the trailhead, take the Piute Pass trail into Humphreys Basin and the lakes at the base of the southwest face of Mt. Humphreys.

To reach the east side of this area, follow the Buttermilk road (dirt) from Highway 168 past the excellent bouldering at the Buttermilk Boulders. Continue up the rough road and turn off on the four-wheel drive road to the McGee Creek trailhead. The east arête of Mt. Humphreys is west of the trailhead; Mt. Locke and Peak 13,112 are the rugged peaks to the south. The Checkered Demon is the steep ice gully on the north face of Peak 13,112. To reach the north face of Mt. Emerson, continue on the Buttermilk road, then follow the rough road to the site of the abandoned "Bishop Bowl" ski area, at the eastern end of the colorful Piute Crags.

Mt. Humphreys Area

Mt. Emerson (13,225 ft.)
North Face
Class 4 snow and ice

F.A. Norman Clyde; July, 1926
Mt. Humphreys Area Map: Page 182
USGS Quad Map: Mt. Tom

Mt. Emerson was named by John Muir during a trip into the area in 1873. The name commemorates the philosopher and essayist Ralph Waldo Emerson, who visited Muir in Yosemite Valley in 1871. The summit of the peak has been incorrectly marked on some maps; it is the eastern peak. The white granite of the peak contrasts strongly with the colorful reds of the nearby Piute Crags.

Splitting the 1,000-foot high north face of Mt. Emerson is a narrow snow and ice couloir that is more than 40 degrees in places. This bold line, first climbed by Norman Clyde, was accomplished in the style of the day: "An ice axe was seldom or never seen," he said, "Any ice cutting was usually done with some sort of wood axe. As to foot gear, there was a tendency to wear at least moderately high boots. Often they were provided with Hungarian nails or hobnails, although somewhat later I changed to Tricouni nails. These were better on snow and ice, but not too satisfactory on smooth hard rock."

Route:
Follow the dirt Buttermilk Road, which leaves Highway 168 west of Bishop. Continue past the turnoff to the McGee Creek trailhead to the road leading to the old rope tows in Bishop Bowl. Travel cross country into the cirque between Peak 13.112 and Mt. Emerson. Scramble up the moraine to the base of the wall and climb the obvious gully on the north face to the east ridge of the peak. The summit is a short scramble to the west.

Alternative Routes:
Nearby Peak 13,112 has two fine ice gullies on its north face. The steep central gully is known as the Checkered Demon and was first climbed by Doug Robinson and John Fischer in blizzard conditions in October, 1970.

Descent:
Retrace your steps.

The North Face of Mt. Emerson

Allan Pietrasanta

Mt. Humphreys (13,986 ft.)
Northwest Face
Class 4

F.A. George Bunn and party; August, 1919
Mt. Humphreys Area Map: Page 182
USGS Quad Map: Mt. Tom

John Muir described Mt. Humphreys: "(It is) a grand wide-winged mountain at the head of the San Joaquin. Its head is high above its fellows and its wings are white with ice and snow." He first visited this region in 1873 and quite possibly made the first ascent, as his notes recount having "climbed the highest peak at the head of the San Joaquin." Minor details – like exactly which peak this was – were often less important to Muir than the natural history of the area. Mt. Humphreys was named by the Whitney Survey for Andrew Humphreys, a Civil War hero who became the chief engineer of the U.S. Army after the war.

James and Edward Hutchinson made the first recorded ascent of Mt. Humphreys in July, 1904. Their climb up the southwest face was quite difficult, and the other members of the party decided against climbing the final tower (rated 5.4). Those not risking the summit attempt built a cairn and named the secondary summit "Married Men's Point." Hutchinson described the final climb: "The summit of Mt. Humphreys is not more than eight feet square . . . It is one mass of cracked and broken blocks, thrown loosely together in such a way as to warn one to move cautiously lest the whole top should break off and fall into the great abyss to the eastward."

Route:
From North Lake, take the Piute Pass trail to Humphreys Basin. Above the lakes at the base of the great southwest face, a number of scree gullies come down off the peak. Take the left-hand gully and follow it to the notch just northwest of the summit tower. A shallow trough (Class 3-4) leads up the northwest face to a steep wall with good holds. Follow this (Class 4) to the summit.

Descent:
Rappel or downclimb the face and retrace your steps down the gully.

John Moynier

Mt. Humphreys over the Humphreys Basin; with the northwest ridge on the left skyline and the East Arête on the right skyline.

Mt. Humphreys (13,986 ft.)
East Arête
II 5.4

F.A. Norman Clyde; June, 1935
Mt. Humphreys Area Map: Page 182
USGS Quad Map: Mt. Tom

The east arête of Mt. Humphreys is a long, exposed and continuously interesting climb ending at Humphreys' secondary summit, which is known as Married Men's Point. Norman Clyde made the first ascent of this airy route and considered Mt. Humphreys a classic mountaineering challenge: "The mountain possesses an unusually stern and almost forbidding aspect and is generally rated one of the most difficult of the higher peaks of the Sierra Nevada."

Many parties shorten the route up the east arête by climbing a steep scree and talus gully to the notch at the base of the final ridge. Although it saves time, this shortcut eliminates much of the knife-edge traverse that gives this route its charm. The complete route to the summit from the saddle joining Peak 12,241 (locally known as "Peaklet") is highly recommended and offers one of the classic ridge climbs of the Sierra.

Route:
From the McGee Creek trailhead, scramble up to the saddle on the east arête between Mt. Humphreys and Peak 12,241. Follow the arête west, negotiating gendarmes, to a prominent tower on the ridge. Downclimb into the notch and scramble up ledges to a steep headwall. A ledge leads left to an exposed crack (5.2), which reaches easier ground and Married Men's Peak. Traverse to the notch on the right side of the steep summit tower. A right-slanting crack (5.4) is followed to the top of Mt. Humphreys.

Descent:
Rappel or downclimb the tower, then downclimb the east ridge to the prominent notch. A steep scree gully leads down into the cirque below Peak 13,112 and the Checkered Demon ice climb; follow this drainage back to the trailhead. It also is possible to descend the northwest ridge and the northeast couloir to the glacier under the north face of Mt. Humphreys. Follow McGee Creek back to the trailhead.

John Moynier

Mt. Humphreys, East Arête

Seven Gables Area

The Seven Gables area is home to the granite spires of Granite Park, the imposing walls of Merriam Peak and Feather Peak, the Seven Gables and the south face of Bear Creek Spire. This rocky scenery is enhanced by the numerous small lakes and meadows scattered through the region. Climbers who also have a weakness for golden trout may think this is heaven. Bob Harrington recalled, "The biggest trout I've ever seen in the Sierra was caught by a guy who was fishing the Royce Lakes the day we arrived there."

Theodore Solomons made an early visit to the area, making the first ascent of the Seven Gables from the west with Leigh Bierce on September 20, 1894. The pair spent ten frustrating days trying to find a way over the Bear Creek Divide for their stock. As they prepared to attempt the crossing on foot, an early winter storm overtook them. The next day, they awoke to four feet of new snow! Solomons and Bierce shot their mules to spare them starvation and abandoned their new view camera, along with several dozen exposed glass plates. Shouldering their loads for a forced march out, they reached Fresno on October 8 after an epic journey.

Approaches

There are few trails through the Seven Gales region. The John Muir Trail makes a major detour to the west to avoid this rugged area. The trail through Granite Park and over Italy Pass has not been maintained in decades. Most climbers approach the region from the east side. Heading north from Bishop on Highway 395, take the spur road past the small mining community of Rovanna (no services) to the Pine Creek trailhead, located just below a large tungsten mine. A short trail accesses an abandoned mining road leading up the steep canyon, the road eventually becomes a trail again. The trail forks just past Upper Pine Lake. The left fork leads to Pine Creek Pass and the right fork leads to Granite Park.

Take the left fork to the pass and head west up ledges to the outlet of Royce Lakes. The three stunning peaks on the left are Merriam Peak, Royce Peak and Feather Peak. To reach the Seven Gables, ascend the small glacier to the col (Class 3) between Merriam and Royce Peaks. From the col, traverse to the saddle west of La Salle Lake (Class 3); this leads into the Bear Creek drainage and around to the Seven Gables Lakes.

Seven Gables (13,075 ft.)
Direct East Face
IV 5.9

F.A.: Claude Fiddler and Vern Clevenger; August, 1981
Seven Gables Area Map: Page 190
USGS Quad Maps: Mt. Tom and Mt. Hilgard

Theodore Solomons made the first ascent of this double-summited peak in 1894 with Leigh Bierce. The many buttresses on the north side of the peak inspired its name. "The south wall of the gap we found to be the side of a peak," wrote Solomons, "the eccentric shape of which is suggested in the name Seven Gables, which we hastened to fasten upon it . . . We climbed the Seven Gables on the afternoon of our arrival at the head of the valley – September 20. There was a dash of snow on its chimney-like pinnacle, which must be upwards of 13,600 feet above the sea."

The most impressive feature of this complex peak is the great east face of the north summit. Vern Clevenger described the route up the center of the face as: "Probably the most significant backcountry climb that I've done." They were inspired to make this ascent by a description of the "unclimbed east face" in Steve Roper's Climber's Guide to the High Sierra. *Apparently, the route was repeated in 1988 by Dick Duane and Sebastian Letemendia, who thought they had done the first ascent – a common situation with many backcountry climbs.*

Route:
Approach from Pine Creek to the Royce Lakes, then go on to Seven Gable Lakes. The twin-summited peak is the jagged backdrop for these lakes. The main summit is to the south; the route lies directly up the east face of the north summit. From the lowest of the lakes, head up to the base of the triangular face. Follow cracks up the central pillar in the middle of the face. At the top of the face, the pillar becomes a knife-edged arête leading directly to the north summit.

Descent:
Drop down talus and ledges to the saddle between the peaks. Cross the main (south) summit and descend easier terrain to Seven Gables Lake.

The Seven Gables above Seven Gables Lakes

Merriam Peak (13,077 ft.)
North Buttress
III 5.10

F.A. Bob Harrington and Vern Clevenger; August, 1976
Seven Gables Area Map: Page 190
USGS Quad Maps: Mt. Tom and Mt. Hilgard

Merriam Peak is the eastern-most of the trio of granite peaks overlooking the beautiful Royce Lakes. This peak was named in 1929 for Dr. Clinton Hart Merriam, who was chief of the U.S. Biological Survey in the late 1800s and later chairman of the U.S. Geographic board. Other names for this peak have included "Isosceles Peak," due to its appearance when viewed from the north, and "Bastille Peak," in honor of the first ascent of the peak made by Sierra Club climbers Lewis Clark, Julie Mortimer and Ted Waller on Bastille Day, 1933.

The north buttress of Merriam Peak is an impressive sight from Royce Lakes. The steep buttress ends on a narrow arête leading to the summit. High-quality rock and excellent climbing characterize the route. Clevenger recalls that he and Bob Harrington had underestimated the route's length and difficulty. Thinking it would be about 5.5 in difficulty, they expected be back in camp by mid-afternoon. After a leisurely breakfast, they strolled over to the wall and began climbing unroped.

Almost immediately, their progress was halted by a difficult crack. A number of hard pitches led the pair to an intimidating corner on the prow of the final tower. An intense thunderstorm was building as Clevenger made the final lead. They reached the summit in late afternoon and made it back to camp just before darkness fell.

Route:
From Pine Creek, take the trail to Pine Creek Pass and climb to the lower Royce Lake. Hike around the lake and ascend broken rock to the toe of the buttress. Climb more or less straight up the buttress, aiming for a left-facing corner about halfway up the route. Climb a crack (5.8) left of the corner to a large flake, and continue up to the base of a left-facing dihedral. The last pitch is the crux, involving a steep lieback (5.10) up the dihedral and ending at a notch behind a block on top of the buttress. Moderate climbing along the knife-edged ridge leads to the summit.

Descent:
Climb down the east face (Class 3) to the lake.

Merriam Peak from Royce Lakes

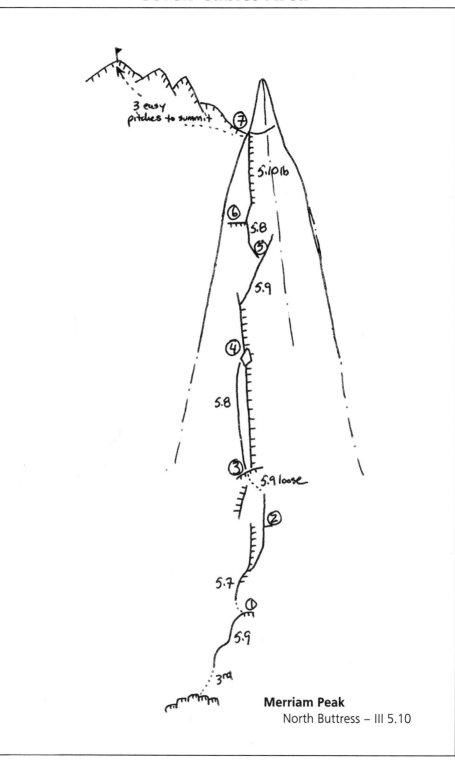

3 easy pitches to summit

⑦

5.10 lb

⑥

5.8

⑤

5.9

④

5.8

③

5.9 loose

②

5.7

①

5.9

3rd

Merriam Peak
North Buttress – III 5.10

Bob Harrington on Merriam Peak

Vern Clevenger

Feather Peak (13,242 ft.)
North Couloir
Class 4-5 ice

F.A. Michael Graber and Alan Bartlett; December, 1976
Seven Gables Area Map: Page 190
USGS Quad Maps: Mt. Tom and Mt. Hilgard

David Brower had made the first ascent of the peak in July, 1933 on his first long backcountry trip. He had promised to name the peak after a young boy, Otis Jasper, but unfortunately (for the boy at least), Brower did not record the name. Norman Clyde called this Feather Peak after he climbed it in 1935, and his appellation has become official.

Over the past twenty years, Mike Graber and Alan Bartlett have climbed a number of fine backcountry routes as members of the loose-knit "Buff Alpine Club." This club also included Dennis Hennek, Rob Dellinger, Allan Pietrasanta, Alan Roberts, Bill St Jean and Gail Wilts. Graber was a confident leader on steep ice, but Bartlett was known to grumble about "wasting his time" on snow and ice routes, or on long approaches. This couloir on Feather Peak was his first backcountry ice climb and Bartlett recalled that Graber "led him up the thing."

Route:
From the trailhead at Pine Creek, follow the route to Pine Creek Pass and climb to Royce Lakes. As seen from the upper lake, the couloir is just west of the slabby north face. Follow the steep couloir to the notch, where a short Class-3 pitch leads to the summit.

Alternative Routes:
The north face also has been climbed (II 5.8; F.A. Gary Colliver, Edward Keller, Mark Waller and Andy Lichtman; August, 1966). Climb up slabs to a headwall, then climb a dihedral that is followed by a steep jam crack (5.8) to the top.

Descent:
Head down ledges on the southeast side to the col between Feather and Royce Peaks. A short, steep couloir leads back to the lake.

Feather Peak from the north

John Moynier

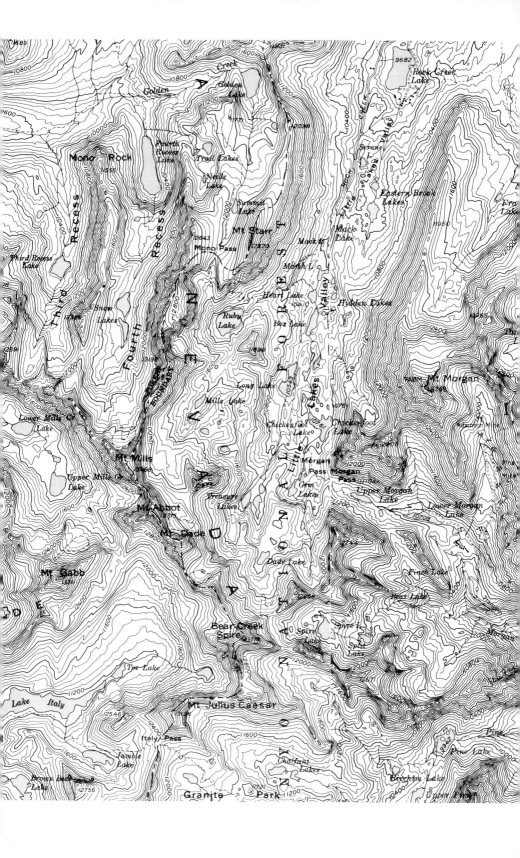

Rock Creek Area

The Rock Creek region offers some of the most accessible backcountry climbing in the Sierra. The paved road from Tom's Place on Highway 395 ends at Mosquito Flats, at an elevation of 10,200 feet. The trail through the canyon was once an old mining road, climbing over Morgan Pass and descending to the tungsten mines in Pine Creek Canyon. Six of the peaks ringing the canyon are more than 13,000 feet, and three (Mt. Morgan, Mt. Abbot and Bear Creek Spire), reach more than 13,700 ft.

Of special interest to hard core climbers is the 1,000-foot Ruby Wall, located above Ruby Lake. This wall is actually a series of spectacular buttresses, corners and faces on which there are currently four routes, with Galen Rowell and Robert "S.P." Parker having each climbed two. All four routes are rated Grade IV, 5.10.

In August, 1971, Rowell made first ascents of both the north arête and the south face of Bear Creek Spire. A direct route (IV 5.9) up the center of the south face was climbed by Robert Parker and Bill Kerwin in February, 1988. There are at least two other routes on the broad face.

Mt. Morgan, the tallest peak in the area, was first climbed by the Wheeler Survey party in 1870. Like many other ascents by the Whitney and Wheeler surveys, the peak was climbed more for its expansive views and topographic value than for any particular interest in mountaineering. James Hutchinson, J.N. LeConte and Duncan McDuffie made the first ascent of Mt. Abbot in July, 1908 from a camp at Lake Italy. They climbed the steep and loose southwest chute from Gabbot Pass.

Approaches

Turn off Highway 395 at the whistle-stop of Tom's Place, where there are accommodations, a small cafe and a general store, but no gas. Take the Rock Creek Road past Rock Creek Lake to the trailhead at Mosquito Flat. There are a number of campgrounds along the road, including a walk-in campground at the trailhead.

The main trail leads up the Little Lakes Valley toward Morgan Pass. From Long Lake, an unmaintained trail leads past Treasure Lakes to the base of Bear Creek Spire. To reach Mt. Abbot, follow the Mono Pass trail to Ruby Lake. A faint climber's trail continues up the drainage past Mills Lake to the glacier at the base of Mt. Abbot.

Rock Creek Traverse
Mono Pass to Morgan Pass
V 5.9

F.A. Rick Wheeler, 1976
Rock Creek Area Map: Page 200
USGS Quad Maps: Mt. Morgan, Mt. Abbot and
Mt. Hilgard

As seen from near the trailhead at Mosquito Flat, the Rock Creek crest forms a jagged skyline of massive peaks and rugged gendarmes. The wild traverse of this crest involves nearly four miles of mostly fourth- and fifth-class terrain, and stays above 13,000 feet for much of its length. The rock is generally very sound and the exposure is quite spectacular in spots.

The Rock Creek crest was first traversed by Rick Wheeler, a prominent figure in the Sierra climbing scene. For many years he lived the life of a prototypical climbing bum, but in the late 1970s, he opened up a climbing shoe repair shop in Bishop. Wheeler's first employee was Bob Harrington, and many other east-side climbers have spent time working there. One such climber was James Wilson, who eventually took over the business, which is now called Wilson's Eastside Sports.

During his traverse, Wheeler climbed around the most difficult sections of the crest. In 1981, Vern Clevenger attempted to stay on the crest the entire way, which involved downclimbing some very exposed 5.9 moves without a rope. Claude Fiddler and Rick Cashner repeated Clevenger's route in 1987, as did Peter Croft and Andrew Stevens in July, 1992. Both of these teams were impressed with the quality of the climbing on the traverse.

Route:

From the trailhead at Mosquito Flat, follow the trail to Mono Pass. The route traverses the knife-edged crest above the Ruby Wall, over Ruby Peak and on to Mt. Mills. One of the cruxes involves downclimbing into the notch between Mt. Mills and Mt. Abbot, and another occurs in the traverse between Mt. Abbot and Mt. Dade. The route eases as it traverses Bear Creek Spire to Pyramid Peak. The rock quality deteriorates as the route reaches Rosy Finch Peak. It ends in a steep loose gully leading down to Morgan Pass and the trail back to Mosquito Flat.

John Moynier

The Ruby Wall in Rock Creek Canyon

Mt. Morgan (13,748 ft.)
Southwest Ridge
Class 4

F.A. Chester Versteeg; 1942
Rock Creek Area Map: Page 200
USGS Quad Map: Mt. Morgan

This is the southern-most of the two Mt. Morgans in the Rock Creek area. Named for J.H. Morgan, a member of the Wheeler Survey party who explored the area in 1878, this massive peak is the tallest mountain north of Mt. Humphreys, and there is an especially extensive view of the Sierra from its summit.

The route begins at Morgan Pass and traverses over the summit of Little Lakes Peak, which was named by Chester Versteeg on the first ascent. Versteeg, a lawyer by profession, devoted much of his free time to exploring the High Sierra, and climbed hundreds of peaks; many of these climbs were first ascents. He also researched and proposed names for many of the features of the Sierra, some of which were accepted and some which were not.

During Versteeg's 1942 traverse of Mt. Morgan, he gave the names "Little Lakes Peak," "12 Flags Peak" and "Mt. Paiute" to subsidiary summits. For his numerous contributions, the U.S. Board of Geographic Names honored Versteeg by naming a peak for him. Mt. Versteeg is located on the Sierra Crest between Mt. Tyndall and Trojan Peak. Trojan Peak was named by Versteeg in honor of the athletic teams of his beloved University of Southern California.

Route:
From Mosquito Flat, follow the trail through the Little Lakes Valley to Morgan Pass. Climb steep slabs onto the crest of the ridge leading to the summit of Little Lakes Peak. Descend the ridge to the narrow saddle between Little Lakes Peak and Mt. Morgan. The ridge leading to the summit of Mt. Morgan is long, and involves steep blocks and loose talus.

Descent:
Continue down the northwest ridge of Mt. Morgan until it is possible to descend a steep, loose talus gully to Eastern Brook Lakes and the trailhead.

Mt. Morgan and Little Lakes Peak

Bear Creek Spire (13,713 ft.)
East Arête
IV 5.8

F.A. Bob Harrington; July, 1980?
Rock Creek Area Map: Page 200
USGS Quad Maps: Mt. Morgan, Mt. Abbot and Mt. Hilgard

The northern aspect of Bear Creek Spire commands the view for those traveling in the Little Lakes Valley. From the Pine Creek drainage, the great south face and razor-thin east arête of the spire are an impressive sight as well.

It is surprising that the first ascent of the classic east arête was made so recently. There is some confusion about exactly who made that ascent, especially considering the description in Steve Roper's 1976 guidebook: "This is the spectacular step-like ridge which rises from the col between Bear Creek Spire and the peaklet southwest of Spire Lake. It is an enjoyable and lengthy climb. F.A. Unknown."

After some detective work, Galen Rowell believed the route had not actually been climbed and set off to make the "first ascent" with John Martinek in August, 1982. They spent a long day on the route, climbing 22 pitches, but it is recorded in R.J Secor's guidebook, The High Sierra – Peaks, Passes and Trails, that they were beaten to the first ascent by Jim Lucke and David Stevenson, who climbed it in July, 1981.

Bob Harrington casually mentioned to the authors that he had soloed the route sometime before that, "I probably climbed the route in the summer of 1980. Since I was soloing, I avoided the harder parts by traversing out onto the north face." He also said that he was pretty sure he wasn't the first to climb it. Maybe Roper was right after all.

Route:

From the trailhead at Mosquito Flat, take the Morgan Pass trail to Long Lake, and then follow the unmaintained trail to Dade Lake. Cross the northeast ridge of Bear Creek Spire and traverse to the base of arête. Gain the crest at the lowest point and climb the very narrow arête, passing a number of gendarmes and finishing at the summit boulder. The rock is excellent on this route.

Descent:

About 100 feet north of the summit boulder is a short Class-4 section, which is either rappeled or downclimbed to a sloping ramp. Below this, steep sand and talus lead to the northern shoulder of the peak. From here, drop down ledges and a small glacier to Dade Lake.

The East Arête of Bear Creek Spire   Dave Nettle

Bear Creek Spire (13,713 ft.)
Northeast Ridge
Class 4

F.A. Norman Clyde; May, 1932
Rock Creek Area Map: Page 200
USGS Quad Maps: Mt. Morgan, Mt. Abbot and Mt. Hilgard

Norman Clyde described Bear Creek Spire: "(It is) an unusually impressive mountain of the Matterhorn type. On all sides, except the west, it drops away in almost vertical walls hundreds of feet in height. The summit itself is a single monolith, only a few feet in diameter, from which these jagged arêtes radiate." Clyde's route up the northeast ridge is an enjoyable scramble to an exhilerating summit.

Clyde made this first ascent from one of his annual spring ski base camps at the head of Rock Creek Canyon. A few years later, Clyde worked with David Brower to compile the Sierra Club's Manual of Ski Mountaineering. *Their "office" for this project was Clyde's spring base camp below Bear Creek Spire.*

Route:
From the trailhead at Mosquito Flats, take the Morgan Pass trail to Long Lake, then follow the unmaintained trail to Dade Lake. Climb up talus and slabs to the saddle at the base of the northeast ridge of Bear Creek Spire. Ascend the ridge, traversing around the south side of a tower. The ridge steepens just before it merges with the north arête. Two short Class-4 pitches up cracks lead to the crest of the arête, which is followed over large steps to the tiny summit block.

Descent:
About 100 feet north of the summit boulder is a short Class-4 section, which is either rappeled or downclimbed to a sloping ramp. Below this, steep sand and talus lead to the northern shoulder of the peak. From here, drop down ledges and a small glacier to Dade Lake.

John Moynier

Bear Creek Spire from the north. The East Arête is the left skyline; the Northeast Ridge rises to the left of the North Arête.

Bear Creek Spire (13,713 ft.)
North Arête
III 5.8

F.A. Galen Rowell and Jeanne Neale; August, 1971
Rock Creek Area Map: Page 200
USGS Quad Maps: Mt. Morgan, Mt. Abbot and
Mt. Hilgard

The north arête of Bear Creek Spire is a fine moderate alpine rock route. Chris Keith described it: "(The route involves) ten pitches of varied, sometimes strenuous, sometimes easy, but completely fun climbing on fine high-country granite. It is an impressive line." This climb is deceptively long, as the view from below is foreshortened.

Throughout his long and successful career climbing in the Sierra, Galen Rowell has made many fine ascents. Vern Clevenger and Claude Fiddler accompanied Rowell on many of these adventures. Fiddler recalled an especially memorable trip: "Vern, Galen and myself had just finished a difficult new route on a huge wall in the remote Dumbbell Lakes area. We were topping out at dusk and the long walk back to camp ensured a night out. Galen's tennies had fallen out of the haulbag on the climb and he would have to make the 25-mile hike back to the car in his EB's.

"We started marching as fast as we could, but darkness soon overtook us. We kept walking, trying to find drinking water. Galen found a lively little stream by stumbling into it. At this point we thought it might be prudent to fish the flashlight out of the pack. Galen jiggled, tapped and fidgeted with the thing trying to get it to work. Vern and I offered no assistance; after all Galen was a mechanic. Finally, Galen hefted a more than adequate-sized rock and pulverized our non-functioning salvation into small bits of plastic.

"At this point, we decided to settle down and spend a brisk, long night of shivering, hugging and calisthenics. The next day we got back to camp, packed, and hiked out. Although our late return would cause Galen to miss an important appointment, he did not mind at all. His adventures in the mountains meant a lot more to him, and all of us."

Route:
From the trailhead at Mosquito Flat, take the Morgan Pass trail to Long Lake, then follow the unmaintained trail to Dade Lake. Climb talus and slabs to the small glacier at the toe of the arête. A short slab leads to the base of the route. Begin in a hand crack (5.8) next to a left-facing corner. Climb up and right over flakes (5.7) to a ramp. Moderate climbing up the arête ends at a steep headwall. An awkward offwidth crack on the left leads to a notch above the headwall. Tunnel through to the other side and continue up the arête, weaving around exposed gendarmes. Higher up, another steep headwall is climbed via knobs. Many Class-4 pitches follow the top of the nearly horizontal arête to the summit boulder.

Descent:
About 100 feet north of the summit boulder is a short Class-4 section, which is either rappeled or downclimbed to a sloping ramp. Steep sand and talus lead to the northern shoulder of the peak. From here, drop down ledges and a small glacier to Dade Lake.

The North Arête of Bear Creek Spire   John Moynier

Rock Creek Area

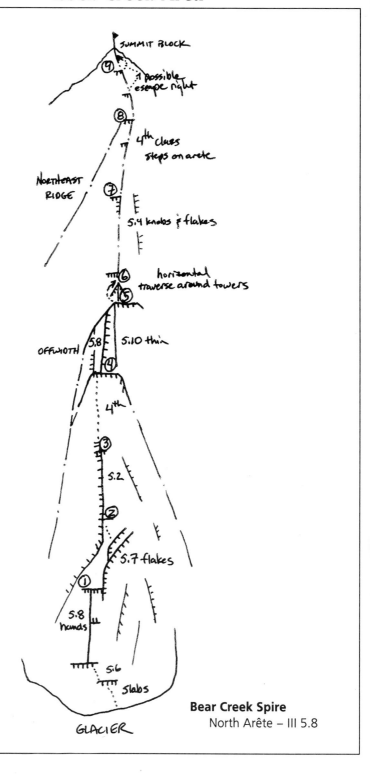

SUMMIT BLOCK

⑨

possible
escape right

⑧

4th class
steps on arete

NORTHEAST
RIDGE

⑦

5.4 knobs & flakes

⑥ horizontal
traverse around towers

⑤

OFFWIDTH 5.8 5.10 thin

④

4th

③

5.2

②

5.7 flakes

①

5.8
hands

5.6

slabs

GLACIER

Bear Creek Spire
North Arête – III 5.8

John Moynier on Mt. Abbot   Lance Machovsky

Mt. Dade (13,600+ ft.)
North Face
Class 4

F.A. Al Green, Dave Brown and Bill Stronge; 1972
Rock Creek Area Map: Page 200
USGS Quad Maps: Mt. Morgan and Mt. Abbot

Partially hidden by the colorful "Treasure Peak," the impressive north face of Mt. Dade is often overlooked by climbers heading for Mt. Abbot or Bear Creek Spire. The first ascent of Mt. Dade was made in August, 1911 by Liston and McKeen. They described themselves as "Locators of this fine peak," and left their record on a torn scrap of Ladies' Home Journal.

The first ascent of the north face of Mt. Dade was made by three members of the China Lake Search and Rescue Group. Their 1972 route climbed the steep snow couloir above the glacier to a rock rib in the center of the face. This rib was followed to the summit. To the authors' knowledge, the impressive pillar and arête to the left of the face has not been climbed.

Tim Forsell and John Moynier, guides at Rock Creek Winter Lodge, made a winter ascent of the north face in January, 1986. They cached their skis on the east side of the peak and postholed around to the base of the north face. Moynier described their adventure as a typical winter climb, combining hard ice, snow-covered ledges, heavy gloves, frozen feet and a short, cold day. The trip was completed by skiing down the steep Hourglass Couloir to the Treasure Lakes.

Route:
From the trailhead at Mosquito Flat, take the Mono Pass trail to Ruby Lake. On the east side of the lake, a faint climbers' trail follows the drainage past Mills Lake to the glacier below Mt. Abbot and Mt. Mills. Cross the glacier to the base of the north face of Mt. Dade. At the top of the glacier, cross the bergschrund and gain the ice slope above. At the top of the ice, continue up the rock face above to the summit buttress (Class 4).

Descent:
Descend talus on the southeast side to the top of the broad Hourglass Couloir. Descend this to the Treasure Lakes and the trail to Mosquito Flats.

John Moynier

The North Face of Mt. Dade

Mt. Abbot (13,704 ft.)
North Couloir
Class 4

F.A. David Brower, Hervey Voge and Norman Clyde; July, 1934
Rock Creek Area Map: Page 200
USGS Quad Maps: Mt. Morgan and Mt. Abbot

Henry Abbot was a surveyor and engineer who worked on the Pacific railroad through California and Oregon and later participated in the planning of the Panama Canal. The Whitney Survey party named Mt. Abbot during the busy summer of 1864. The first ascent was made by Joseph N. LeConte, James Hutchinson and Duncan McDuffie in July, 1908 from Lake Italy by way of the steep and loose southwest chute: "Then the rope was brought into play, and after two or three ugly places, we finally climbed over the edge once more, this time on the extreme summit, and Mount Abbot was conquered."

The route up the lower part of the north couloir of Mt. Abbot was first ascended by Brower, Voge and Clyde during their peak-bagging expedition of 1934. They left the snow at the halfway point and climbed up ledges on the right to the narrow north-west ridge, following it to the broad summit plateau. This route is the easiest and most popular route to Mt. Abbot's summit. In August, 1984, John Moynier continued up the steep ice of the upper couloir and then ascended a blocky chimney to the summit plateau for a more challenging finish.

Route:
From the trailhead at Mosquito Flats, take the Mono Pass trail to Ruby Lake. On the east side of the lake an unmaintained trail follows the drainage past Mills Lake to the glacier below Mt. Abbot and Mt. Mills. From the glacier, climb halfway up the couloir, exit onto Class-3 ledges on the right, then gain the northwest ridge. It is possible to continue up the couloir (**50 degrees near the top**). A loose chimney provides access to the summit plateau.

Alternative route:
The attractive spire in the Mills-Abbot Col is known locally as the Petit Griffon. It was first climbed by Pat Callis in 1966 via Class-4 cracks on the east side. The north face offers an excellent three pitch route up a prominent left-facing corner (5.9). This was climbed by Moynier and Andy Selters in July, 1990.

Descent:
Follow the narrow northwest ridge toward Mt. Mills, then descend Class-3 ledges on the north face to the lower couloir.

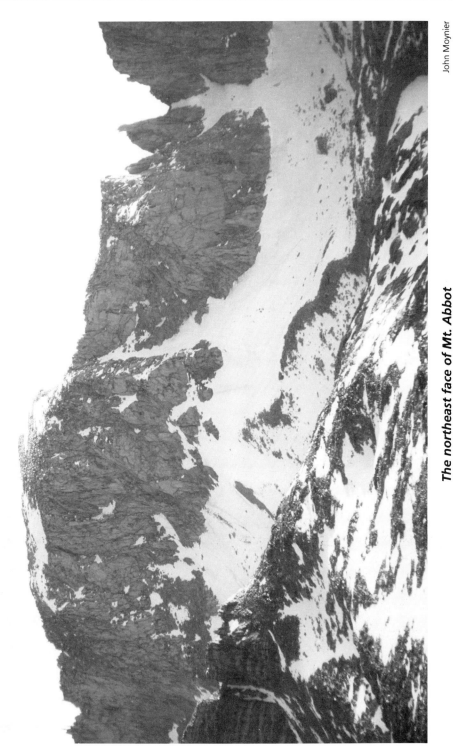

John Moynier

The northeast face of Mt. Abbot

Mt. Morrison
Area

In contrast to the abundant granite of the bulk of the Sierra, the Mt. Morrison area is comprised of ancient metamorphic rocks – primarily shales, dolomites and limestones. These rocks are part of the "Morrison roof pendant," the oldest rocks in the Sierra. They are a remnant of the original rock material that was deposited as sediment in a shallow inland sea. The uplifting that led to the present Sierra twisted and folded these rocks into fantastic shapes, spectacular towers and colorful cliffs.

These ancient rocks can be frightfully loose, and the great walls, so attractive from below, offer potentially dangerous ascents. The north face of Mt. Morrison, in particular, is more reminiscent of a route in the Canadian Rockies than the Sierra. Bruce Lella, a well-travelled local climber, called it: "A suicide climb, yet one of the most unique and satisfying routes in the range." This wall has been called the "Eiger of the Sierra." Perhaps this appellation has only made the wall more intriguing.

Some of the finest mountaineers in the history of the range have attacked this wall, with varying degrees of success. The slabby north buttress was first climbed in September, 1946 by Chuck Wilts and Harry Sutherland (IV 5.7), who avoided the steep lower section. Jim Wilson, Allen Steck and Ron Hayes made the first direct ascent of the north buttress (IV 5.8, A2) in July, 1960. The north face was first tackled via circuitous climbing (IV 5.8) by Tom Higgins and Charlie Raymond in May, 1967. The cleanest and most direct line on the north face (IV 5.10) was climbed by Dean Hobbs and Gary Slate in 1987.

The character of the dark, metamorphic rock in this area requires a level of commitment not usually associated with other Sierra rock types. Lacking the continuous, defined crack systems associated with Sierra granite, this type of rock presents the climber with a different kind of challenge. Extreme care must be taken, as even Class-3 routes are serious affairs.

It is generally accepted that the first proper roped climb in the Sierra was made when John Mendenhall and James Van Patten ascended the northeast face of Laurel Mountain (on the opposite side of Convict Lake from Mt. Morrison) in September, 1930. Their route is rarely repeated, and then usually as an early season snow and ice climb.

The following spring, Mendenhall climbed the steep snow gully to the right of the north face of Mt. Morrison. An avalanche cone at the base of the couloir provided moderate access to the upper gully, and he rated the route Class 3. Forty years later,

Yvon Chouinard, Doug Robinson and Dennis Hennek attempted the route as a winter ice climb. The avalanche cone at the base had not formed in many years and access to the couloir was blocked by a 200-foot cliff of rotten rock. Each of the climbers described this as the most dangerous climb of their careers, and named the route the Death Couloir.

Approaches

The two main approaches to the area are by way of the Convict and McGee Creek trails. Both are accessed off Highway 395 in the Crowley Lake area, near the Mammoth Lakes airport. To reach the trailhead for the Nevahbe Ridge and Red and White Mountain, drive up the McGee Creek Road to the parking lot just past the pack station. The Nevahbe Ridge is to the east across the creek. The McGee Pass trail follows an old mining road up the canyon to the McGee Lakes, and continues on to McGee Pass, which lies between Red and White Mountain and Red Slate Mountain.

To reach the Convict Creek trailhead, take the road opposite the Mammoth Lakes Airport to Convict Lake. The trail skirts the west side of the lake to a rough trail leading into the hanging valley at the base of Mt. Morrison's north face. To reach Red Slate Mountain, continue up the Convict Creek trail to Mildred Lake. An unmaintained trail continues up the drainage to Constance Lake at the base of the peak.

Climber near the top of the Red Slate Couloir   Allan Pietrasanta

Mt. Morgan North (13,005 ft.)
Nevahbe Ridge
Class 3-4

F.A. Unknown
Mt. Morrison Area Map: Page 218
USGS Quad Map: Convict Lake

The sweeping crest of the Nevahbe Ridge is a dramatic and colorful backdrop for the community of Crowley Lake. This route is a long, airy ridge climb, rising nearly a vertical mile from McGee Creek to the summit. The climbing is continually interesting and involves a wide range of rock types and quality.

The peak is named for J.P. Morgan, the prominent banker who was involved with the "Big Four" in the development of the transcontinental Central Pacific Railroad. The four – Leland Stanford, Charles Crocker, Mark Hopkins and Collis Huntington – all have nearby peaks named for them in the nearby Pioneer Basin.

Route:
Cross McGee Creek just before the pack station, and hike up brushy slopes to the base of a couloir that leads to the ridge crest. Climb the steep couloir and ascend the ridge. Along the way, short steep steps on less than perfect rock force one out onto the greatly exposed east face, directly overlooking the town of Crowley Lake. From the top of the Nevahbe Ridge, sandy granite slopes lead to the summit of Mt. Morgan.

Descent:
Descend colorful Esha Canyon back to the pack station.

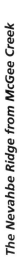

John Moyner

The Nevahbe Ridge from McGee Creek

Red and White Mtn. (12,850 ft.)
Northeast Ridge
Class 3

F.A. Norman Clyde; July, 1928
Mt. Morrison Area Map: Page 218
USGS Quad Maps: Convict Lake and Mt. Abbot

The first ascent of Red and White Mountain was made by James Hutchinson, Lincoln Hutchinson and Charles A. Noble in July, 1902. Their route up this colorful peak ascended the loose and exposed knife-edged west ridge. In 1928, Norman Clyde climbed the northeast ridge from near McGee Pass. This route is steeper than the west ridge, but the rock is less shattered and offers a safer ascent.

Prior to this ascent, Clyde had resigned his post as principal of Independence High School. On Halloween night in 1927, Clyde learned that some rowdy students were planning to vandalize his school. In an attempt to protect the school, Clyde ambushed the students and fired some warning shots over their heads. The parents demanded his arrest, but the sheriff refused to press charges. He told them that if Clyde had wanted to hit the kids, he would have, as he was the best pistol shot in the county. Unsatisfied, the parents demanded and received Clyde's resignation. Clyde never returned to a permanent job, and spent the next forty years as a writer, guide and caretaker at various resorts along the eastern Sierra.

Glen Dawson, Jules Eichorn and John Olmstead made the second ascent of Clyde's route in July, 1930. It was the first time Dawson and Eichorn had climbed together and marked the beginning of their lifelong friendship and climbing partnership.

Route:
From the trailhead in McGee Creek, follow the McGee Pass trail past Big McGee Lake and Little McGee Lake. From Little McGee Lake, go west up a shallow gully (often snowfilled) to a small glacier just below the crest. Climb the glacier, or the scree to its right, and gain the crest. Careful routefinding on the crest is needed to pass some sharp, loose sections at the base of the northeast ridge. Traverse onto the south side of the ridge and ascend a steep gully to the summit.

Descent:
Retrace your steps.

John Moynier

Red and White Mountain on the left and Red Slate Mountain on the right (from Mt. Mills)

Red Slate Mtn. (13,163 ft.)
North Couloir
Class 4 snow and ice

F.A. Unknown
Mt. Morrison Area Map: Page 218
USGS Quad Map: Convict Lake

Red Slate Mountain is the tallest and most massive peak in this part of the Sierra. There is a tremendous view of the northern High Sierra from the summit, and this led James Gardiner of the Whitney Survey party to make the first ascent in 1864. Although the peak is perhaps the most dominant mountain along this section of the crest, it is hidden from travelers on Highway 395 and does not receive as much attention as its more visible neighbors.

An attractive couloir splits the north face of the peak. In the spring, this gully has become something of a testpiece for extreme skiers and snowboarders. Later in the year, the couloir makes an excellent introduction to Sierra snow and ice climbing.

Route:
From the trailhead at Convict Lake, hike up the Convict Creek trail to Mildred Lake. An unmaintained trail leads to Constance Lake, at the base of the Red Slate Mountain. From the small glacier at the base of the peak, climb the 40-degree couloir to the top. If a cornice blocks the exit onto the summit, the rocks on the left side (Class 4) can be climbed to the top.

Descent:
Descend loose shale on the west side of the peak to the saddle on the crest. From there, scree and snow slopes lead to Constance Lake.

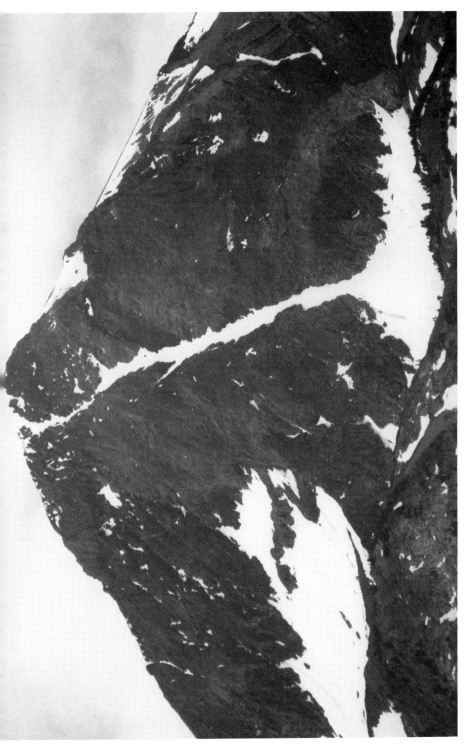

John Moynier

Red Slate Mountain from Mildred Lake

Mt. Morrison (12,268 ft.)
North Face
IV 5.10+

F.A. Gary Slate and Dean Hobbs; July, 1987
Mt. Morrison Area Map: Page 218
USGS Quad Map: Convict Lake

The north escarpment of Mt. Morrison holds an almost "fatal attraction" for climbers. The wall, which looks solid and climbable from the road, is shattered and dangerously loose. Mike Strassman described his climb up the neighboring north buttress route: "(It's) a vertical scree field. Protection was not worth placing, and retreat was not a possibility." Finishing the climb under the light of a failing headlamp, Strassman's team stumbled back to the car just before dawn, where they were surprised to find two climbers packing up to tackle the face.

Dean Hobbs and Gary Slate's route up the north face offers the cleanest rock and the finest line on the face. Hobbs and Slate were both active in the east-side climbing scene for many years, with Slate helping to introduce the 5.12 standard to the Owens River Gorge.

Bruce Lella and Dave Nettle, both very experienced alpinists, each have repeated this route and both describe it as a serious but satisfying climb. It is one of the longest routes in the Sierra, and recommended in spite of the considerable objective hazards.

Route:
From the Convict Creek trailhead, follow the trail around Convict Lake and hike up the brushy moraine to the hanging valley at the base of Mt. Morrison. From the toe of the north buttress, scramble up and right about 200 feet to a prominent area of yellowish rock. A difficult hand crack (5.10) zigzags up and right to a ramp. Traverse right (5.10) on runout face moves to a flake and climb cracks to a scree-covered ledge below a wide chimney. Climb this on its left side, then traverse left onto an exposed arête. Double cracks above gain the base of a crackless corner. Difficult face climbing (5.10) leads up and right to a big ledge and easier climbing. Ascend a steep right-facing corner (5.10) to a gully that leads into the prominent notch at the top of the north buttress. A steep, clean crack (5.8) gives way to the final scramble to summit.

Descent:
Scramble down blocks to the chute on the northeast side. Follow this to the saddle between Mt. Morrison and the peak to the northeast, descend into the hanging valley, then follow the valley over a moraine to Convict Lake.

The North Face of Mt. Morrison   John Moynier

Mt. Morrison Area

Mt. Morrison
North Face – IV 5.10+

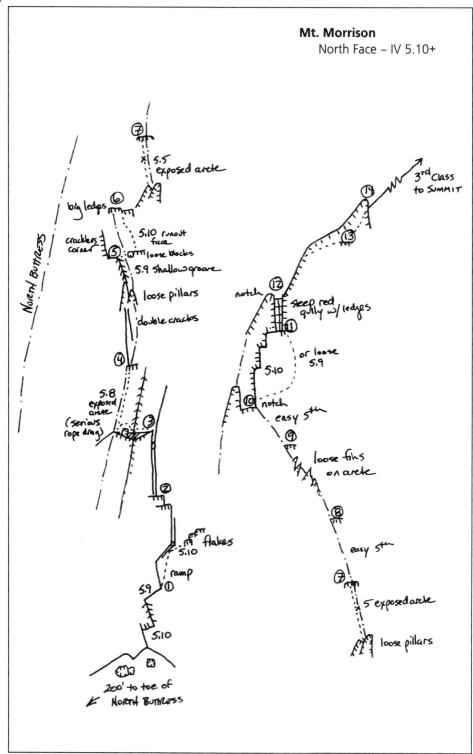

NORTH BUTTRESS

⑦
x| 5.5
exposed arete

big ledges ⑥

crackless
corner ⑤
5.10 runout
face
loose blocks
5.9 shallow groove

loose pillars

double cracks

④

5.8
exposed
arete
(serious
rope drag) ③

②

flakes
5.10

ramp
5.9 ①

5.10

200' to toe of
← NORTH BUTTRESS

3rd Class
to SUMMIT

⑭

⑬

notch ⑫
steep red
gully w/ledges
⑪
or loose
5.9
5.10

⑩ notch
easy 5th

⑨

loose fins
on arete

⑧
easy 5th

⑦
5 exposed arete
x
loose pillars

Tim Forsell at the top of the Red Slate Couloir in winter   John Moynier

Ritter Range Area

"One of the most exciting pieces of pure wilderness was disclosed that I ever discovered in all my mountaineering...Looking southward along the axis of the range, the eye caught a row of exceedingly sharp and slender spires, which rise openly to a height of about a thousand feet, above a series of short, residual glaciers that lean back against their bases; their fantastic sculpture and the unrelieved sharpness with which they spring out of the ice rendering them particularly wild and striking. They are 'The Minarets.'"

– John Muir

The Ritter Range is composed of highly fractured meta-volcanic rock, the weathered core of an ancient volcano. Steep pocket glaciers cling to the sides of these impressively sharp peaks, lending the area an alpine character. These are truly "mountaineering" peaks, as only a few summits can be reached by Class 3 or easier routes.

The Whitney Survey party studied this area in 1864 and named Mt. Ritter. James Gardiner, a member of the survey, observed Mt. Ritter from the summit of Mt. Clark in 1866 and described it as, "One of the most striking peaks in the Sierra, from its great size and from the needle-like peaks that rise from a mountain at its southern end. King names them the Minarets." Gardiner and Clarence King attempted Mt. Ritter later that year, but the first ascent was left to John Muir in 1872.

Charles Michael made the first recorded ascent in the Minarets in 1923 when he climbed (solo) the difficult spire that now bears his name. Most of the Minarets have been named after the leaders of their first-ascent teams: Charles Michael, Norman Clyde, Glen Dawson, Jules Eichorn, Jack Reigelhuth, Ted Waller, Walter A. Starr, Jr,

Ritter Range Area

Oliver Kehrlein, Kenneth Davis, Kenneth Adam, May Pridham, John Dyer, Richard Leonard, Ed Turner, William Rice, Torcom Bedayn, Carl Jensen, and Ansel Adams. Many of these spires received their first ascents during an organized search for the body of Walter A. Starr, Jr, who had fallen to his death while attempting a solo climb of Michael Minaret in August, 1933.

Approaches

The resort town of Mammoth Lakes is three miles west of Highway 395. Climbing and backpacking supplies are available at Pat's Backcountry Shop. To reach the Ritter Range, drive west from town to the ski area at Mammoth Mountain. A mandatory shuttle bus service leads to the various trailheads. The first trailhead is Agnew Meadows. From here, trails lead north along the San Joaquin River to Shadow Lake, Thousand Island Lake and Yosemite National Park via the John Muir Trail. The Red's Meadow trailhead provides access to Minaret Lake and the southern end of the Ritter Range.

Michael Minaret

Vern Clevenger

The Minaret Traverse
South Notch to Ritter Pass
VI 5.9

F.A. Vern Clevenger and Claude Fiddler, August, 1982
Ritter Range Area Map: Page 232
USGS Quad Map: Mt. Ritter

The traverse of the Minarets involves more than a linear mile of continuously difficult, exposed and committing climbing. It was first done by active Tuolumne Meadows climbers Vern Clevenger and Claude Fiddler in 1982. The second traverse of this jagged ridge was made ten years later by legendary Yosemite solo climber Peter Croft. Croft was impressed by the difficulty and exposure of the route.

In 1978, Fiddler and Clevenger made their first climb together – the first ascent of the route Out of Gas in Tuolumne Meadows. Fiddler described their unique partnership: "We climbed well together and never had to think too much about what the other was doing. We also managed to bring out the best in each other's climbing ability, either by words of encouragement or reassurance. In the mountains we third-classed a lot; we were familiar with the climbing, so we rarely used the rope until the climbing got to about 5.9."

Their traverse was not without incident. Fiddler recalled, "Jules Eichorn once told me that, 'Strange things happen in a mountaineer's life'. His words were brought to mind during a rappel off Rice Minaret. Vern had anchored the rope to a large block and asked if it looked okay. I said yes, and began the rappel. Suddenly, Vern called down that the anchor was pulling out and that I should get my weight off the rope. As I looked about for a ledge, Vern shouted that he had it under control. He simply put his back to the block and held it in place!"

Route:
From the trailhead at Agnew Meadows, follow the trail past Shadow Lake to Lake Ediza. A trail leads south past Iceberg Lake and up a steep slope to Cecile Lake. The summits of the Minarets are traversed in the order: Reigelhuth, Pridham, Kehrlein, Ken, Clyde, Eichorn, Michael, Rice, Bedayn, Dawson, Dyer, Jensen, Turner, Leonard and Waller. A complete traverse of the Ritter Range from Iron Mountain in the south to North Glacier Pass has probably never been done, and rivals the Palisades Traverse in terms of difficulty, length and commitment.

Descent:
From Ritter Pass, descend to Lake Ediza and follow the trail to Agnew Meadows.

The Minarets from the east; with Clyde Minaret on the left, and Dawson and Dyer Minarets on the right

John Moynier

Clyde Minaret (12,281 ft.)
Southeast Face
IV 5.8 (Direct route: IV 5.9+)

F.A. Allen Steck, John Evans, Dick Long and Chuck Wilts; June, 1963
Ritter Range Area Map: Page 232
USGS Quad Map: Mt. Ritter

Rising above Minaret Lake, the attractive southeast face of Clyde Minaret is one of the most impressive and visible walls in the range, yet it remained unclimbed until the early 1960s. Norman Clyde made the first ascent of this peak, the highest of the Minarets, in June, 1928. His steep and exposed route on the north face was accomplished solo.

The members of the team that accomplished the first ascent of the southeast face were very experienced climbers, and had been involved with many difficult ascents in Yosemite Valley and at Tahquitz Rock. In spite of their experience, their confidence faltered at the sight of the imposing southeast face, but once on the rock, they found an abundance of square-cut holds that helped connect discontinuous crack systems.

Many route options have given this climb a reputation for difficult routefinding. The original route made a number of traverses to avoid more difficult climbing. Peter Mayfield, an experienced Yosemite climber and guide, pointed out that the nature of the rock allows for climbable routes almost anywhere on the face. Mayfield recommended the direct start; although this is technically more difficult than the original route, it can be easily followed and provides enjoyable climbing.

Route:
From Red's Meadow, follow the trail to Minaret Lake. Continue up the inlet creek to Cecile Lake, then traverse to the face below an obvious area of reddish rock. At the highest point of the talus, ascend a thin crack in a prominent right-facing corner system (5.9+); this takes you up two long pitches to the top of a tower. From the highest of the ledges above the tower, climb up and right for three pitches via moderate (5.7) corners to a big ledge that is just left of the prominent left-facing dihedral. A difficult traverse leads into the corner. Climb the corner through a blocky roof (5.8) and the face above to a square-cut ledge. Continue in the upper dihedral (5.8) to a notch on the right-hand skyline ridge, where a large ledge leads left across the face. Continue up the broken upper face (5.7), to the spectacular summit arête. From here, several hundred feet of moderate climbing leads to the summit.

Descent:
Descend the exposed ledges of the southwest face (Class 3) to Amphitheater Lake, then traverse around the west side of Ken Minaret to South Notch. This leads down a small glacier to Cecile Lake. It is also possible to descend the Ken-Clyde Couloir to the base of the route. This involves some loose downclimbing and at least one rappel.

Jim Stimson

The southeast face of Clyde Minaret

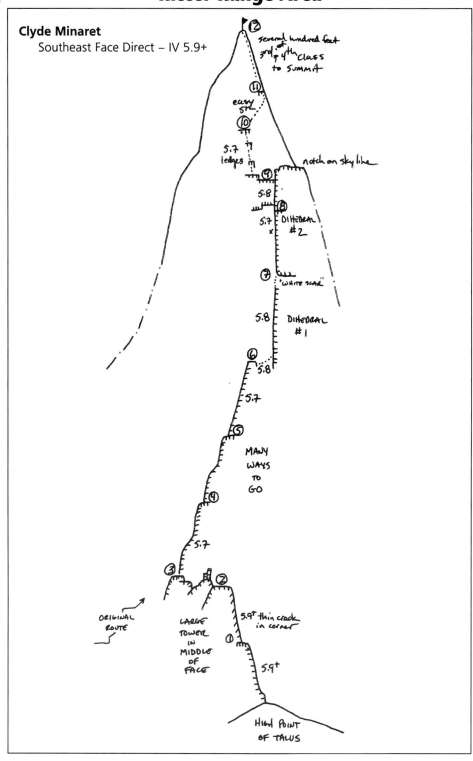

Clyde Minaret
Southeast Face Direct – IV 5.9+

several hundred feet
3rd & 4th class
to summit

easy 5th

5.7
ledges

notch on sky line

5.8

5.7
x

DIHEDRAL #2

"WHITE SCAR"

5.8

DIHEDRAL #1

5.8

5.7

MANY WAYS TO GO

5.7

ORIGINAL ROUTE

LARGE TOWER IN MIDDLE OF FACE

5.9+ thin crack in corner

5.9+

HIGH POINT OF TALUS

Southeast Face of Clyde Minaret   Vern Clevenger

Michael Minaret (12,240+ ft.)
Eichorn's Chute
Class 4-5

F.A. Jules Eichorn, Glen Dawson and Richard Jones; August, 1933
Ritter Range Area Map: Page 232
USGS Quad Map: Mt. Ritter

The first ascent of Michael Minaret was made by Charles Michael in September, 1923. Michael's wife, Enid, accompanied him up "Michael"s Chute" to the last difficult section, which he termed: "The ladder with the lower rungs missing." Another active solo climber, Walter "Pete" Starr, Jr., fell to his death on this peak in 1933. Starr, author of Starr's Guide to the John Muir Trail and the High Sierra Region, *was famous for his weekend escapes from his law practice. These trips often involved 30-mile hiking days and the ascents of many peaks.*

When Starr was late returning from a trip into the Minarets in August, 1933, his friend Francis Farquhar organized a search involving the top climbers of the day. During the search, many of the Minarets were climbed for the first time. After several days, the initial search proved unsuccessful and was called off.

Unwilling to give up, Norman Clyde remained and continued to search for his friend. Clyde eventually found "the earthly remains of Peter Starr" on a ledge near Eichorn's Chute. Jules Eichorn returned to the Minarets to help inter Starr's remains on the ledge, and later recalled the event: "We placed Pete in a crevice, or I should say that I did. Norman did not touch the body, he just started handing me rocks to cover him with. During this solemn task, I glanced over at Norman and he was weeping. Well, I can't tell you how deeply this affected me."

Route:
From the trailhead at Agnew Meadows, follow the trail past Shadow Lake to Lake Ediza. From the lake, hike into the cirque between Leonard and Clyde Minarets to North Notch. Cross the notch (Class 3) and descend to the west side, before traversing south to Michael Minaret. Eichorn's Chute is the left-most of the two chutes leading to the ridge north of Michael Minaret. After reaching the notch between Michael and Eichorn Minarets, traverse on a ledge to the Portal. Tunnel under a large chockstone, then follow ledges up and left to the top.

Descent:
From the Portal, descend an obvious chute (one rappel) to Amphitheater Lake, then go around the west side of Ken Minaret to the South Notch. From the notch, traverse to Cecile Lake and follow the trail to Lake Ediza.

Vern Clevenger

The Minarets from the west; with North Notch on the left, and Michael Minaret on the right

Mt. Ritter (13,157 ft.)
Southwest Ridge
VI 5.9

F.A. Vern Clevenger and Claude Fiddler; July, 1984
Ritter Range Area Map: Page 232
USGS Quad Map: Mt. Ritter

Mt. Ritter is the highest peak in the Ritter Range and has been the target of moun-taineers since the days of Clarence King and John Muir. A large glacier above the Ritter Lakes is bordered by the massive west face of Mt. Ritter. The long and jagged southwest ridge, which rises from the canyon of the north fork of the San Joaquin River, was first climbed by Claude Fiddler and Vern Clevenger on a day trip from Agnew Meadows. The pair started climbing low on the jagged ridge and reached the summit late in the day. Of the long hike out, which lasted into the night, Clevenger remembers practically crawling the final miles of trail to Agnew Meadows.

Clevenger returned with John Moynier in 1990 and traversed Peak 12,344 ft. This prominent tower on the southwest ridge was one of the last summits in the Sierra to be reached. After safely reaching the glacier, Clevenger looked at the rest of the tra-verse and said, "How did Claude and I ever survive those adventures?"

Route:

From Agnew Meadow, follow the trail past Shadow Lake to Lake Ediza, and climb grassy slopes to Ritter Pass. Cross the pass and descend talus to the lakes on the west side. Gain the southwest ridge at the low saddle to the west, and climb over the summit of Peak 12,344. The route continues over towers and into deep notch-es, climbing many significant peaklets on its way to the main summit.

Descent:

From the summit, descend the broad southeast slopes to an obvious chute. Descend the chute, or the ledges on the side, to the east slopes of the peak. Continue past the southeast glacier to Lake Ediza and the trail to Agnew Meadows.

John Moynier

The Southwest Ridge of Mt. Ritter

Mt. Ritter (13,157 ft.)
North Face
Class 3

F.A. John Muir; October, 1872
Ritter Range Area Map: Page 232
USGS Quad Maps: Mt. Ritter and Mammoth Mtn.

Mt. Ritter was named by the Whitney Survey party in 1864 for Karl Ritter, the noted German geographer. Josiah Whitney, the leader of the survey, had been a student of Ritter's at the University of Berlin in the 1840s. Clarence King made an attempt on the peak in 1866 with his friend James Gardiner. After being turned back by foul weather, King described the peak as "inaccessible."

John Muir made the first ascent of Mt. Ritter by way of the north face. While climbing the steep face, Muir reached a point where he could neither move up or down. His arms and legs outstretched on tiny holds, Muir began to panic: "Suddenly my danger broke upon me. Faith and hope failed, suffered eclipse. Cold sweat broke out. My senses filled as with smoke. I was alone, cut off from all affinity. Would I fall to the glacier below? Well, no matter . . .

"Then as if my body, finding the ordinary dominion of mind insufficient, pushed it aside, I became possessed of a new sense. My eyes became preternaturally clear and every rift, flaw, niche and tablet in the cliff ahead were seen as through a microscope. At any rate the danger was safely passed, I scarce know how, and shortly after noon I leaped with wild freedom upon the highest crag of the summit. Had I been born aloft upon wings, my deliverance could not have been more complete."

Route:
From Agnew Meadows, follow the trail past Shadow Lake to Lake Ediza. A trail leads around the lake toward the saddle between Mt. Ritter and Banner Peak. At the top of the small glacier, a steep, icy chute (Class 3) climbs to the saddle. Above the saddle, climb the far right-hand chute on the steep face to the northwest arête. Follow a ledge left to the summit.

Descent:
From the summit, descend the broad southeast slopes to an obvious chute. Descend the chute (often snow- or ice-filled), or the ledges on either side of the chute, to the east slopes of the peak. Stay on the southern side of the slope as it descends past the southeast glacier and down to Lake Ediza.

John Moynier

The North Face of Mt. Ritter

Banner Peak (12,945 ft.)
East Corner
Class 4

F.A. Jules Eichorn and Robert Underhill; August, 1931
Ritter Range Area Map: Page 232
USGS Quad Maps: Mt. Ritter and Mammoth Mtn.

Banner Peak is the impressive mountain just north of Mt. Ritter. The convoluted east face is a spectacular sight when viewed from Garnet and Thousand Island Lakes. Comprised of a series of steep arêtes, the face culminates at Banner's sharp summit. The route up the east corner was made by Jules Eichorn and Robert Underhill during the Sierra Club's 1931 "Underhill Camp."

Robert Underhill was a prominent member of the Appalachian Mountain Club. On a 1930 trip to Selkirk Mountains in Canada, the Sierra Club's Francis Farquhar had learned the techniques of proper roped climbing from Underhill, and invited him out to the Sierra to instruct at the 1931 Annual Outing in the Ritter Range. On his way to the Sierra that summer, Underhill made first ascents of the Underhill Ridge and the North Face routes on the Grand Teton. Upon arriving at the Garnet Lake camp, Underhill organized a regular climbing school, instructing the Sierra Club climbers in the use of roped belays.

John Mendenhall and Ruth Dyar climbed the route on July 4, 1939. They had a bit of an epic, but it turned out well, as Ruth later wrote: "Due to inexperience and over-optimism, we thought we could make an afternoon climb of the Underhill-Eichorn route on Banner Peak. The approach seemed long, but we moved fast when we got on the rock. The difficulty increased as we climbed and by 6 p.m. the summit was still far above us and we decided to bivouac...We were teased for years about this bivouac, as a couple of weeks later we announced our engagement."

Route:
From Agnew Meadows, follow the trail past Shadow Lake to Garnet Lake. The east corner of Banner Peak is the skyline ridge rising between Banner and the small peaklet to the east. Gain the ridge crest via a steep, loose chute above the saddle between the peaks, and climb the ever-steepening arête. At an overhang, climb up and right into a steep chute leading to the summit.

Descent:
Head south down ledges and scree to the saddle between Mt. Ritter and Banner Peak, then descend the glacier west to Catherine Lake and the low saddle of North Glacier Pass. Contour around Thousand Island Lake, cross the ridge to Garnet Lake and follow the trail back to Agnew Meadows.

The East Corner of Banner Peak

Banner Peak (12,945 ft.)
North Buttress
III 5.7

F.A. David Harden and Kevin Sutter; August, 1973
Ritter Range Area Map: Page 232
USGS Quad Maps: Mt. Ritter and Mammoth Mtn.

The first ascent of Banner Peak's spectacular north skyline was made by Dave Harden and Kevin Sutter. A decade later, the route caught the attention of Claude Fiddler. Unaware that it already had been climbed, Fiddler excitedly made plans to meet his partner, Vern Clevenger, at the Silver Lake Store in June Lake.

Their story was a classic case of misunderstanding. Fiddler recalled: "I wondered why Vern had said we would not need a rope for the climb. I guess he thought we were just climbing the peak. When we got to the base of the buttress and I started climbing, Vern asked if I had lost my marbles. I replied that it was his idea not to bring a rope. Needless to say, we finished the route and had a grand climb."

Route:
From Silver Lake on the June Lake Loop, follow the Rush Creek trail over Gem Pass to the outlet of Thousand Island Lake. From the north shore of Thousand Island Lake, ascend the pass north of the peak. Access the ridge from the east and climb to the summit of a small peaklet on the crest. A number of towers on the crest are passed on the east side of the ridge. From the notch above the tallest of these towers, climb a steep ramp on the east face of the arête to the low-angled summit ridge.

Descent:
Descend ledges and scree to the saddle between Banner Peak and Mt. Ritter. Follow the glacier west to Lake Catherine, then head north over North Glacier Pass to Thousand Island Lake. Follow the Gem Pass trail back to Silver Lake.

Banner Peak from the north   Claude Fiddler

Mt. Lyell
Area

Mt. Lyell is the highest point in Yosemite National Park. Draped in glaciers, Mt. Lyell and its companion peak Mt. Maclure form an alpine skyline at the head of the Lyell Fork of the Tuolumne River. Every year, hundreds of backpackers pass beneath them as they climb over Donohue Pass on the John Muir Trail. In winter and spring, dozens of backcountry skiers follow the same route below these magnificent peaks on a popular ski tour from Mammoth Mountain to Tuolumne Meadows.

William Brewer and Charles Hoffmann attempted to climb Mt. Lyell in 1863, but were stopped by a difficult-looking wall above the glacier. They described the final tower as "inaccessible." The peak was climbed in 1871 by John B. Tileston, who found the wall a rather straightforward scramble. Since the first ascent, Mt. Lyell has become popular and is climbed hundreds of times each year. The first winter ascent of Mt. Lyell was made on a Sierra Club ski mountaineering trip led by David Brower in 1936. An avid skier who had learned to ski at Badger Pass in Yosemite, Brower went on to make winter ski ascents of many Sierra peaks during the 1930s and 40s.

Approaches

From either Lee Vining on the east side of the Sierra or Yosemite Valley on the west, take Highway 120 through Yosemite Park to Tuolumne Meadows. Groceries and climbing supplies are available at the general store and mountain shop in Tuolumne Meadows. Wilderness permits are available at the kiosk at Puppy Dome. From the backcountry parking lot at Tuolumne Meadows, follow the John Muir Trail up the Lyell Fork of the Tuolumne River.

An alternate approach to this area is from the June Lake Loop road. The Rush Creek Trail climbs past Gem and Waugh Lakes, crossing the John Muir Trail and continuing up to Marie Lakes at the base of the east face of Mt. Lyell.

Mt. Lyell (13,114 ft.)
East Ridge
Class 3 (Class 4 from Marie Lakes)

F.A. Unknown
Mt. Lyell Area Map: Page 252
USGS Quad Maps: Mt. Lyell and Vogelsang Peak

Mt. Lyell, the highest peak in Yosemite National Park, was named by William Brewer of the Whitney Survey Party: "As we had named the other (nearby) mountain Mount Dana, after the most eminent of American geologists, we named this Mount Lyell, after the most eminent of English geologists." Brewer, accompanied by Charles Hoffmann, attempted the peak in 1863, but soft snow weakened them. "We toil on for hours; it seems at times as if our breath refuses to strengthen us, we puff and blow so in the thin air. After seven hours of hard climbing we struck the last pinnacle of rock that rises through the snow and forms the summit – only to find it inaccessible."

The "inaccessible" peak was eventually climbed in August, 1871 by John B. Tileston. He later wrote, "I was up early the next morning, toasted some bacon, boiled my tea, and was off at six. I climbed the mountain, and reached the top of the highest pinnacle before eight. I came down the mountain and reached camp before one, pretty tired."

Route:
From the trailhead near the Tuolumne Meadows Lodge, follow the John Muir Trail up Lyell Canyon. Scramble up slabs to the Lyell Glacier, passing to the right of the prominent rock ridge dividing the glacier. Cross the glacier to the saddle on the east ridge and climb the crest of the east ridge to the summit.

Alternative Routes:
The east ridge also can be gained lower down, either from the Lyell Canyon side or from the Marie Lakes at the head of Rush Creek. The lower part of the east ridge is Class 4.

Descent:
Head west toward the saddle between Mts. Lyell and Maclure before descending onto the glacier. Continue down slabs to the John Muir Trail.

Mt. Lyell and Mt. Maclure

Mt. Maclure (12,960+ ft.)
North Ridge
Class 4

F.A. Unknown
Mt. Lyell Area Map: Page 252
USGS Quad Maps: Mt. Lyell and Vogelsang Peak

The elegant Mt. Maclure usually is climbed as an afterthought to those mountaineers intent on the summit of Mt. Lyell. The north and northwest ridges both offer excellent Class-4 routes on reasonably good rock, and the view from the summit is nearly as impressive as that from Mt. Lyell.

Mt. Maclure was named by the Whitney Survey Party during their trip to the Tuolumne region in 1863. Whitney dedicated the summit: "To the pioneer of American geology, William Maclure, one of the dominating peaks of the Sierra Nevada is very properly dedicated." Maclure was responsible for the first geologic map of the United States, which he produced in 1809.

Route:
From the trailhead near the Tuolumne Meadows Lodge, follow the John Muir Trail up Lyell Canyon to the point where the trail takes a turn to the east. Continue up the drainage past some small lakes and climb slabs toward the peak. Gain the toe of the north ridge and follow it as it climbs steeply to the summit.

Alternative Route:
The northwest ridge is also a fine climb, providing a longer and more exposed route to the summit. This route, first climbed by George and Allen Steck, ascends the north glacier of Maclure to a small pyramidal peak on the northwest ridge. This narrow ridge is followed past a number of towers to the final arête leading to the summit.

Descent:
Descend ledges and talus to the saddle (Class 3) between Mts. Lyell and Maclure, and then head down the glacier to the lakes.

John Moynier climbing in the Mt. Lyell area Chris Libby

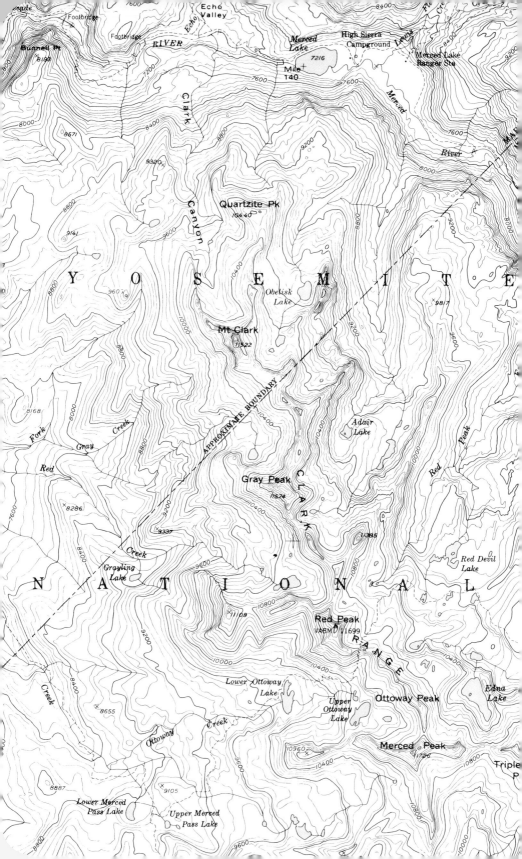

Mt. Clark
Area

Mt. Clark is an impressive granite peak standing near the southern border of Yosemite National Park. When viewed from the north, this striking peak is seen as a narrow fin of granite and was once known as "Gothic Peak" and "The Obelisk." Mt. Clark is the high point of the Clark Range, a major ridge on the divide between the Merced and San Joaquin River drainages. The peak is named for Galen Clark, who became the first guardian of Yosemite State Park in 1864, and who lived in the neighboring Mariposa Grove of Giant Sequoias for over 40 years.

Clarence King and James Gardiner of the Whitney Survey party made the first ascent of the peak in 1866. After a somewhat precarious ascent, they were able to make a detailed survey of the southern portion of Yosemite Park from its summit. Josiah Whitney later wrote of their efforts: "Mr. King, who with Mr. Gardiner, made the ascent of the peak, says that its summit is so slender, that when on top of it they seemed to be suspended in air."

Approach

The approach to Mt. Clark begins on the east end of Yosemite Valley. From the trailhead at Happy Isles, follow the John Muir Trail to Little Yosemite Valley, and then continue on the Merced Lake trail to Echo Valley. Scramble up brushy slabs, following the course of the Clark Canyon Creek to the cirque to the north of Mt. Clark, just west of Quartzite Peak.

Mount Clark (11,522 ft.)
Northwest Arête
Class 4

F.A. Neil Ruge and Douglas Olds; October, 1934
Mt. Clark Area Map: Page 258
USGS Quad Maps: Merced Peak and Half Dome

This stunning fin is the highpoint of the Clark Range in Yosemite National Park. The sharp profile of this feature inspired its early name: The Obelisk. Clarence King was obsessed with climbing Mt. Clark. "From every commanding eminence around the Yosemite," he wrote, "No distant object rises with more inspiring greatness than The Obelisk of Mt. Clark . . . From the north this peak is a slender needle, jutting two thousand feet from a pedestal of rocks and snow-fields." While in the area to map the region for the Whitney Survey Party, King and his companion James Gardiner made an ill-fated attempt to climb Mt. Clark in late fall of 1864. An early winter storm swept in on their camp at the base of the peak, leaving the slopes covered with a foot and a half of snow.

Two years later, King and Gardiner returned, determined to make the ascent. "There was in our hope of scaling this peak," King wrote, "Something more than a mere desire to master a difficult peak. It was a station of great topographical value, the apex of many triangles, and, more than all, would command a grander view of the Merced region than any other summit." The final steps to the summit were spectacularly exposed, and involved an insecure leap onto a ledge.

Gardiner wrote: "It was, I think, duty's call that nerved us. That leap, like most dangers, seemed more perilous after it was made than before; it was not the length of the spring – that was easy – but to light in exact balance on a projecting rock that scarcely held half of one foot, while the remainder of the body hung over a precipice 1500 feet deep, was a thing requiring most exact judgement."

Route:
From the trailhead at Happy Isles in Yosemite Valley, follow the trail through Little Yosemite Valley to near Merced Lake. Ascend the steep drainage of Clark Canyon to the base of the northern cirque of Mt. Clark. Gain the northwest ridge and follow it along its steep eastern drop-off to a point just below the summit, where it steepens dramatically. A short Class-4 arête leads to the exposed summit.

Descent:
Retrace your steps.

Mt. Clark from the north

John Moynier

Cathedral Area

The Tuolumne Meadows area of Yosemite National Park is world famous for exciting climbing on glacially polished domes. Most climbers are content to climb the many roadside routes in Tuolumne, but those willing to make the relatively short approaches to the granite peaks of the Cathedral Range will find excellent climbing on clean cracks, prolific knobs and steep flakes.

Cathedral Peak, a landmark of the Tuolumne region, offers accessible and varied climbing on rock of exceptionally high quality. John Muir made the first ascent of this peak in 1869. His route remains a popular climb and features fourth-class slabs, followed by a short, vertical crack leading to the tiny summit. This exposed route was considered the most difficult climb of its time. There are a variety of climbs on the south and west sides of the peak. The most notable are Chuck Wilts and Spencer Austin's 1945 climb of the Southeast Buttress and Gary Colliver and Mike Cohen's 1972 route up the spectacular west pillar of the Eichorn Pinnacle.

The other summits of the region are no less enticing and have a great history of their own. Francis Farquhar and James Rennie made the first ascent of the slender summit of Unicorn Peak in 1911. Norman Clyde and Carl Sharsmith climbed the tallest of the Echo Peaks in 1931. Glen Dawson and Jules Eichorn also were very active in the Cathedral Range, making the first ascents of the airy Eichorn Pinnacle, the Matthes Crest and the west face of the Cockscomb.

Approaches

From either Lee Vining to the east, or Yosemite Valley to the west, take Highway 120 through Yosemite Park to Tuolumne Meadows. Groceries and climbing supplies are available at the general store and mountain shop in Tuolumne Meadows. Wilderness permits are available at the kiosk at Puppy Dome.

There are two approaches to the peaks of this area. Both start from the Cathedral Lakes parking area, a few miles west of the Tuolumne Meadows store. The Budd Lake trail provides access to Unicorn Peak, the Cockscomb, the Matthes Crest, the Echo Peaks and the southeast buttress of Cathedral Peak. About a half mile from the parking lot, a significant unmaintained trail breaks off to the left and follows Budd Creek to Budd Lake, which lies below these peaks. To reach the Matthes Crest, climb the broad scree gully between Echo Peaks #7 and #8, and traverse across slabs to the base of the crest. The second approach to the area is by way of the Cathedral Lakes trail, which takes you just below Cathedral Pass.

Cathedral Range Traverse
Unicorn Peak to Cathedral Peak
IV 5.7

F.A. Unknown
Cathedral Area Map: Page 262
USGS Quad Map: Tenaya Lake

This enjoyable traverse is often a welcome respite from the unnerving, runout climbs commonly found on the domes of Tuolumne Meadows. The traverse is a peak-bagger's dream as well, with the possibility of climbing as many as 15 summits in one long day, including Unicorn Peak, the Cockscomb, Matthes Crest, Echo Ridge, the nine Echo Peaks, Cathedral Peak and Eichorn Pinnacle. The Matthes Crest, Echo Peak # 9, the southeast buttress of Cathedral Peak and Eichorn Pinnacle all involve exposed Class-5 climbing. Climbers looking for a less-committing day can omit these, and concentrate on the enjoyable fourth-class routes on the other peaks.

Route:

From the Cathedral Lakes trailhead, start up the Cathedral Lakes trail, then follow the unmaintained trail to Budd Lake. Climb slabs on the northwest side of Unicorn Peak to the north summit (Class 4). Head south along the ridge to the Cockscomb, where a fourth-class route leads up cracks on the northwest side. The high point of the traverse is the knife-edged Echo Ridge (11,120+ ft.). Climb Class-4 flakes on the east ridge and traverse down to the Echo Peaks.

There are nine Echo Peaks, and most of the summits are Class 4. The exception is Echo Peak #9, which is 5.7 via its southwest side. Further north along the ridge is Cathedral Peak. Either climb the southeast buttress (5.7), or scramble up the eastern slopes to the east ridge and contour west across slabs to the short summit crack (Class 4). If there is time, the north face of Eichorn's Pinnacle (5.3) provides an exciting finale.

Descent:

Head down steep slabs north to the Cathedral Lakes trail, or scramble down the sandy east slopes to the Budd Lake trail.

The Echo Peaks and Cathedral Range

John Moynier

Cathedral Peak (10,940 ft.)
Southeast Buttress
III 5.6

F.A. Chuck Wilts and Spencer Austin; 1945
Cathedral Area Map: Page 262
USGS Quad Map: Tenaya Lake

Named by the Whitney Survey Party in 1863, Cathedral Peak is one of the most beautiful peaks in the range. John Muir made the first ascent of this peak in 1869, declaring, "This, I may say, is the first time I have been at church in California." Muir's ascent was perhaps the most difficult rock climb of the time; the exposed jam crack on the final summit tower involves a short section of fifth class climbing. Characteristically, Muir understated the difficulties of the climb: "I made my way up to its topmost spire, which I reached at noon, having loitered by the way to study the fine trees."

Chuck Wilts and Spencer Austin were rock climbers at Tahquitz Rock in southern California in the mid-forties and early fifties. Wilts, an engineer who designed the first knife-blade piton, was involved with the first ascents of a number of other technical routes in the High Sierra, including the southeast face of Clyde Minaret, the traverse of the Matthes Crest and the southwest face of Echo Peak #9.

The popularity of this route seems to grow each year, and has led to some obvious impacts to the wilderness surroundings; particularly erosion on the sandy descent route and overcrowding on the climb.

Route:
From the Cathedral Lakes trailhead, start up the main trail, then follow the unmarked trail to Budd Lake. Scramble up sand and scree slopes to the base of the buttress. There are many options on the lower part of the route: most climbers start up and right of the very toe of the buttress, climbing a left-facing corner-and-flake system to a ledge with a small tree. Continue up and right to another ledge with a tree. Two more pitches lead to a large ledge at the base of a prominent chimney. Climb the chimney (5.6), which leads to a small ledge perched above the south face. Follow a series of left-facing corners and ledges up the prow to a huge ledge at the base of the final tower. Climb a wide crack to a flake at the top of the ridge. Step across to the final jam crack that gains the tiny summit.

Descent:
Downclimb the crack on the west side and traverse to the east ridge. Descend sand and scree slopes to the base of the buttress and the Budd Lake trail.

The Southeast Buttress of Cathedral Peak   John Moynier

Cathedral Area

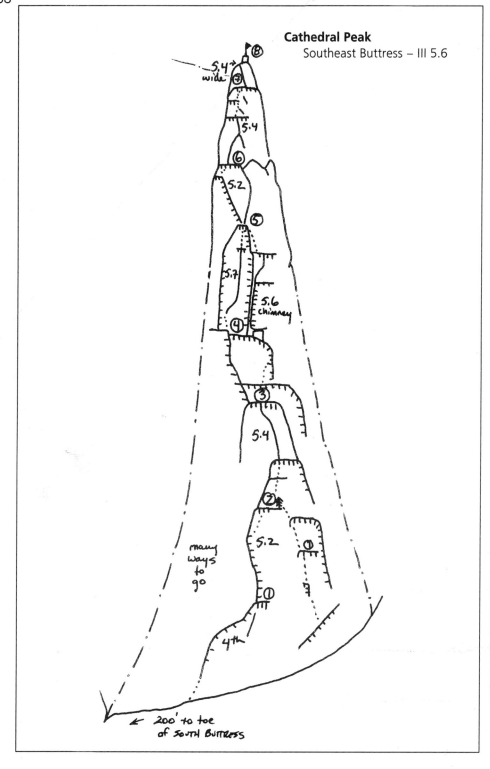

Cathedral Peak
Southeast Buttress – III 5.6

Clean Sierra Granite

Eichorn Pinnacle (10,700 ft.)
West Pillar
III 5.10b

F.A. Gary Colliver and Mike Cohen; July, 1972
Cathedral Area Map: Page 262
USGS Quad Map: Tenaya Lake

The spectacular summit of Eichorn's Pinnacle is an enticing sight from the summit of Cathedral Peak, but few climbers actually venture there. Jules Eichorn and Glen Dawson made the first ascent of the pinnacle in July, 1931, climbing cracks on the north face. The climb took place while the climbers were on their way to the Sierra Club's Underhill Camp in the Ritter Range. As Eichorn and Dawson did not learn proper belay techniques until the next week at the camp, the ascent of Eichorn Pinnacle was a daring adventure. The leader of the camp, Robert Underhill, described the enthusiastic pair: "(They are) young, natural-born rock climbers of the first water."

The west side of Eichorn Pinnacle is a thin pillar rising dramatically from the northeast side of the Cathedral Lakes. This pillar attracted Yosemite guides Mike Cohen and Gary Colliver, who in their careers established many fine routes throughout the range. Cohen and Colliver were known as "elder statesmen" to the generation of younger climbers who came to live in Tuolumne Meadows during the late 1970s and early '80s.

In 1979, two young climbers, Alan Bartlett and Don Reid, attempted to repeat the original route. Struggling up a steep crack, Bartlett called down to Reid, "This is hard – are you sure we're on route?" At the top of the crack, they regained the original line. Their popular direct variation is rated 5.10b.

Route:
From the trailhead, follow the Cathedral Lakes Trail to Cathedral Lake, and scramble up to the toe of the pillar. Begin by climbing an obvious wide crack (5.9) to a ledge, then ascend double cracks (5.9) to another ledge. Traverse right to a left-facing flare (5.8), then traverse right again to a hidden hand crack (5.8) that leads to the crest of the pillar. Easy climbing on the west side of the crest leads to a steep headwall. Stem/chimney between flakes (5.9) to the top of the headwall, then finish with an easy pitch to the top of the pillar.

Alternative Routes:
At the top of the double cracks, a difficult left-facing corner (5.10b) leads straight up to the crest of the pillar.

Descent:
A rappel off the summit leads to slabs on the northwest side, and the trail.

Vern Clevenger

The Eichorn Pinnacle

Eichorn Pinnacle
West Pillar – III 5.10b

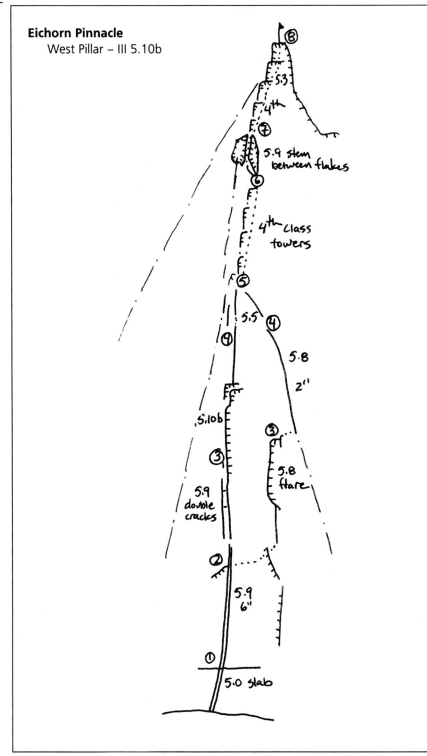

⑧

5.3

4th

⑦

5.9 stem
between flakes

⑥

4th class
towers

⑤

5.5   ④

5.8

2"

④

5.10b

③   ③

5.8
flare

5.9
double
cracks

②

5.9
6"

①

5.0 slab

John Moynier climbing in the Yosemite high country   Robert "SP" Parker

Matthes Crest (10,880 ft.)
Traverse from South to North
III 5.6

F.A. Chuck and Ellen Wilts; June, 1947
Cathedral Area Map: Page 262
USGS Quad Map: Tenaya Lake

The Matthes Crest is a dramatic sharp fin of rock with twin summit towers. It is named for Francois Matthes, author of The Incomparable Valley, *an excellent introduction to geomorphology of the Sierra, particularly that of Yosemite Valley. He coined the term "Cockscomb" and named the nearby peak as a definitive example. When told that this crest had been named after him (by Reid Moran, a Yosemite National Park Ranger), Matthes was reported to be greatly pleased and said, "He knew of no other unnamed feature in the Sierra which he would rather have chosen."*

Many of the climbers who helped with this book cited this as their favorite climb. It offers enjoyable climbing on excellent rock, tremendous exposure and a thrilling summit. The first ascent of the crest was made via the knife-edged north ridge by Jules Eichorn, Glen Dawson and Walter Brem in July, 1931 while the climbers were en route to the Underhill Camp in the Ritter Range. Their route ended with a steep 5.3 pitch to the summit. The south-to-north traverse was first done by Chuck Wilts and his wife, Ellen. Climbing the southern part of the knife-edged ridge adds many enjoyable pitches to the route.

Route:
From the Cathedral Lakes trailhead, start up the main trail, then follow the unmaintained trail to Budd Lake. Scramble up the sandy gully between Echo Peaks #7 and #8, then drop down to Echo Lake. Climb slabs at the southern end of the fin, and ascend a number of moderate pitches to the ridge top. This delicate knife edge is followed around pinnacles and notches to the base of the main summit. Traverse around the west side and climb steep cracks to the summit. A rappel brings you back onto the north ridge, which is followed to the slabs south of the Echo Peaks.

Descent:
Traverse across slabs to the saddle between Echo Peaks #7 and #8 and return past Budd Lake to Tuolumne Meadows.

The Matthes Crest   John Moynier

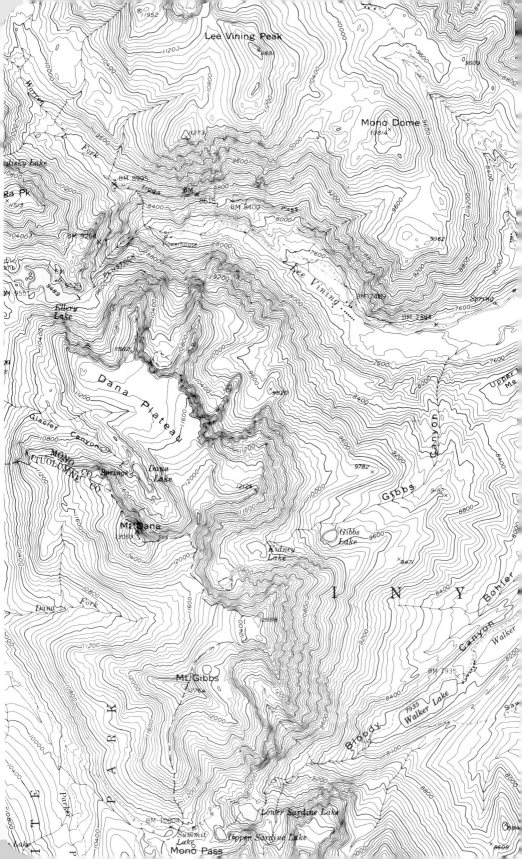

Mt. Dana
Area

The Mt. Dana region offers a good representation of the variety of Sierra climbing. This scenic area offers a fine ice route, an excellent rock route and a long history of climbing, as well as great skiing in the springtime.

Mt. Dana is accessible from Highway 120 and Tioga Pass, and is a forbidding sight from Glacier Canyon. To the left of the northeast face of Mt. Dana is the Dana Couloir, a popular 1,000-foot ice climb that ends on the south ridge of the peak.

On the other side of Glacier Canyon is the broad Dana Plateau. This peneplain terminates at its eastern margin in a series of precipitous couloirs and rock buttresses. The most striking of these buttresses is the Third Pillar. The gullies descending from the plateau, as well as the Dana Couloir, are enjoyable spring ski descents. Yosemite climbers Bob Locke, Chris Falkenstein and Dale Bard made many of the first ski descents of these steep couloirs in the late 1970s.

In winter and early spring, the steep cliffs on the south side of lower Lee Vining Canyon are home to the finest waterfall ice climbing in California. There are three main section of cliffs in the canyon that form nearly vertical falls, as well as a number of thin smears and free-standing ice columns. Doug Robinson, Tom Frost and Yvon Chouinard spent a great deal of time here in the late 1960s perfecting their techniques and developing the Chouinard ice tools.

Approaches

Take Highway 120 west from the small town of Lee Vining on Highway 395. Drive past the forest service ranger station, Tioga Pass Resort and the turnoff to Saddlebag Lake to the parking lot at the west end of Tioga Lake. Ahead is the Tioga Pass entrance to Yosemite National Park.

An unmaintained trail follows the outlet stream of Glacier Canyon. At the mouth of the canyon, either head left, up onto the Dana Plateau, or continue to Dana Lake at the base of Mt. Dana's north face. To reach the top of the Third Pillar from Glacier Canyon, head up the dry drainage to the east and aim for the crest. The top of the pillar is obvious and overhangs the climbing route. To reach the base of the climb, descend the steep ridge (Class 3-4) just north of the pillar.

Mt. Dana (13,053 ft.)
Dana Couloir
Class 4 ice

F.A. Unknown
Mt. Dana Area Map: Page 276
USGS Quad Map: Mt. Dana

The first ascent of Mt. Dana was made by William Brewer and Charles Hoffmann, members of the Whitney Survey Party, on June 28, 1863. Josiah Whitney accompanied Brewer for an ascent the following day. They named the peak for a professor of natural history and geology at Yale during the middle and late 1800s, declaring, "We give the name of Mount Dana to it in honor of James D. Dana, the most eminent American Geologist." This ascent was one of the survey's first in the Sierra and they speculated that Mount Dana might be the highest peak in the range. The view from the summit, however, showed that Mt. Lyell, at least, was higher, and that there were many tall peaks to consider to the south.

The ascent of the 1,000-foot Dana Couloir is an excellent introduction to Sierra gully ice, offering about seven pitches of moderately angled ice. This also is a fine spring ski descent and has become something of a pilgrimage for many skiers. It is possible to ski from the top of Mt. Dana to the couloir, then ski the couloir, thenclimb onto the Dana Plateau and ski down one of the steep couloirs above Ellery Lake.

Route:
From the parking lot at the west end of Tioga Lake, follow the unmaintained trail into Glacier Canyon and up to Dana Lake. The couloir is to the left of the steep northeast face. Ascend the glacier to the small bergschrund at the base of the couloir. The gully consists of about 1,000 feet of 40-degree ice and snow. At the top of the couloir, a short section of loose rock leads to a saddle on the southeast ridge. Climb up the ridge to the summit.

Descent:
A trail leads from the summit of Mt. Dana down to Tioga Pass.

The Dana Couloir

John Moynier

Dana Plateau, Third Pillar (11,500 ft.)
East Face

III 5.10

F.A. Phil Bircheff and Bill Bonebrake;
July, 1969
Mt. Dana Area Map: Page 276
USGS Quad Map: Mt. Dana

Although the Third Pillar is a striking formation when viewed from the east, it can hardly be described as a peak. As an alpine rock climb, however, this feature is an undeniable classic. Each pitch is interesting, and a wide variety of climbing techniques are used on the route. The pillar narrows to a slightly overhanging prow near its top. The last pitch is a perfect hand crack leading to a mantel onto the summit. The exposure is tremendous and the rock is perfect granite. As Richard Leversee said, "It's the best 5.9 pitch in the universe!"

Route:

From the parking lot at the west end of Tioga Lake, follow the unmaintained trail into Glacier Canyon, then take the dry drainage to the east onto the Dana Plateau. The non-descript top of the Third Pillar is on the northeastern margin of the plateau. To reach the base, scramble down the steep ridge to the north (Class 3-4). At the base, cross the snow gully and traverse onto the highest ledge, rather than dropping to the very toe of the pillar. The route begins with a moderate crack (5.7). The second pitch is less obvious and ascends a hand crack to a ledge with a boulder and a small tree. The third pitch makes an inobvious traverse left (5.9) to a crack that widens to an awkward size (5.9) at the top before reaching a good ledge. A long moderate pitch leads to a large flake that can be tunneled behind or liebacked on its left side (5.8). Difficult face climbing (5.10a) above leads past a fixed piton and up to a ledge on the prow. The final pitch (5.9+) offers strenuous jams, tricky mantels and hard face moves, finishing with a mantel onto the summit block.

Descent:

Retrace your steps down Glacier Canyon.

The Third Pillar of Mt. Dana

Robert "SP" Parker

Mt. Dana Area

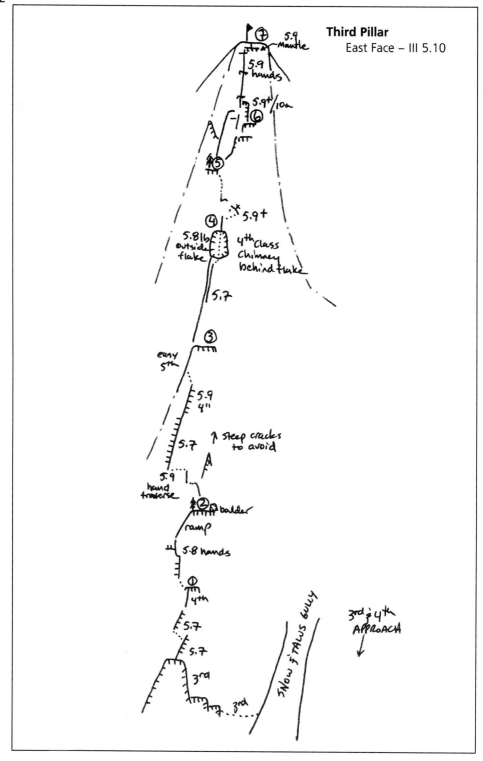

Third Pillar
East Face – III 5.10

5.9 Mantle

5.9 hands

5.9+/10a

5.9+

5.8 lb outside flake

4th Class Chimney behind flake

5.7

easy 5th

5.9 4"

↑ steep cracks to avoid

5.7

5.9 hand traverse

boulder

ramp

5.8 hands

4th

5.7

5.7

3rd

3rd

SNow STALUS GULLY

3rd & 4th APPROACH

Richard Leversee on the Third Pillar

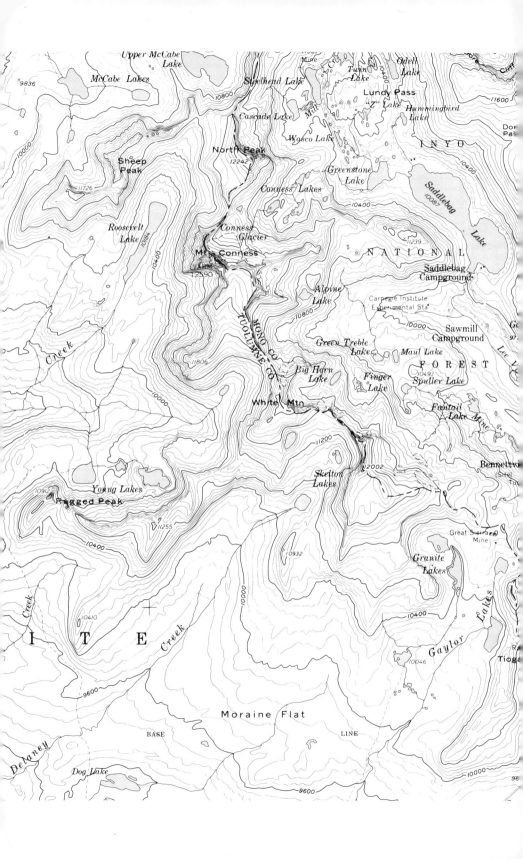

Mt. Conness Area

The area surrounding Mt. Conness has many charming features. Scattered through-out the area, a number of fine alpine lakes colored a bright green by suspended glaci-er flour lie at the feet of bold granite peaks. The northern portion of Yosemite National Peak lies west of the crest. Much of the area east of the crest is protected as the Hall Natural Area. Ansel Hall was Chief Naturalist for Yosemite National Park dur-ing the 1920s and '30s. In 1932, Sierra Club climber Dick Leonard accompanied Hall and geologist Francois Matthes on a ten-week trip into the Yosemite high country with a group of Eagle Scouts.

Clarence King and James Gardiner made the first ascent of Mt. Conness in 1866, using the fine view from the summit to continue their efforts mapping the Yosemite region. Later, this summit was frequently used as a triangulation station for mapping the northern Sierra. The Wheeler Survey Party climbed Mt. Conness in 1878. During the summers of 1879, 1887 and 1890, the U.S. Coast and Geodetic Survey built a semi-permanent camp just below the summit, and erected a shelter for their instru-ments on the very summit. These surveying efforts were made at great peril, due to periodic and violent afternoon thunderstorms.

Professor George Davidson, who was in charge of the U.S.Coast and Geodetic Survey, wrote of these electrical storms: "Early in the day magnificent masses of cumulus formed along the line of the Sierra as far north and south as was visible. When form-ing over such masses as Mt. Lyell and its neighbors, the magnificent volumes of clouds would become very black and flatten at the base, and gradually settle down enough to envelop the tops of the mountains, and heavy thunder peals would rever-berate through the canyons at frequent intervals."

The Tioga Road was built in 1892 and 1893 to serve the many mining camps along the east side of the crest in this region. Most of these mines closed soon thereafter, and the road fell into temporary disuse. The ruined camp of Bennettville still exists beside Mine Creek, about a mile west of the Tioga Pass Resort (TPR).

Approaches

Follow Highway 120 west from the small town of Lee Vining, passing the forest ser-vice ranger station, and take to the turnoff to Saddlebag Lake, just east of the Tioga Pass Resort. Follow the road to the parking lot at Saddlebag Lake. Although it is possi-ble to hike around the lake, it is much quicker (and more fun) to buy a boat ride across. From the docks, a trail leads up to Steelhead Lake and the Conness Lakes, at the base of North Peak and Mt. Conness, respectively. Note: No overnight camping is allowed in the Hall Natural Area.

Mt. Conness (12,590 ft.)
West Ridge
II 5.6

F.A. Dick Long and friends; 1957
Mt. Conness Area Map: Page 284
USGS Quad Map: Tioga Pass

Mt. Conness was named in 1863 by the Whitney Survey party in honor of John Conness, the survey's benefactor in the U.S. Senate. The western side of the peak is a series of convoluted ridges and gullies rising above the deep blue waters of Roosevelt Lake. The west ridge is the southern-most of these, and forms the border with the great southwest face.

Dick Long, a talented Yosemite climber of the 1950s and '60s, spotted this line on the west ridge and made the first ascent with a group of friends. Long often climbed with Allen Steck, and was involved in many other notable Sierra climbs, including ascents of the southeast face of Clyde Minaret and the south face of the Angel Wings. He was also a member of the first-ascent team that climbed the Hummingbird Ridge on Mt. Logan.

TM Herbert, another longtime Yosemite climber, described this route: "Peter Croft came back to camp one evening last summer and said that he had just climbed the best route he had done in the Sierra backcountry. I figured it must have been Cathedral or the Matthes Crest, but he said it was the west ridge of Conness. Not only that, but most of it was fourth class! So I hiked in and climbed it the next week and he was right! It was great fun, like two Cathedral Peaks stacked on top of each other."

Route:
From Lee Vining, follow Highway 120 west to the Saddlebag Lake road and park at the Sawmill walk-in campground. Easy cross-country travel leads past the Carnegie Institute to Alpine Lake. Climb the south side of the ridge above Alpine Lake to the broad plateau south of the summit of Mt. Conness. Head west down sandy slopes before turning north to the toe of the west ridge. Climb the steep ridge to the summit, staying fairly close to the edge of the southwest face. An alternate approach goes from Tuolumne Meadows up Conness Creek to Roosevelt Lake.

Descent:
Descend the old surveyors trail to the plateau, and retrace your steps to the Saddlebag Lake road.

Mt. Conness from the southwest　　　John Moynier

Mt. Conness (12,590 ft.)
Southwest Face
V 5.9 A2 or 5.10c

F.A. Warren Harding, Glen Denny and Herb Swedlund; Sept, 1959
F.F.A. Galen Rowell and Chris Vandiver; July, 1976
Mt. Conness Area Map: Page 284
USGS Quad Map: Tioga Pass

The great southwest face of Mt. Conness is an impressive sight from many places in the Tuolumne Meadows area. This wall was first attempted by a group of Bay Area climbers, led by Don Goodrich. Goodrich's attempt ended in tragedy when he pulled off a loose block while leading the second pitch; he was mortally injured in the fall. A memorial plaque was placed at the base of the route.

Subsequently, Warren Harding led the first ascent of the route. Having completed both The Nose route on El Capitan and the east face of Washington Column the previous year, Harding was in great shape. The following summer, Harding made his other great Sierra wall climb: The east face of Keeler Needle.

During the first ascents of both the routes on Keeler and Conness, Harding was forced to make several aid bolt placements while he struggled up the wide cracks. His determination on climbs was epitomized by his legendary all-night effort in placing the bolt ladder on the headwall at the top of The Nose.

Harding's "apprentice," Galen Rowell, made the first free ascent of the southwest face of Mt. Conness with Chris Vandiver in 1976; the route is now regarded as one of the finest free climbs in the High Sierra.

Route:
From Lee Vining, follow Highway 120 west to the Saddlebag Lake road and park at the Sawmill walk-in campground. Easy cross-country travel leads past the Carnegie Institute to Alpine Lake. Climb the south side of the ridge above the lake to the broad plateau south of the summit of Mt. Conness. Head west down sandy slopes, then turn north into the cirque below the southwest face. The southwest face route follows the crack system on the left side of the wall, and begins at the Goodrich memorial plaque. Twin cracks lead up and right from the base. Climb the left crack (5.10a), then traverse right to a stance below a small roof. A long pitch surmounts the roof on the right, then steps left into a crack (5.10). A short pitch leads to a good ledge; from here, climb a moderate face (5.6) to a chimney with a chockstone.

Belay in an alcove and climb into a right-facing corner that begins as a hand-and-fist crack (5.9), widens to an offwidth (5.10a), and eventually widens to a squeeze chimney (5.9). The crack ends at a big ledge. From the right end of the ledge, climb a short left-facing corner (5.9) and make a difficult traverse right past a bolt to a finger crack (5.10). Continue up and right to a hand crack (5.9) that ascends for a few pitches, ending at a ramp that leads right to easier ground and the top.

Alternative Routes:
The Rosy Crown route (IV 5.9 A2) climbs the right side of the wall up through a prominent right-facing dihedral. The first ascent was made by Chris Vandiver and Gary Colliver in June, 1974. Urmas Franosch and Malcolm Jolley climbed this route free in the summer of 1990, and rated it 5.10c.

Descent:
Descend the old surveyor's trail to the plateau, and retrace your steps.

Chris Falkenstein

The Southwest Face of Mt. Conness

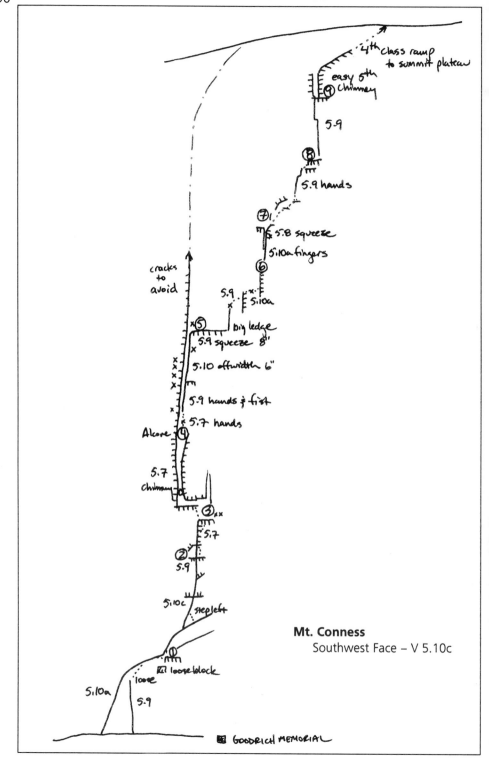

4th class ramp
to summit plateau

easy 5th
⑨ chimney

5.9

⑧

5.9 hands

⑦

5.8 squeeze

5.10a fingers

⑥

cracks
to
avoid

5.9   5.10a

⑤ big ledge

5.9 squeeze 8"

5.10 offwidth 6"

5.9 hands & fist

5.7 hands

Alcove ④

5.7
Chimney

③

5.7

② 5.9

5.10c step left

① loose block
loose

5.10a 5.9

Mt. Conness
Southwest Face – V 5.10c

GOODRICH MEMORIAL

Peter Croft on the North Ridge of Mt. Conness   Chris Falkenstein

Mt. Conness (12,590 ft.)
North Ridge
II 5.6

F.A. Galen Rowell and Barry Hagan; July, 1969
Mt. Conness Area Map: Page 284
USGS Quad Map: Tioga Pass

The north ridge of Mt. Conness is an enjoyable climb that involves dramatically exposed climbing on excellent rock at a moderate grade. The crux is a tower high on the ridge, which is either downclimbed (5.6) or rappelled. The route can be extended by making a traverse of the entire Conness crest from North Peak to Tioga Pass – a fine, moderate traverse similar to the traverse of the Cathedral Range.

This long traverse was first done in 1985 by Claude and Nancy Fiddler. Nancy, a member of the U.S. Cross Country Ski Team for many years, pointed out that throughout the history of Sierra mountaineering, women like Lucy Brown, Helen Gompertz, Ruth Dyar Mendenhall, Marjory Bridge and May Pridham have been active making first ascents. Nancy feels a vicarious kinship with these other women mountaineers through their entries in summit registers, especially with Barbara Lilley, whose signature appears in remote summit registers throughout the range.

Route:
Take the boat across Saddlebag Lake (or walk around) and follow the trail past Greenstone Lake to the Conness Lakes. Scramble up to the saddle between Conness and North Peak. Stay near the top of the ridge as it climbs to a tower at the junction with the west face. From the top of the tower, either make a short rappel or downclimb (5.6) into the notch and climb the steep face just right of the crest to the summit.

Alternative Routes:
Starting at McCabe Pass, climb the north ridge (5.3) of North Peak and continue over the summit to the saddle between Mt. Conness and North Peak. Climb the north ridge of Mt. Conness and follow the crest over White Mountain, Peak 12,002 and Gaylor Peak to Tioga Pass.

Descent:
Descend the old surveyor's trail to the summit plateau, then descend the east ridge past Alpine Lake to the Saddlebag Road.

John Moynier

The North Ridge of Mt. Conness

North Peak (12,242 ft.)
North Couloir
Class 4-5 ice

F.A. Unknown
Mt. Conness Area Map: Page 284
USGS Quad Map: Tioga Pass

The vertical north wall of North Peak is cut by three prominent ice couloirs. These gullies offer excellent ice climbs and can be climbed easily in a day from Saddlebag Lake. The right-most of the three is the easiest and is the most dependable in late season; the left-hand gully is the steepest. It is rare for such fine ice climbs to be so accessible, which helps explain their popularity.

North Peak was first climbed in 1937 by Smoke Blanchard, Hubert North and Gary Leech. Blanchard was a long-time eastern Sierra climber and a frequent climbing companion of Norman Clyde's. Blanchard was perhaps the first crag climber in the eastern Sierra, climbing many difficult routes (often solo) in the Wheeler Crest crags and the Buttermilk Country above Bishop.

Blanchard was also a mountain guide and influenced many young Sierra climbers, including the "Armadillos," a loose-knit group of young climbers and guides that included Doug Robinson, John Fischer, Jay Jensen, Gordon Wiltsie and Galen Rowell.

Robinson and Rowell wanted to find a climb to serve as a memorial to Blanchard, but he refused to let them name anything after him. Blanchard was not to win this battle, for after the first ascent of the east face of a prominent tower on the Wheeler Crest (IV 5.9), Robinson and Rowell named it the "Smokestack."

Route:
Take the boat across Saddlebag Lake (or walk around), then follow the old mining road to Steelhead Lake. Cross over to Cascade Lake and ascend a ramp leading to the glacier at the base of the north face. There are three couloirs to the left of the summit. Scramble up the glacier and cross the bergschrund at the left side of the base of the right-most couloir. Cross back to the right side of the couloir, and climb the ice for five pitches. The summit is reached by way of the Class-3 wall above.

Descent:
Descend scree and sand slopes on the southeast side of the peak to the Conness Lakes and the trail around Saddlebag Lake.

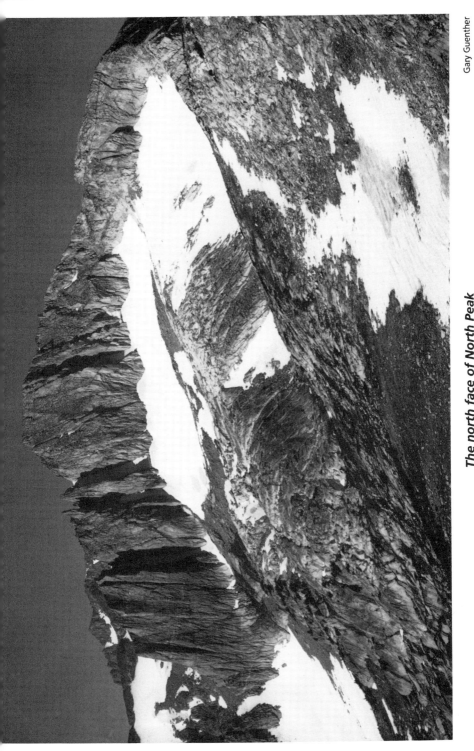

The north face of North Peak

Gary Guenther

Sawtooth Ridge Area

This dramatic section of the Sierra crest has long received the attention of Sierra mountaineers. Matterhorn Peak, the highest peak in the area, was first climbed in 1899 by James and Lincoln Hutchinson, Charles A. Noble and M.R. Dempster. The granite of the Sawtooth Ridge is of high quality, and there are a number of fine technical routes. The Sierra Club's Rock Climbing Section was active in this region, and between 1930 and World War II, members climbed virtually all of the summits and prominent spires. These climbers also made many short climbs and traverses of sections of the crest, particularly in the region of the Three Teeth.

The first major climb of the post-war era was the ascent of the north arête of Matterhorn Peak by Yosemite climbers Jerry Gallwas, Wally Kodis and Don Wilson in 1954. The striking granite spires of Little Slide Canyon also have attracted a number of climbers. The Incredible Hulk, in particular, has been the sight of considerable climbing activity by climbers from the Yosemite Valley and Tuolumne Meadows.

Approaches

The small town of Bridgeport, on Highway 395, offers the basic essentials of gas, food and accommodations. Wilderness permits are available at the forest service ranger station just south of town. Follow the Twin Lakes road to the private parking lot at Twin Lakes. The Matterhorn Peak area of the crest is reached by way of the Horse Creek trail, which leads south from the parking lot. To reach Blacksmith Peak, head west from the trailhead and follow Blacksmith Creek up to either Avalanche Lake or Glacier Lake. Little Slide Canyon is accessed from the Robinson Creek trail. Beaver ponds make crossing the creek difficult. A faint trail leads up the east side of the canyon to Maltby Lake.

Sawtooth Ridge Traverse

Cleaver Peak (11,760 ft.)
to Matterhorn Peak (12,264 ft.)
VI 5.9

F.A. Vern Clevenger and Claude Fiddler; July, 1984
Sawtooth Ridge Area Map: Page 296
USGS Quad Maps: Matterhorn Peak and Buckeye Ridge

Most of the peaks of the jagged Sawtooth Ridge were climbed and named by Sierra Club climbers in the early 1930s. In 1931, Jules Eichorn, Glen Dawson and Walter Brem traversed from the Dragtooth to Matterhorn Peak. Henry Beers, Bestor Robinson and Richard Leonard made the first traverse of the Three Teeth from the northwest to southeast (III 5.5, with rappels) in 1933. That same year, Oliver Kehrlein and Henry Beers climbed Cleaver Peak. The Doodad was climbed by Howard Twining and Kenneth May on July 7, 1934. On July 25th, Glen Dawson and Jack Riegelhuth traversed the Three Teeth from the southeast to the northwest (III 5.6, with rappels). That same day, Dave Brower and Hervey Voge made the first traverse of the Sawblade (Class 5).

A continuous traverse of the central section of the Sawtooth Ridge was not made until 1984. Vern Clevenger and Claude Fiddler took two days, with a bivouac on the crest. Fiddler and Clevenger began their traverse by ascending the Cleaver, a long, sharp arête dividing Horse Creek from Blacksmith Creek. Their route involved nearly two horizontal miles of technical climbing with heart-stopping exposure and free-hanging rappels.

Route:

From the trailhead at Twin Lakes, follow the Horse Creek trail up the switchbacks to the mouth of the canyon. The first-ascent team followed the long knife-edged ridge of the Cleaver to Cleaver Peak. From Cleaver Peak, continue along the spectacular Sawblade, traversing the Three Teeth to the Col de Doodad. Climb the wildly exposed Doodad, and drop down to Polemonium Pass at the base of the Dragtooth. Traverse over the Dragtooth to the summit of Matterhorn Peak and continue along the crest to Horse Creek Pass, descending Horse Creek Canyon to Twin Lakes.

The Sawtooth Ridge from Bridgeport

John Moynier

Matterhorn Peak (12,279 ft.)
North Arête
II 5.6

F.A. Jerry Gallwas, Wally Kodis and Don Wilson;
Spetember, 1954
Sawtooth Ridge Area Map: Page 296
USGS Quad Maps: Matterhorn Peak and Buckeye
Ridge

The Wheeler Survey Party was responsible for give Matterhorn Peak its somewhat inappropriate name. Of the first ascent of the peak, Lincoln Hutchinson wrote: "That the name is a poor one there can be no doubt, as there is only the barest suggestion of resemblance to the wonderful Swiss mountain after which it is called." The most striking feature on the peak is the distinctive north arête, rising above the small glacier at its base to the sharp summit.

The first ascent of this arête involved two of the leading climbers of the post-War generation: Jerry Gallwas and Don Wilson. The pair were Tahquitz regulars and had accompanied climbing legend Royal Robbins on his first visit to Yosemite Valley the year before. Two years after their route on Matterhorn Peak, Gallwas and Wilson accompanied Mark Powell on the first ascent of Spider Rock in New Mexico. In 1957, Gallwas capped off his climbing career by accompanying Royal Robbins and Mike Sherrick on the historic first ascent of the northwest face of Half Dome.

Route:

From the trailhead at Twin Lakes, follow the trail up the switchbacks into Horse Creek Canyon. Hike up slabs to the small glacier at the toe of the arête. Scramble up the couloir east of the arête a short way, then climb a left-facing corner to a broken area, trending up and right to a terrace on the prow of the arête. Continue up cracks on the right side of the prow (5.6) to a ledge. Traverse left around the prow of the arête and belay at the base of the summit corner. Lieback and jam the progressively wider crack (5.6) up the steep corner onto the summit ridge. Easier climbing leads to the top.

Descent:

Drop down ledges on the east side of the peak to a notch on the crest. The steep east couloir (Class 3) leads down onto the glacier below.

Matterhorn Peak from Horse Creek

Andy Selters

Sawtooth Ridge Area

Blacksmith Peak (11,680 ft.)
Northwest Face
III 5.8 A2 or 5.11

F.A. Lito-Tejada Flores and Chris Jones; July, 1973
F.F.A. Dave Nettle and Jim Howle; July, 1992
Sawtooth Ridge Area Map: Page 296
USGS Quad Maps: Matterhorn Peak and Buckeye Ridge

Blacksmith Peak is the granite fin guarding the northwest end of the Sawtooth Ridge. There are four summit towers; the northwest pinnacle is the highest and is rated 5.6. The peak was first climbed by way of a slabby gully on the southwest face by Bestor Robinson and Richard Leonard in July, 1933. Robinson returned three years later to climb the northeast gully (II 5.6), which rises above the glacier between Blacksmith and Cleaver Peak.

The northwest face is a great expanse of granite that attracted Yosemite climbers Lito Tejada-Flores and Chris Jones. Dave Nettle described their route: "(It is) the most striking line on the biggest face on the peak." Unaware that Tejada-Flores and Jones were on the route, Doug Robinson, Keith Bell and John Fischer also headed into the area to climb the face. Arriving at the base of the climb, they were amazed to see Tejada-Flores and Jones bivouaced midway up. Disappointed, Robinson and Bell climbed a new route on the left side of the face, while Fischer (who was feeling ill) went up the back way to meet his friends on top.

Route:
From Twin Lakes, head up and right into Blacksmith Canyon, following the creek to Glacier Lake and the small glacier at the base of the route. Scramble up to the right side of the face and climb a serrated crack above a slab to a rounded roof (5.10). The second pitch is the crux and climbs a thin crack to a difficult roof (5.11), then up an obvious left-facing corner below a square-cut roof. Surmount the roof (5.10) on its right side and lieback the right-facing corner above (5.9). Continue up the corner system to a small ledge. Stem and jam up the left side of the prow above to the Class-4 summit ridge.

Alternative Routes:
The face to the left of this route offers an excellent, moderate free climb (II 5.8; F.A. Doug Robinson and Keith Bell; July, 1973). Start on the left side of the face and continue up and right over broken rock to the summit.

Descent:
Rappel off the summit block, then descend the Class-3 southwest face to the notch, and traverse around to the base of the peak.

Dave Nettle

The Northwest Face of Blacksmith Peak

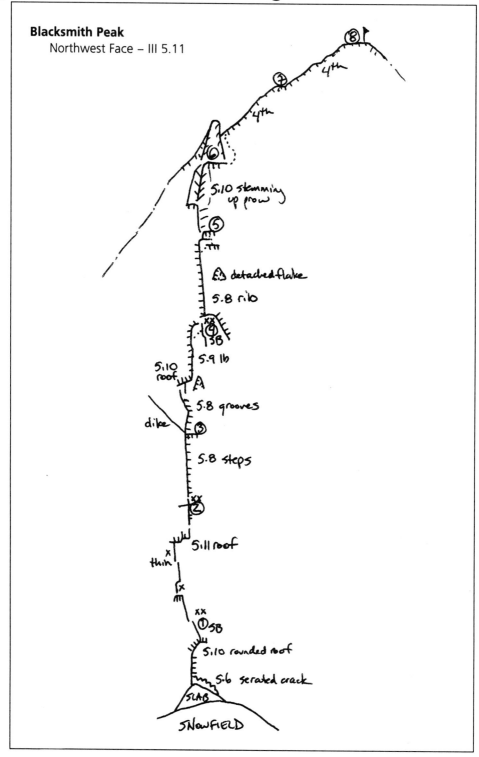

Blacksmith Peak
  Northwest Face – III 5.11

Climbing on the North Arête of Matterhorn Peak

The Incredible Hulk (11,040 ft.)
West Face: Red Dihedral (aka "Ygdrasil")
IV 5.10

F.A. Dale Bard, Mike Farrell and Bob Locke; June, 1975

Sawtooth Ridge Area Map: Page 296

USGS Quad Maps: Matterhorn Peak and Buckeye Ridge

Due to its excellent rock and relative accessibility, the Incredible Hulk has been the sight of considerable climbing activity. In the late 1970s, Tuolumne Meadows climbers would make furtive trips to the Hulk for first ascents. Mike Farrell, Dale Bard, Rick Wheeler and Bob Harrington were the most keen of these climbers, putting up many new routes.

Bob Harrington described his first view of the peak in 1976: "Rick Wheeler and I had just attempted a traverse of the Sawtooth Ridge, but bailed off to the south from the Doodad. We bivouaced west of Burro Pass and decided to walk out Little Slide Canyon. Wheeler had already been there, having climbed the Macedonian Route with Dave Bircheff. Dale Bard, Mike Farrell and Bob Locke had climbed Ygdrasil and Dale was being so transparently secretive about the place, I wanted to have a look at it. When I got my first saw the Hulk, my jaw dropped. It is about 1,200 feet high and has a classic pyramidal shape. We returned a few weeks later and climbed the Polish Route on the left side of the face."

The name "Ygdrasil" stems from Norse mythology and refers to the tree at the center of the earth that holds Heaven, Hell and Earth together with its roots and branches. The route Ygdrasil lies in the center of the broad west face of the Hulk and is the most enjoyable climb on the peak.

On the first ascent of the route, the climbers were trying move quickly in the face of an approaching storm. High on the face, Bard finished seconding a pitch at a ledge, but before he could clip into the anchors, a strong gust of wind knocked him off balance. Farrell managed to catch Dale's gear sling as he went over the edge, wrenching Farrell's shoulder, but saving Bard from a possibly fatal fall.

Route:
From Twin Lakes, hike up the Robinson Creek trail until it is possible to cross the creek and head up into Little Slide Canyon. A faint trail leads up the left side of the canyon toward Maltby Lake. The route ascends the middle of the broad wall to the right-most of the prominent corners. Scramble up ledges, then climb moderate cracks to a chimney (5.9). Continue up this and cracks (5.9) to the prominent left-facing Red Dihedral. Climb the corner, exiting over a roof (5.10) to the right. Moderate face climbing leads to a "splitter" crack (5.9+) in a smooth face. Three more pitches of face and crack climbing (5.8) lead past a shattered pillar to the top of the face, just right of two standing pillars. To reach the summit, continue up the arête to the base of a blocky chimney. Two pitches of dirty climbing (5.8) lead to a "keyhole" exit. The top is 100 feet above.

Descent:
Downclimb and rappel the southeast face, then contour around to the base of the wall.

The West Face of the Incredible Hulk   Dave Nettle

The Incredible Hulk (11,040 ft.)
West Face: Positive Vibrations
V 5.10 A2 or 5.11

F.A. Bob Harrington and Alan Bartlett; August, 1981
F.F.A. Dale Bard and Bobbie Bensman; August, 1986
Sawtooth Ridge Area Map: Page 296
USGS Quad Maps: Matterhorn Peak and Buckeye Ridge

A number of prominent left-facing corners are on the left side of the Incredible Hulk; a prow dominates the center of the face. Bob Harrington recalled his first attempt to climb the prow: "Dale Bard and I hiked in to the wall in July, 1977. We climbed to the bivy ledge and realized that we would never make it up the prow that day. I voted for going down, but Dale wanted to do a route, so we started up cracks to the right of the ledge.

"The higher we got, the harder the climbing got; some of it scary 5.10 with horrible pro. With an hour of light left, the crack system we had been following ended. I made a pendulum into another crack, but couldn't climb it. I brought Dale over to the belay and he flew up it without any hesitation (or gear for that matter). By the time the light ran out, we were pretty unhappy with each other. We suffered an awful bivouac and finished off the route the next day – glad to get off the wall."

Harrington had a hard time finding partners to do the route after word of his and Bard's epic reached the climbing community. He eventually convinced Alan Bartlett to attempt it with him in 1981.

"There had been thunderstorms the day before," he said, "We wanted to climb fast. Starting early, we reached the previous high point in about two hours, and blazed onto the summit by 11 a.m. Positive Vibrations was one of those rare times when I felt I was on the right route, with the right partner, on the right day, with the right gear. "

Route:
From the trailhead at Twin Lakes, hike up the Robinson Creek trail until it is possible to cross the creek and head up into Little Slide Canyon. A faint trail leads up the canyon toward Maltby Lake; the wall is on the left.) The route follows the prow in the middle of the face. Begin by climbing to the large ledge shared by the Macedonian and Donaldson routes. From the left side of the ledge, climb a left-facing corner (5.9), then lieback a thin crack past a bolt. Escape right before a left-facing arch, and climb moderate rock to the base of the faint oval above the prominent triangle. A steep hand crack (5.9) leads to the crux: disconnected thin cracks (5.11) on a very steep headwall. Continuously difficult climbing leads up the headwall four more pitches to the summit ridge. To reach the summit, continue up the arête to the base of a blocky chimney. Two pitches of dirty climbing lead to a keyhole exit. The top is 100 feet above.

Descent:
Downclimb and rappel the southeast face and then contour around to the base of the wall.

The Incredible Hulk
    left - Polish Route – III 5.10
    center - Positive Vibrations – IV 5.11
    right - Red Dihedral Route – IV 5.10

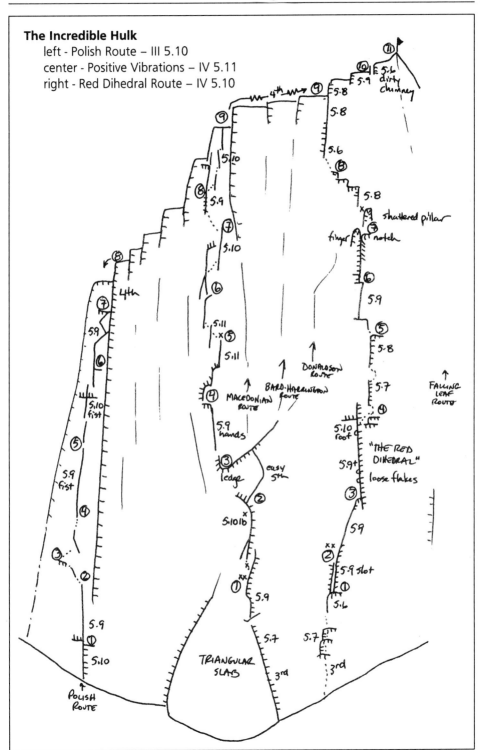

Tower Peak
Area

Tower Peak represents the northern terminus of the High Sierra. It lies to the north-west of the Sawtooth ridge on the northern border of Yosemite Park. To the north the peaks change character in height, appearance and geology. It is a rather remote peak and is best accessed by way of the West Walker River and Leavitt Meadows from the historic pioneer route over Sonora Pass.

The first recorded ascent of Tower Peak was made in 1870 as part of the final map-ping efforts of the Whitney Survey Party. The team found a small cairn and an arrow on the summit, and presumed that the first ascent had been made by an adventurous Indian brave. Tower Peak is the dominant peak in the area and can be seen from many peaks in the northern Sierra. Stretching out to the south of the peak are a num-ber of impressive, glacially carved canyons draining into the Grand Canyon of the Tuolumne River at the heart of Yosemite National Park.

Approach

From the town of Bridgeport, take Highway 395 north to the turnoff to Highway 108. Head west towards Sonora Pass on Highway 108 to the trailhead at Leavitt Meadows. From the meadows, follow the trail along the West Walker River to Upper Piute Meadows. At the junction with Kirkwood Creek, take the trail up West Tower Canyon to Tower Lake at the base of the crest.

Tower Peak (11,755 ft.)
Northwest Face
Class 3

F.A. Charles Hoffmann, William Goodyear and Alfred Craven; 1870
Tower Peak Area Map: Page 310
USGS Quad Maps: Buckeye Ridge and Tower Peak

Tower Peak is the northernmost sentinel of the High Sierra and can be seen from many peaks in central Yosemite National Park. North of this peak, the range changes dramatically in composition, from tall granite peaks to lower volcanic and metamorphic ridges that are less interesting to the climber.

The first ascent of Tower Peak was made via the northwest face. The survey team of Charles Hoffmann, William Goodyear and Alfred Craven were undertaking the final explorations of the Whitney Survey Party and set up their instruments on the summit to survey the northern Yosemite region.

The northeast face of Tower Peak recently has attracted climbers willing to make the long trek in. In 1988, Tuolumne locals Alan Swanson and John Nye climbed a five-pitch route (II 5.9) up a corner system to the right of the impressive pillar on the face. This party also climbed a nine-pitch route (III 5.9) on the west face of nearby Hawksbeak Peak.

Route:
From Leavitt Meadows on the Sonora Pass road (Highway 108), take the trail to Piute Meadows. Follow the trail up West Tower Canyon to Tower Lake, then climb to the saddle on the crest. Follow the crest of the ridge until blocked by towers. Cross over to a gully on the west side, which is followed up the northwest face (Class 3) to the summit.

Descent:
Retrace your steps.

Gary Guenther

Tower Peak from the northeast

Index

Index

Index

About the Authors

John Moynier has lived in the High Sierra since 1978, working as a climbing and ski mountaineering guide for much of that time, and currently teaches skiing at Mammoth Ski Area. He is active with the American Mountain Guides Association (AMGA), serving as a clinician/examiner for their ski mountaineering committee. He is also a member of the American Association of Avalanche Professionals (AAAP) and sits on the board of directors for the Professional Ski Instructors of America – Western Division (PSIA–W). John is also a freelance photographer and writer published in numerous outdoor magazines and author of *Backcountry Skiing in the High Sierra,* as well as *The Basic Essentials of Mountaineering* and *The Basic Essentials of Cross Country Skiing.* He lives in Mammoth Lakes, California with his wife Rose and daughter Kathrynne.

Claude Fiddler has been a prominent member of the Sierra climbing community since the early 1970s. He has participated in numerous first ascents in Yosemite Valley, Tuolumne Meadows and the High Sierra, as well as other ranges throughout the world. Claude participated in the 1983 American Expedition to the West Ridge of Mt. Everest, climbing to over 27,000 feet. For many years, Claude worked the winter seasons as a professional ski patroller, and the summers as a mountain guide. He is currently pursuing a career in large-format fine art photography, and has had a number of articles published in national outdoor magazines. He lives in Crowley Lake, California with his wife Nancy and their dog Chester.